The Peoples of Philadelphia

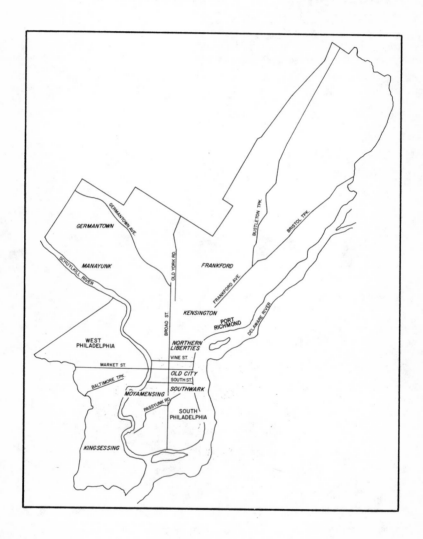

Philadelphia in 1854

Edited by
Allen F. Davis and Mark H. Haller

The Peoples of Philadelphia

A History of Ethnic Groups and Lower-Class Life, 1790–1940

Temple University Press
Philadelphia

Temple University Press, Philadelphia 19122
© 1973 by Temple University. All rights reserved
Published 1973
Printed in the United States of America

International Standard Book Number: 0-87722-053-0
Library of Congress Catalog Card Number: 72-95879

For Merle Curti
Pioneer in Social History

Contents

Preface

This book had its origin in a conference on the History of the Peoples of Philadelphia held at Temple University April 1–2, 1971, and sponsored by the Committee for Urban Studies and the Center for the Study of Federalism. The idea for the conference emerged when we learned that many young scholars, as well as a few older scholars, were engaged in studying various aspects of the history of lower-class life in Philadelphia during the nineteenth and early twentieth centuries. We invited twelve of them to prepare papers, and some other scholars to offer comments and criticism. Because the papers were of such high quality and treated common themes, we decided that they were worthy of publication in book form in order that a wider audience might share the advantages of those who attended the conference.

All the papers have been revised, many of them extensively. Taken together they offer some stimulating insights and ask provocative questions about the nature of crime, violence, mobility, ethnic communities, and the quality of life not only in Philadelphia but in all American cities.

We would like to thank the following people who participated in the conference and who helped to improve the quality of the essays in this book: Philip S. Benjamin, Daniel J. Elazar, Nathan Glazer, Herbert G. Gutman, Samuel P. Hays, Roger Lane, Roy Lubove, August Meier, Humbert S. Nelli, Elliott Rudwick, Seth M. Scheiner, Rudolph J. Vecoli, Richard C. Wade, and Sam Bass Warner, Jr. We would also especially like to thank Lane Johnson for his aid with the maps and Russell F. Weigley, who has an essay in this volume and who also played an important role in planning the conference, offering perceptive criticism, and in many other ways making this a better book.

The Peoples of Philadelphia

Introduction

Allen F. Davis

Philadelphia has been curiously neglected by historians. It is true that the "greene countrie towne," founded and laid out in a gridiron pattern by William Penn in 1682, has been described many times. The Colonial and Revolutionary city of Benjamin Franklin, site of the signing of the Declaration of Independence and the Constitutional Convention, is also the familiar subject of many scholarly and popular studies.[1] But the later Philadelphia seems to disappear from the history books. The city has of course produced its share of filiopietistic accounts, even though its citizens have had a long ingrained habit of downgrading their city. But when we think of the problems and opportunities created by the industrial city, we most often use Chicago as an example. If we deal with immigration and acculturation, it is to Boston and New York that we turn. Even the story of the reform movements which emerged in response to the problems of political corruption, poor housing, urban poverty and crime is most often told from the perspective of Boston, Chicago, and New York—even from the point of view of Cleveland, Rochester, or Detroit—and Philadelphia again is ignored or given scant attention. Only when it comes to the habits and the foibles of the rich does Philadelphia hold its own. Books such as Edward Digby Baltzell's *The Philadelphia Gentlemen: The Making of a National Upper Class* (New York, 1958) and Nathaniel Burt's *The Perennial Philadelphian: The Anatomy of an American Aristocracy* (Boston, 1963) document the life of the upper class in the city, but no comparable analysis has been made of lower-class life.

It is interesting to speculate as to why Philadelphia has been so neglected. Perhaps it is because its own resident scholars have been too fascinated with the city's Colonial and Revolutionary

3

heritage and the life of the upper class. Perhaps it is because the University of Pennsylvania (and other local institutions) failed to provide the same stimulus for historical and sociological studies of the city that Harvard and the University of Chicago encouraged. The one important study of lower-class life in Philadelphia done before the 1960s was William E. B. DuBois' *The Philadelphia Negro* (Philadelphia, 1899), written while he was on a temporary fellowship at the University of Pennsylvania.[2] His book was the first systematic and scholarly account of a Negro community in an urban environment, and is still well worth reading, but it did not stimulate further analysis along similar lines, at least not in Philadelphia. The city did not even produce popular or auto-biographical accounts of life among the poor during the progressive era; nothing in any way comparable to Jacob Riis' *How the Other Half Lives* (New York, 1890) or Jane Addams' *Twenty Years at Hull House* (New York, 1910). With the exception of the DuBois study, there was nothing even resembling Robert Woods' books on Boston, *The City Wilderness* (Boston, 1898) and *Americans in Process* (Boston, 1902). Philadelphia produced nothing to compare with the sociological and community studies written on Chicago in the 1920s, such as Louis Wirth's *The Ghetto* (Chicago, 1928), or Harvey Zorbaugh's *The Gold Coast and the Slum* (Chicago, 1929). There has been nothing in a more recent period resembling Oscar Handlin's *Boston's Immigrants* (Cambridge, 1941), or Moses Rischin's *The Promised City: New York Jews, 1870–1914* (Cambridge, 1962).[3] Philadelphia had no multivolume history such as Blake McKelvey prepared for Rochester and Bessie Pierce for Chicago.[4] Even in the 1960s, a decade when historians finally discovered the city, Philadelphia received little attention. Kansas City, for example, was much more fortunate.[5]

Happily, the neglect of Philadelphia's other history, the story of its lower-class life and ethnic communities, is now being remedied. Sam Bass Warner, Jr., has made an important beginning in his provocative book, *The Private City: Philadelphia In Three Periods of Its Growth* (Philadelphia, 1968), but it is only a beginning, for Warner deals very selectively and tentatively with the economic, political, and social forces which influenced the lives of the ordinary people who lived in the city.[6]

The essays in this volume represent a further beginning in the task of examining Philadelphia's other history. Most of the essays are by young scholars at work on larger studies dealing with some aspect of the history of the city. Many of them write in the tradition of the "new urban history." Until quite recently, cities and urban development have been ignored by American historians, who have preferred to stress the frontier and rural heritage of the American people. Even much of the urban history written in the last two decades has focused on established institutions, and community leaders, rather than on mass behavior and social process. Gradually, a new urban history has emerged which seeks to tell the story of the ordinary people who make up the life of a city, but who leave no autobiographies or manuscripts and rarely even get into the newspapers. Who were these people? Where did they come from? How long did they stay? What work did they do? Where did they live? What can we learn about their families, their clubs and neighborhoods, their churches and schools? In other words, mass behavior and social process is the subject of the new urban history.[7]

In order to attempt to answer some of these questions, historians are forced to use a different kind of source material—census schedules, court records, city directories, tax records—in addition to newspapers and manuscripts. Because of the nature of the questions they ask and the sources they use, many of these new urban historians borrow insights and techniques from social scientists, especially sociologists. Because of the statistical nature of their data, some have found the computer helpful in organizing and analyzing their material. Of course these new sources and techniques raise as many questions as they answer, and it would be unfair to suggest that this new urban history is completely separate from old methods of studying the city. Indeed, some historians have for years been trying to tell the story of ordinary men and women and how they lived. Often the only way to get a glimpse of the life of the lower class in a particular period is through the eyes of the upper class, or through the distorted view of the press. Many of the essays in this book effectively combine new and old approaches to the study of the city.

Recent studies make possible a few tentative conclusions about the nature of life in American cities. It may seem like an obvious statement, but historians are discovering that cities are not alike.

Of course there are similarities, but what is true for New York or Chicago may not be true for Boston, Philadelphia, or Kansas City. The Italian community in Boston may have different problems from the Italians in Buffalo or Chicago. To be Irish and Catholic in Philadelphia may have different meaning from being Irish and Catholic in Boston. Historians of immigration and ethnicity are discovering that they must make careful studies of each ethnic group in each city before they can generalize about the Italian experience or the Polish or Jewish point of view.

Cities also change over time. The Colonial city of Philadelphia, with a population of about 24,000 on the eve of the Revolution, has little in common with the booming industrial city of 1860 which contained more than half a million people, or with today's sprawling metropolis with a population of almost five million in the metropolitan area. Colonial Philadelphia was a walking city extending from the Delaware River to Seventh Street, from South to Vine. All parts of the city, and the rich farm lands on the outskirts, were within easy walking distance. Artisan, businessman, and day laborer all lived close together and worked in or near their residences. They met each other on the street and frequented the same taverns. By 1860 over half a million people (about 30 percent foreign-born) lived crowded together in a city which covered more than six square miles. Carriages and wagons mingled with pedestrians and street cars. No longer was it possible to walk across the city, and already Philadelphia was becoming a railroad city, with eight companies using eight different terminals to serve the rapidly growing urban area. Textile, locomotive, furniture, and other factories operated in the outlying areas of the city, some of them employing more than a hundred workers. No longer could most people live and work in the same neighborhood. Thousands were forced to commute many miles each day. The city was not yet separated into rich and poor areas, but Germantown was on its way to becoming a well-to-do suburb, and the process of residential segregation and the desertion of the center city by the wealthy had begun.

The twentieth century brought the automobile, which gradually replaced the railroad, the streetcar and the horse-drawn carriage as the dominant method of transportation, and the automobile once again, as the railway had before it, transformed the appearance of the city and the habits of its residents (though not to the extent that Los Angeles and Detroit were transformed). The city continued to grow in size. There were nearly two million people in 1930, with close to another million living in the metropolitan region. Residential segregation by income, race, or ethnic group had become the rule. A central business core was surrounded by an area of poverty, then came a ring of working-class and middle-class homes. The wealthy, with a few exceptions, lived in a few favored suburbs.

The patterns of urban growth, the creation of the massive problems that now seem synonymous with the city, have been similar in most major metropolitan areas, but each city also has its own special blend of influences. Few comparative studies have been attempted, but the essays in this book provide the beginning for an analysis of just how Philadelphia was similar and how it differed from other cities.

Philadelphia has always been one of the largest cities in the country, for example. That fact may be obvious, but it is often overlooked. It has been much larger than Boston, for example, to which it is often compared. The largest city in North America during the Colonial period, Philadelphia fell to second place behind New York in 1810, was eclipsed in population by Chicago in 1890, but remained the third largest city until passed by Los Angeles in 1960 (see table 1). It still remains, of course, one of the major metropolises in the country. And size was important in many ways. Philadelphia lost its unity, its "walking-city" quality faster than did most other cities, fostering the need for urban transportation as well as for clubs and gangs to substitute for neighborhoods. Its large size and early industrialization also enabled Philadelphia to provide greater opportunity for immigrants than did many cities.

After the mid-nineteenth century, Philadelphia ranked near the top of large cities in the proportion of economic activity devoted to various forms of manufacture. Of course, for many years manufacture was carried on in small shops or even in homes, but increasingly it took place in large factories and this meant opportunity for a great number of unskilled workers, though it often also meant downward mobility for skilled artisans. Philadelphia's strength as a center for manufacturing had important implications for the adjustment of immigrants in the city. Most cities offered an array of unskilled jobs in the nineteenth century and most Ameri-

TABLE 1 Comparative Population of American Cities (Pop. in Thousands)

	1800	1820	1840	1860	1880	1900	1920	1940	1960
New York	60	124	313	806	1,206	3,437	5,620	7,455	7,782
Philadelphia *	68	98	258	566	847	1,274	1,824	1,931	2,003
Chicago	—	—	4	299	503	1,699	2,702	3,397	3,550
Detroit	—	1	9	46	116	286	994	1,623	1,670
Los Angeles	—	—	—	4	11	102	577	1,504	2,479
St. Louis	—	10	16	161	351	575	773	816	750
Cleveland	—	1	6	43	160	382	797	878	876
Baltimore	27	63	102	212	332	509	734	859	939
Boston	25	43	93	178	363	561	748	771	697
Pittsburgh	2	7	21	49	235	452	588	672	604
Washington, D.C.	3	13	23	61	178	279	438	663	763
San Francisco	—	—	—	57	234	343	507	635	740
Milwaukee	—	—	2	45	116	285	457	587	741
Buffalo	—	2	18	81	155	352	507	576	532

* Population figures for Philadelphia and New York vary in various accounts depending on which geographic boundaries are used. The figures used here for Philadelphia for 1800 and 1820 are the old city plus Southwark and Northern Liberties (considered part of the city by most Philadelphians). The figure used for 1840 is for Philadelphia County, the boundary of the city after 1854.

can cities were built using cheap immigrant labor to dig the ditches and foundations, carry the bricks and steel to construct the buildings and lay the railroads. Philadelphia, however, offered a greater variety of jobs in manufacturing than most cities, in addition to the usual jobs of carrying, pushing, pulling, and digging. This provided greater opportunity for all groups except the blacks, who were systematically prevented from taking jobs in manufacturing. By 1850 they had even been driven from the skilled trades where previously they had a foothold. Opportunity for most immigrant groups in manufacturing also helped to create in Philadelphia larger and more enduring blue-collar neighborhoods than in most cities. Southwark, Kensington, and Manayunk have remained relatively stable, blue-collar neighborhoods for more than 150 years.

The number and kind of immigrants who came to Philadelphia was also important. Although hundreds of thousands of immigrants poured into the city, the proportion of foreign-born in the city was relatively low compared with other major cities. In 1870 Philadelphia was the second largest city in the country with a population of more than 700,000, but a little less than 30 percent of its population was foreign-born, well below the median (34 percent) for all cities. Chicago and San Francisco had close to 50 percent, while New York had 45 percent foreign-born. St. Louis, Boston, Cleveland, Detroit, Milwaukee, and Rochester all had a larger percentage of foreign-born than did Philadelphia, but Baltimore, New Orleans, Washington, and Kansas City had a smaller percentage. In 1910 Philadelphia with a population of more than a million and a half had a foreign-born population of about 25 percent, still well below the median for all cities (29 percent). New York had 40 percent foreign-born in 1910 and Chicago had 36 percent. Boston, Cleveland, Detroit, San Francisco, Milwaukee, even Pittsburgh, had a larger percentage of foreign-born than did Philadelphia, but St. Louis, Baltimore, Cincinnati, Los Angeles, New Orleans, Washington, and Kansas City had a smaller proportion.

When we look at specific ethnic groups we find that like most Northeastern cities, Philadelphia had more Irish (about 14½ percent) than Germans (about 7½ percent) in 1870. While about 23 percent of the population in Boston in the same year were Irish-born, only about 2½ percent were German-born. New York had something over 20 percent Irish and 16 percent German. Philadelphia had a larger proportion of Irish than Chicago, St. Louis, Cleveland, Detroit, and Milwaukee, but a smaller proportion of German-born than all these cities. By 1910 the percentage of Irish-born had dropped to just over 5 percent, and the German-born to about 4 percent. Boston and a number of small New England cities had a larger proportion of Irish-born than did Philadelphia, but New York, which had a slightly higher proportion of German-born, had about the same percentage of Irish as Philadelphia. Chicago, Detroit, and St. Louis continued to have a smaller percentage of Irish but more Germans than Philadelphia.

Looking for a moment at other ethnic groups, it is interesting to note that Philadelphia had a smaller percentage (about 3½ percent) of combined Russian and Italians by birth in 1910 than did Cleveland, Chicago, Pittsburgh, New York, Detroit, and Milwaukee, but more than Boston, Baltimore, Los Angeles, and Kansas City. Philadelphia had fewer people of Austro-Hungarian birth in 1910 than Boston, Providence, and New York, but more than Chicago, Pittsburgh, Detroit, St. Louis, and Milwaukee.

Yet Philadelphia was a city of immigrants. There were over 110,000 Irish-born in the city in 1890, nearly 75,000 German-born in the same year, over 90,000 Russian-born in 1910 and over 45,000 Italian-born in that year, but the proportions were less than in many of the other large cities. Just how the particular mix and proportions of immigrants coming to Philadelphia affected the political, economic and aesthetic development of the city is a subject that needs study, but tentatively at least it seems that some groups found more opportunity for advancement in Philadelphia than they did in other large cities.[8]

Philadelphia's location was also significant. It was a major inland port and rail center, though it was not as important a port as New York, Boston, or even New Orleans in 1830. Philadelphia's natural trade routes were with the South, which affected attitudes and also resulted in the largest black population of any northern city in the decades before the Civil War. Much has been made of Philadelphia's Quaker heritage, and for the development of a ruling elite this heritage may well be important, but the Quaker background seems to have made little difference for the ordinary citizen in most periods. One might expect that the Quaker influence would have produced a city friendly to free blacks and abolitionists, but the opposite was true. Of all the northern cities, none treated abolitionists and blacks worse than did Philadelphia.

Philadelphia long had the reputation of being a "City of Homes" rather than a city of tenement houses and apartments, and to a certain extent this reputation was justified; it did have a larger percentage of one-family dwellings than Boston, Chicago, or New York, but it also had its share of slums, with disease and despair and overcrowding. It is obvious from the essays in this book that the "City of Brotherly Love" has been a city of poverty, crime, and violence, of racial and ethnic tensions which often flared into riots. It has been a city which provided opportunity for Italian, Irish, Jew, Pole, and black, but the opportunity was often illusive and for many the urban experience was shattering and devastating.

No single generalization, no catch phrase, can sum up the total experience of life in Philadelphia over many decades, of course. The essays in this book explore some of the complexities and contradictions that make up life in a large city. The authors in many cases admit that their conclusions are tentative, their data incomplete. But taken together these essays begin to fill a void, they begin to tell the story of all the people of Philadelphia. It is a fascinating story, even though it is not always reassuring.

NOTES

1. See for example Frederick Tolles, *Meeting House and Counting House: The Quaker Merchants of Colonial Philadelphia, 1682–1783* (Chapel Hill: Univ. of North Carolina Press, 1940); Carl and Jessica Bridenbaugh, *Rebels and Gentlemen: Philadelphia in the Age of Franklin* (New York, 1942).
2. Now available in several reprint editions including a paperback published by Schocken Books.
3. The last full-scale history of the city was J. Thomas Scharf and Thompson Westcott, *History of Philadelphia,* 3 vols. (Philadelphia: L. H. Everts, 1884).
4. Edwin Wolf 2nd and Maxwell Whiteman, *The History of the Jews of Philadelphia from Colonial Times to the Age of Jackson* (Philadelphia: Jewish Publication Society of America, 1957) is a scholarly study, but one which concentrates on the upper class.
5. A. Theodore Brown, *A History of Kansas City,* vol. 1 (Columbia, Mo.: Univ. of Missouri Press, 1963); Charles N. Glaab, *Kansas City and the Railroads* (Madison, Wis.: State Historical Society of Wisconsin,

1962); Lyle Dorsett, *The Pendergast Machine* (New York: Oxford Univ. Press, 1968); William Wilson, *The City Beautiful Movement in Kansas City* (Columbia Mo.: Univ. of Missouri Press, 1964). There are a number of dissertations and many articles on various aspects of life in Philadelphia.

6. See also his article "If All the World Were Philadelphia: A Scaffolding of Urban History, 1774–1930," *American Historical Review* 74 (Oct. 1968): 26–43.

7. See Philip M. Hauser and Leo Schnore, eds., *The Study of Urbanization* (New York: John Wiley and Sons, 1965); Stephen Thernstrom, "Reflections on the New Urban History," *Daedalus* 100 (Spring 1971): 359–75.

8. Comparative statistics are from David Ward, *Cities and Immigrants: A Geography of Change in Nineteenth Century America* (New York: Oxford Univ. Press, 1971), pp. 76–81.

John K. Alexander

1

Poverty, Fear, and Continuity
An Analysis of the Poor in Late Eighteenth-Century Philadelphia

Sam Bass Warner in his important study of eighteenth-century Philadelphia maintained that the city had an "open society and economy" and that "prosperity" was "commonplace." [1] In addition, because "every rank and occupation lived jumbled together" the city had a strong sense of "community" and "suffered none of the communications problems of later Philadelphias." [2] Maybe. But, as we continue to learn more about late eighteenth-century Philadelphia, it is possible that we will discover that it is closer to the facts of the case to see Philadelphia not as an open society but as a city deeply divided against itself. [3] Elite Philadelphians were, in many ways, fearful of the present and anxious about the future. And much of their fear was a fear of the poor.

Philadelphia was a city steeped in fear in part because by the late years of the eighteenth century, Philadelphia was a cosmopolitan city. Walking through her streets and alleys, one could hear a mixture of languages and dialects. The number of German-speaking Philadelphians was large enough to necessitate the printing of signposts in both German and English. The Irish immigrants and the descendants of Irish stock also formed a large segment of Philadelphia's population. [4] Toward the end of the period, refugees from the French Revolution and the revolt of blacks at Port au Prince in 1794 turned the city into "one great hotel or place of shelter for strangers." [5]

Many Philadelphia leaders wanted immigrants in order to increase the city's population and economic activity. Throughout

This is a revised version of a chapter that appeared as "The City of Brotherly Fear: The Poor in Late-Eighteenth-Century Philadelphia," in *Cities in American History,* Kenneth T. Jackson and Stanley K. Schultz, eds. (New York: Alfred A. Knopf, 1972). We wish to thank the publisher for permission to print the chapter here.

13

this period Philadelphia boosters painted a picture of glorious opportunities awaiting immigrants to the city and to Pennsylvania, and they carefully pointed out the dangers of settling in other parts of America.[6] But at the same time the booster literature made it quite clear that Philadelphia wanted only the right kind of immigrants. Tench Coxe, one of Philadelphia's leading boosters, pointed out that since the Revolution the state's policy was to receive all "sober" immigrants with open arms. The *Pennsylvania Journal* agreed, proclaiming its hope that the Pennsylvania area would always be "the asylum of peacable [*sic*] and honest emigrants." In tune with this view, the first arrival of the French "peasantry" in 1790 was applauded because of their "sobriety, honesty and industry." [7]

Well before the end of the eighteenth century many Philadelphians were not at all sure that living in an "asylum" was desirable. For these Philadelphians, there were clearly dangers in accepting immigrants unless their character and political views were carefully scrutinized. Charles Biddle, when he was Vice-President of Pennsylvania, claimed that the state needed a system for admitting "the industrious and honest" while excluding "the idle and profligate" immigrant.[8] And it was not only the idle and profligate who were viewed with alarm. Irish and French immigrants—even when industrious—often came under attack for their politics. In a time of great political ferment, Philadelphians who feared democrats knew that these two national groups would rarely be their allies. And they did not hesitate to paint the Irish and French as bloody Jacobins who wanted nothing more than to subvert any political system that stressed order and stability.[9]

If some questioned the wisdom of calling for immigrants to choose Philadelphia as their new home, no one questioned the fact that the boosters had done their work well. From the end of the Revolution to the start of the nineteenth century, the city boomed in population. In the first federal census (1790), Philadelphia's population was listed as slightly more than 42,500; by 1800 the population was almost 70,000.[10] And probably 30 percent of Philadelphia's growth in the period 1790 to 1800 was due to the arrival of immigrants.[11]

As the city's population increased, so did her total wealth. But many observers felt that far too much of Philadelphia's wealth was being squandered on needless luxuries which weakened the city's moral fiber. Calls for economy constantly appeared in print. The same critics were often quick to point out that poverty too was on the increase.[12] Thus, while many Philadelphians basked in luxury, many others lived in want.

Side by side with the growth of population and the increase in total wealth stood the fear of decline. After the great yellow fever epidemic of 1793 and with the regular reappearance of the yellow death, Philadelphians lived in fear of each approaching autumn. Each new bout with yellow fever seemed to lessen the city's chance for urban dominance.[13] Also, while Philadelphia was the nation's capital during the 1790s, in 1800 the capital would move to the banks of the Potomac. Many established Philadelphians may have feared that economic and political dominance would move with the capital.[14]

The fear of economic decline and ruin reached into even the best Philadelphia homes. A constant theme of the period was how easily one could fall from the pinnacle of prosperity to the depths of the debtor's prison.[15] It is no accident that calls for charity were often couched in statements such as "it is a prudent foresight of the disasters which may happen to our selves, which induces us to assist others: that they may be willing to return the favor to us on a similar occasion." The concept of charity as insurance was an organic part of the whole scheme of poor relief.[16] When even the most prosperous of Philadelphia's citizens looked around them, they saw much to fear, and a special focus of their fear and anger was the poor.

For the Philadelphians of this period, as for most Americans of the time, the disadvantaged were of two types. There were, first, the "industrious" or "deserving" poor. Their chief characteristics were industry and, hopefully, sobriety. These people worked when employment was available, but lived close to the subsistence level. They were the citizens who, if unemployed for long were at most a few weeks from needing to enter the city's Almshouse. The industrious poor were the people for whom subscription charities were almost annually established during the winter when the weather deprived them of work. They were the Philadelphians who were especially hard hit by yellow fever because they could not afford to flee the city, and also could not find work. This necessitated immense relief funds to save them from starvation.[17]

Below the industrious poor, in the estimation of prosperous Philadelphians, were the "indigent" or "vicious" poor. Their chief characteristic was a lack of industry often caused by intemperance or "vicious" upbringing. They were seen as "worthless" and "vagabond" types and as "Drunken; Rioting, Sulking Lazy fellow[s]."[18] Most calls to give charity evidenced the distinction between the two types of poor. Prosperous Philadelphians were constantly reminded of their duty to help the industrious poor while spurning aid to the indolent poor. Despite the rhetoric, when the non-poor Philadelphians wrote of the dangerous actions of the poor, the distinctions between the industrious and the worthless poor tended to melt away.[19]

Given the eighteenth-century definition, how many Philadelphians were "poor"? This is a critical question but, unfortunately, impossible to answer with precision. We can say how many people were in the Almshouse at any given time, but this only shows us the very bottom level of poverty for, as the overseers of the poor noted, "the better sort of poor," the "honest" poor, refused to go there.[20] The essential question is how many industrious poor there were in the city. The poorer element was not listed in city directories, and while census returns usually listed occupations, in lower-class areas occupations often were not given.[21] And many poor people may not have appeared in the census at all. In 1790 an observer noted that the census population of the city was too low because "the smaller and poorer families" often hid members, fearing they would be taxed by the size of their family. Also the poor moved frequently, which made it easier for recording agencies to overlook them. In the winter, country laborers came to the city to find work, which probably increased the number of poor.[22] It is therefore very difficult to say precisely how many poor people were in Philadelphia at any given time.

One of the best sources for determining the number of poor people was the record of charity dispensed in the winter. During the winter of 1783–84, a private subscription fund provided wood and other "necessaries" to "the poorer labouring people" of the city. Approximately 1,600 families, a total of 5,212 people, were relieved. This means one in every seven Philadelphians was relieved by this charity alone. In addition to the number aided by subscription, there were also persons relieved by public funds, immigrant aid societies, and church charity. Finally, some may have been denied aid because they were not "labouring poor." It is reasonable to assume, then, that more than one in every six Philadelphians needed assistance during that winter.[23]

Other indicators suggest an unequal distribution of wealth in the city. In 1793 Philadelphia numbered 7,088 taxables among its population. By 1800 the number of taxables had fallen to 6,625.[24] This decline was even more dramatic when compared to the city's sharp rise in population during the 1790s. If we cannot say precisely how many Philadelphians were poor, we can say that the number was significant.[25]

What did it mean to be a poor person in the Philadelphia of this period? It meant above all else that employment was uncertain. What good were high wages if one could not get a job? When winter came early, many jobs literally ceased to exist. Unskilled day laborers were not the only ones hurt. Mechanics were usually referred to as part of the "common people" and linked with laborers as part of the industrious poor because of the uncertainty of their employment. It was not just chance that appeals to support American manufacturers repeatedly stressed the need to provide employment for the industrious poor.[26] Thus to be poor meant one had to plan ahead, be frugal, and practice the difficult necessity of deferred consumption.[27] And since employment was often uncertain, the poor had to work even under harsh conditions that were clearly dangerous to their health. One commentator noted that "in this climate most who are used to hard labor without doors begin to fail soon after thirty, especially if they have been obliged to live on poor diet." [28]

To be poor was, for many, also to be visible. Before the war, and probably after it, a person's occupation level and rank in society was clearly indicated by his clothing. As late as 1797 Charles Peale could note of a woman walking by him "her dress bespoke that her wants were supplied by industry." Common seamen not only dressed distinctively, they also spoke distinctively. And at least one Philadelphian felt it was helpful to describe a thief as having "a servant like address." [29] Also, because the poor always paid a housing price for their poverty, they were visible in a geographic sense. Since Philadelphia was still a walking city, the least desirable housing areas were at a distance from the center of activity. It should not surprise us that the poor often lived on the outskirts of the city.[30] Certainly Philadelphians of the day were aware that the poor people normally lived at or near the outer edges of the city.[31] In fact, the number of poor people such as laborers who lived in the central part of the city was almost non-existent. Even when laborers lived in the central areas of the city, they usually lived together or next to each other.[32] And the dwellings of the poor were often located in the alleys of the city. In the early 1790's, for instance, 10 of the 23 working adults living on Apple Tree Alley were unskilled day laborers.[33]

Distance was not the only housing price the poor paid. While Philadelphia as a whole was not a clean city, almost everyone agreed that the extremities of the city were the most "noxious" and unhealthy areas.[34] The smaller alleys—again often the home of the poor—were also offensively dirty, as were the cellars that the poor occupied. The stagnant pools and piles of trash that were often located near the poor provided an excellent breeding place for the mosquitos which carried yellow fever. During the yellow fever scourges, the alleys and cellars were death traps that often caught the poor who could not afford to flee the city. Mathew Carey, writing in November of 1793, estimated that seven-eighths of the people who died from yellow fever that year were "poor." [35] For the poor, life in the cellars and alleys could indeed be nasty, brutish, and short.

To be poor also meant the necessity to be deferential and of good character, for charity of all kinds required recommenda-tions. Even in the chaos that marked yellow fever epidemics, people seeking relief were expected to procure a recommendation from a "respectable" person.[36] While it was not explicity stated by participants, the recommendation system probably served as a means of social control. Presumably only the better sort of poor —that is, the industrious, sober, and orderly—could get a recom-mendation. Some groups dispensing charity clearly stated that they intended to "superintend the morals, and general conduct" of the people to whom they gave assistance. And part of this supervision was to see that the recipients of aid gained "a deep impression of the most important, and generally acknowledged moral and religious principles." [37] When winter charity was a regular occurrence, and when even artisans as well as mechanics and laborers were unemployed during yellow fever periods, the ability to receive a recommendation was essential.[38] Certainly having a reputation as an honest poor person and exhibiting a properly deferential demeanor enhanced chances of receiving aid. Thus, it was not surprising that charity-dispensing groups expected and usually received "a becoming deference" from the poor.[39]

But the poor were not always quietly deferential. Self-styled respectable citizens of the city complained constantly of disorder in the streets, especially near the outskirts of the city inhabited by the poor. The streets were filled with vicious children making it "next to impossible in the crouds (sic) of Vice to preserve the morals of children." The district of Southwark found it necessary to establish a Society for the Suppression of Vice and Immorality. But even with such measures, people feared that where the "Vices of *Whoring, drunkenness, swindling, fraud,* and *daring impiety* abound to the extent they do in this city" success against these evils was "not possible." The public press felt the need to denounce the person who "joins in mobs, beats down the watchman, breaks open doors, takes off knockers and disturbs the quiet of honest people." [40]

Not only were the streets scenes of disorder, they were also too often the places of crime. Especially during slack times or during the yellow fever periods, the crime rate was viewed as dangerously high. Philadelphians even felt there were times when people would resort to arson to be able to "plunder" the ruins. It was noted that after each fire, "the ruined buildings are generally overrun with boys and idle people, scrutinizing, not without risque, the scenes of destruction and probably secreting any small article which they find uninjured." [41]

Fear of the poor and of immigrants was not without some foundation. Records from the city court indicate that for the period 1794–1800 at least 68.3 percent of the criminals convicted were either *born* in Ireland or were blacks. Less than 12 percent of the criminals were born in Pennsylvania and less than 6 percent were born in Philadelphia.[42] Not only were the convicted criminals often foreign-born or blacks, they were also from the poorer element of Philadelphia. The vast majority of the blacks in the city were, all observers agreed, members of the lower class and, at best, members of the industrious poor. (The majority of blacks appear to have been laborers, servants, and seamen.)[43] That the blacks accounted for almost 32 percent of all the convictions, indicated that a large number of the criminals came from the poorer classes. The occupations of the criminals also attested

their poverty. Of those convicts who had an occupation listed,
26.7 percent were laborers. The next highest groups of offenders
were mariners, shoemakers, and carpenters. Few men whose occupations indicated a possible high income were convicted in the
city court. Further, the type of items taken were often not of the
type that could be pawned. Richard Butcher stole a salmon;
Oliver O'Harra took one pair of boots; Joseph, a black man, took
two loaves of sugar. In at least half the cases, such items suggested
that hunger or need for clothing was the force that pushed these
people into crime.[44]

The poor did indeed appear to form a dangerous class. Philadelphians clearly saw the link between poverty and crime. Writing in 1797, *Gale's Independent Gazetteer* pointed out that "the
most afflictive and accumulated distress" in Philadelphia existed
"amongst the *Irish Emigrants* and the *French* Negroes," which led
the editor to note that

> it may not perhaps, be unworthy of public attention, to enquire
> how these people are generally supported, and whether many
> acts of depredation, and many scenes of horror which have
> occurred in this and neighboring States, may not, in some de-
> gree, be traced to the extreme poverty of this distressed class of
> people; for, where there is no hope there can be but little
> exertion, and it requires something more than common abilities
> to struggle against the accumulated miseries of Poverty, Sick-
> ness and Contempt![45]

It was not simply the physical and criminal violence of the
poor that made them a dangerous class; their very language was
considered violent. Swearing was far too common, and it was
noted that among "the lower sort of People . . . there is a want
of good manners." [46] Benjamin Rush, a driving force behind
education for the poor, argued that the "ignorance and vices" of
the children of the poor "contaminated" the children who came
from "the higher ranks of society." Only by educating the children of the poor, who form "a great proportion in all communities," could the "profane and indecent language" that abounded in
"every street" be stopped. Moreover, education would reduce the
number of poor and lower the crime rate. It was essential not to
"exhaust" charity funds on health care because "their [the poor's]
morals are of more consequence to society than their health or
lives." [47] Thus the poor were to be educated not so much for

themselves as for society's needs. Rush was not alone in fearing what he called the "vulgar habits" of the poor.[48] Urging the need to educate the poor as well as the rich, one writer maintained that "ignorance, generally speaking, is the cause of almost all the evils we feel or fear." Another observer noted that "seven-eights [sic] of the wretches who suffer punishment for crimes, are destitute of learning." Time and again the point was made that once the children of the poor were educated, "then our streets will be no more crouded [sic] with the votaries of ignorance or vice, nor our persons endangered by the midnight robbers or assassin." [49]

Philadelphia responded to such appeals by establishing numerous charity schools. The Society of Friends increased its already impressive efforts to provide education for blacks. The Sunday School Society opened its first school in March 1791. By 1800 it had provided schooling for more than 2,100 poor children. Church groups also opened their own charity schools. Efforts to educate the poor were truly charitable, but not disinterested. The people who supported these charities were thankful that the children of the "poorer part of the community who would otherwise have been running through the streets habituating themselves to mischief, are rescued from vice and innured [sic] to habits of virtue and religion." These charities seem clearly designed not so much to elevate the poor as to keep them orderly.[50]

Not all Philadelphians agreed that education was the road to a tranquil society. Those who wanted to educate the poor noted that their opponents often "contend that the poor ought to be ignorant —that learning makes them idle, vicious and proud." And some coupled a call for education with a demand that youths who could not pay for their education should be forced to work to learn habits of industry.[51] Still, even the opponents of education were dominated by fear—the fear that an educated but poor person would be discontented with his lot. Clearly the whole public debate on educating the poor reflected the belief that the poor formed a dangerous class. The primary question was how best to keep them in check.

Fear of the poor also clouded politics. Throughout the period almost all public comments on political questions bristled with statements that reveal class antagonisms. Specific appeals to the poor were also commonplace.[52] The governance of the city itself created a political battle liberally sprinkled with appeals to save the poor from oppression. In 1783, when a plan for incorporating the city was before the state legislature, approximately 1,400 Philadelphians signed a petition against incorporation, because it would subject them to "an aristocratic police." When the issue came up again in 1786, citizens noted how "distressed" Philadelphians would be if the people should once again be subjected to "an aristocratic common council, who may extend it[self] at their pleasure." [53]

But in 1789 Philadelphia was incorporated. The basis of the new city government was a 15-man aldermanic council elected by freeholders worth £50 and a 30-man common council elected by all freemen.[54] The protests and attacks on this city government continued loud and long. A non-freeholder urged the freemen to elect common councilmen who "are in your own situation of life—men who will not *betray*, but *feelingly support*, your interest." In a later essay he expressed his fears more explicitly, arguing "as a *freeman*, I abhor the odious distinction which the constitution holds out upon the present occasion. It not only *deprives* the *poor* of a vote in the election of Aldermen, but it places the *Aldermen* in a state of *dependence upon the rich only;* and this *dependence* may induce them to disregard and *oppress the poor*, who have the misfortune to contend for *their rights with the rich*." Throughout the 1790s the poor were told that their interests were being sacrificed to benefit the rich.[55] If the rich feared the language and viciousness of the poor, the poor and even the middle classes feared the political power of the rich.

The experience of Israel Israel as a candidate in Philadelphia offers a clear picture of politics based on class appeals and fear of the poor. During the yellow fever epidemic of 1793, Israel, a leader in the Democratic Societies, was one of the people who stayed in the city and helped distribute relief to the poor. Using this relief work as a key point in his campaigns, he ran for the state legislature in 1793 and 1795, losing each time. In both campaigns he stressed the fact that the Philadelphia government was an aristocratic government which disregarded the needs of the poor. As one of his supporters argued, "let the poor wretch agonized with disease and ab[a]ndoned by the world say whether ISRAEL ISRAEL has not a soul above the common part." [56]

The election of 1797 was a different story. The vote for state senator occurred while many affluent Philadelphians were out of the city because of a reoccurrence of the yellow fever. Israel carried only 2 of the 12 city wards—North and South Mulberry, but these were the wards with the highest percentage of lower class residents. And by winning slightly more than 82 percent of the vote in the Northern Liberties and almost 87 percent of the vote in Southwark, both lower-class suburban areas, Israel was able to win by a margin of 38 votes out of 4,010 cast.[57] The supporters of his opponent, Benjamin R. Morgan, denounced the election and argued that Israel won only because the yellow fever had driven "the freeholders and other respectable inhabitants" away, allowing "the citoyens of Irishtown [in Southwark] and the Northern Liberties" to elect Israel. Only his appeal to the "deluded masses" and chance allowed him to win.[58]

There is no question that Israel used class appeals and his relief work for the poor to achieve victory. As one of his supporters noted, "the *well born*" of Philadelphia opposed Israel because he was a tavern keeper, "but as the right of suffrage is fortunately *not yet* confined to the gentlemen of the *learned professions,* it is not to be [but] imagined, that this objection will have little weight with the useful classes among us, the artisans and mechanics have too much respect for themselves to object to Israel Israel because he is not a merchant or a lawyer." [59]

Morgan's supporters were not to be done in so easily. They petitioned the state senate, claiming Israel's election was illegal because people in the Northern Liberties and in Southwark had been allowed to vote without proving that they had taken the required oath of allegiance. The senate committee agreed, and ordered a new election.[60]

Cries of foul play were rushed into print. From the middle of January 1798 until the new election of February 22, the press was filled with charges and counter-charges. Both sides denounced the violence of the opposition. Both sides claimed the opposition would use fraud, intimidation, and "dark schemes" to win.[61] "A Friend to Justice," claiming he had not voted for Israel in October, declared he would do so now because the committee had proven the right of suffrage "to be of *sportive* value." He argued that since 1790 a certificate of allegiance was unnecessary and not needed to vote "until lately, when party purposes were to be answered by the exaction." And he agreed with Israel's supporters that if such a voting rule was to be uniformly required, not a single legislator could claim to be legally elected. "A Republican" bitterly argued that Israel's election was not put aside for irregularities, but because Israel's opponents objected to "his being a zealous defender of, and advocate for liberty and equality amongst men, disapproving of all distinctions, titles, excises and stamp acts, with every other political measure which lays a burden on the common and poor people for the benefit of the rich." Israel's supporters stressed the fact that he was "a true republican" and a friend to the poor, as his relief work indicated. Using such appeals, the pro-Israel group hammered home the theme that the rights of the common people had been taken away when he was denied the senate seat.[62]

The Morgan forces depicted Israel and his followers as riotous Jacobins. Time and again they charged that Israel's followers used violence to take over or to disrupt Morgan endorsement meetings. The pro-Morgan newspapers carried dire predictions of what an Israel victory would mean. They warned that "the hour of danger is come— . . . our country is struggling in the deadly gripe of disorder and rapine, and the contest is doubtful. Our government and laws totter under the unremitting exertions of ruffians panting for tumult, plunder and bloodshed . . . and in hellish anticipation [they] view your property as already their own." Other Morgan backers urged all to vote for Morgan lest "the lawless sons of anarchy and misrule" steal the people's property. And realizing the appeal of Israel to the poor, the Morgan forces attempted to counter it by reminding the voters that "the enemies of the rich, are the enemies of the poor." They denounced all "demagogues" who drew "a political distinction between the rich and the poor"; since the interests of the rich and the poor were identical and since Morgan was the man who supported the Constitution, Morgan was the only choice.[63]

When the votes were in, Morgan had won by 357 out of 8,723 votes cast. Israel won only a third of the votes cast in the city wards. As in the first election, the only city wards he carried were North and South Mulberry wards. And Israel again won handily in the lower-class areas of the Northern Liberties and Southwark. He won 69 percent of the vote in the eastern Northern Liberties, 76 percent in the western Northern Liberties, and just less than 75 percent of the vote in Southwark.[64] Not without reason did William Cobbett claim that many of "the ignorant and indigent" were won to Israel's cause by his relief work.[65]

When the victory for Morgan was assured, Cobbett gloated that "the friends of government [i.e., Morgan backers] have proved themselves, not only the most rich and the best informed, but also the most *numerous.*" Still he had to concede that Morgan was able to win only because the Quakers, who normally did not vote, had supported him. Had the Quakers, who were among the most prosperous Philadelphians, not supported Morgan, Philadelphia would have had "the mortification to see a grogshop man fixed in the Senate." And with special relish he told his readers an election story that revealed the deep class divisions in the election. A Quaker on his way to vote asked a man walking along the road if he wanted a ride. But he also asked the man for whom he was going to vote. When the man said Israel Israel, the Quaker told him to walk. Cobbett noted "this is a good example. Let no one give them a lift. Let them trudge through the dirt, without shoes or stockings, 'till misery and pain bring them to their senses." [66]

The pro-Israel *Aurora* agreed that the vote was cast along class lines. It argued that Israel had done very well "not withstanding all the influence of wealth was exerted in his [Morgan's] favor." And the editor added that the closeness of the election "must strike terror into the hearts of aristocrats." The *Aurora* closed the books on the election by claiming that Morgan people "have threatened and deprived of bread those who are in their employ if they did not vote with them." [67] To the last, the election of Israel was conducted with an eye to the position of the poor and with bitter class antagonism.

The case of Israel Israel illustrated that many Philadelphians feared the political power of the poor, and also demonstrated that the poor would respond to a man who had helped them in a time of need. Israel was not the equal of the city or ward bosses of the nineteenth century, but he too gave assistance and asked for votes in return. And he got them. [68]

The attempt to control the poor or dangerous class went beyond Sunday schools and alliances to defeat candidates who courted the votes of the poor. The Philadelphia press printed countless items that offered psychological inducements to the poor to suffer their woes quietly, contentedly. These took various forms. Appeals extolled the joys of poverty, labor, and adversity, while pointing out the miseries of being rich. The poor were reminded that "the mind that's contented, from ambition free/Tis that man alone which can happiness see." [69] It was often claimed that "Riches bring Cares," and that while contentment "seldom makes her home/In proud grandeur's gilded dome" she "loves to visit humble cots." [70] To be rich was dangerous, for "Prosperity best discovers Vice, but Adversity, Virtue!" Occasionally the theme was varied to say that while people in "the higher departments of life" had more pleasure, they also had a greater measure of pain.[71]

Tied to the listing of the joys of poverty were reminders "to suffer what we cannot alter and to pursue without repinning [sic] the road which Providence, who directs every thing, has marked to us." Since all men suffer "misery and misfortunes" we should suffer "willing[ly] what we cannot avoid." And there are rewards if one suffers quietly. For "to be good is to be happy" and "Virtue alone, has that to give/which makes it joy to die or live." If one was contented and virtuous, but poor, he would surely receive his reward in Heaven for God loved the poor.[72] Of course if a man was sober, respectable, and industrious, he could expect to advance.[73] And if he suffered misfortunes, such as being out of employment, he could expect to receive charity. Still, one should be contented with his lot and not expect advancement to come quickly.

We cannot be sure that these psychological appeals were caused solely by fear of the poor. Still, the appeals must be examined in the context of the fear of the poor that did exist. Surely, in a city that was fearful of the poor, mere chance did not dictate such a high number of calls to suffer in orderly quiet. And it is revealing that even with the controls the non-poor had over jobs and charity, even with the power of the government to aid them, the established Philadelphians felt the need to add this psychological weapon to their arsenal. A man does not constantly plead with you to be orderly and to stay in your place when he can, without violence, force you to do so. The constant use of these appeals seems to show just how terribly unsure the prosperous were of being able to control the poor.

The Philadelphia we have been examining was still a preindustrial city. Many of the elements we associate with the modern city had yet to make their appearance. Still, Philadelphia of the late eighteenth century seems, in many ways, to be similar to modern cities. Was the preindustrial eighteenth century city really so different from that of the nineteenth or even twentieth century? Certainly we need to examine the story of the poor and their place in early American society far more than we yet have. And certainly before we proclaim that early America was basically a happy, socially open society, we had better do some more excavating. And in excavating the bedrock of the urban social structure in young America, we may uncover some strikingly familiar artifacts. We may find that time has wrought few changes in American urban life. Even this preliminary examination apparently supports historians' claims of continuity in American history.[74] But that continuity may well be far different from what is normally depicted. At least for urban America there is the real possibility that among the most continuing elements have been a high degree of residential segregation, a large measure of poverty, and a deep fear of the poor.

NOTES

1. *The Private City: Philadelphia in Three Periods of Its Growth* (Philadelphia: Univ. of Pennsylvania Press, 1968), pp. 5, 8. Warner is careful to point out that the city did not have an even distribution of wealth, nor did it enjoy "economic democracy" (pp. 9, 45).
2. Ibid., pp. 10–11.
3. Recent studies of Boston during this period point to a society that would hardly be described as "open." See James A. Henretta, "Economic Development and Social Structure in Colonial Boston," *William and Mary Quarterly*, 3rd ser., 22 (Jan. 1965): 75–92; and Allan Kulikoff, "The Progress of Inequality in Revolutionary Boston," ibid., 3rd ser., 27 (July 1971): 375–412. See also n. 25 below.
4. *Eine Acte, zur Incorporiung der zur Unterstützung nothleidender Deutschen beysteurenden Deutschen Gesellschaft in Pennsylvanien* (Philadelphia: Steiner und Kammerer, 1793), p. 4; Philip Padelfond, ed., *Colonial Panorama 1775* (San Marino, Calif.: The Huntington Library, 1939), p. 20; Philadelphia City Archives, Sentence Docket December 2, 1794 to February, 1804, pp. 3, 48, 72 (hereafter, Sentence Docket, 1794–1804). (The city archives will be abbreviated hereafter as PCA.) See also "A Citizen of Pennsylvania," *The Pennsylvania Packet, and General Advertiser*, April 7, 1790 (hereafter, *Penn. Packet*). Henry Wansey, *Journal of An Excursion to the United States of North America* (Salisbury, Eng.: n.p., 1790), pp. 184–85. Cf. PCA, "Minutes of the Board of Health beginning 26th July 1796 and ending the 3rd of May 1798," p. 74. *Aurora General Advertiser*, March 17, 1798 (hereafter, *Aurora*). See also Benjamin Rush to Charles Nisbet, August 27, 1784, in L. H. Butterfield, ed., *Letters of Benjamin Rush*, 2 vols. (Princeton: Princeton Univ. Press, 1951), 1: 336.

5. Samuel Hazard, ed., *Register of Pennsylvania, Devoted to the Preservation of Facts and Documents, and Every Other Kind of Useful Information Respecting the State of Pennsylvania,* 16 vols. (Philadelphia: Hazard, 1828–36), 2: 22–23.

6. Isaac Weld, *Travels Through the States of North America, and the Province of Upper and Lower Canada, During the Years 1795, 1796, and 1797* (London: John Stockdale, 1799), pp. 438–39; *The Pennsylvania Mercury and Universal Advertiser,* June 29, 1787 (hereafter, *Penn. Mercury*). Benjamin Rush to James Currie, November 20, 1801, in Butterfield, *Letters,* 2: 839 and "To American Farmers About to Settle in New Parts of the United States," in *Letters,* 1: 503–505. "Emigration," September 10, 1789, and "A Citizen of Pennsylvania," May 7, 1790, in *Penn. Packet; Aurora,* November 17, 1791; Tench Coxe, *A View of the United States of America* (Philadelphia: Hall and Wrigley & Berriman, 1794), pp. 61, 94–95; "M," *Aurora,* Jan. 7, 1795.

7. Coxe, *A View,* p. 74; *Penn. Mercury,* June 3, 1790; *The Pennsylvania Journal* (hereafter, *Penn. Journal*), and the *Weekly Advertiser,* Feb. 4, 1789.

8. *Penn. Packet,* March 1, 1786.

9. "Charlotte," *The Pennsylvania Evening Post and Daily Advertiser,* August 10, 1785 (hereafter, *Penn. Post*). *Gazette of the United States, & Philadelphia Daily Advertiser,* Nov. 8 and Dec. 17, 1798 (hereafter, *Gaz. of U. S.*). "Irish Rebels," *Porcupine's Gazette,* Nov. 28, 1798; "Comparison," *Porcupine's Gazette,* Dec. 6, 1798. For a relevant study of the Irish and politics in Philadelphia, see Edward C. Carter II, "A 'Wild Irishman' Under Every Federalist's Bed: Naturalization in Philadelphia, 1789–1806," *The Pennsylvania Magazine of History and Biography* 94 (July 1970): 331–46.

10. Philadelphia at that time included the district of Southwark and the township of the Northern Liberties. While not legally a part of the city, they were considered as integral parts of the city by all Philadelphians. For this reason, all population figures are for greater Philadelphia. See *A Century of Population Growth* (Washington, D. C.: Government Printing Office, 1909), pp. 11, 13; Evarts B. Green and Virginia D. Harrington, *American Population Before the Federal Census of 1790* (New York: Columbia Univ. Press, 1932), pp. 117n, 118; *Return of the Whole Number of Persons . . . for the second census . . . One Thousand Eight Hundred* (Washington, D. C.: Apollo Press, 1802), p. 49. It is possible that the population count for 1790 is too low.

11. The question of how the city's population grew is extremely complex and any figure of growth due to immigration is at best a qualified guess. The estimate given is based on the work of Carter, "A 'Wild Irishman'," pp. 340–42.

12. [J. P. Brissot De Warville], *New Travels in the United States of America 1788,* Durand Echeverria, ed. (Cambridge: Harvard Univ. Press, 1964), p. 253; Eugene Chase, ed. and trans., *Our Revolutionary*

*Forefathers: The Letters of François, Marquis de Barbe Marbois
. . . 1779–1785* (New York: Duffield and Company, 1929), p. 133;
"Luxury," *Aurora*, Feb. 15, 1796; "An Admirer of the Ladies," Feb.
17, 1787, "A New Catechism," July 14, 1789, and "X.Y.," Oct. 26,
1793 in *The Independent Gazetteer; or the Chronical of Freedom*
(hereafter, *Indep. Gazetteer*). "On the Times," *The Philadelphia
Minerva*, July 9, 1796 (hereafter, *The Minerva*). *The Pennsylvania
Herald, and General Advertiser*, June 9, 1787 (hereafter, *Penn.
Herald*). *Penn. Packet*, Dec. 9, 1784.

13. John H. Powell, *Bring Out Your Dead* (Philadelphia: Univ. of Pennsylvania Press, 1949) and Richard Folwell, *Short History of the
Yellow Fever, that Broke Out in the City of Philadelphia in July
1797 . . .*, 2d ed. (Philadelphia: Richard Folwell, 1798). *Claypoole's American Daily Advertiser*, Nov. 8, 1798 (hereafter *Am.
Daily Adv.*).

14 *The Freeman's Journal: or the North-American Intelligencer*, April 7,
1784 and Aug. 24, 1791 (hereafter, *Freeman's Journal*). *Penn. Journal*, Aug. 26, 1789; *Gaz. of U. S.*, Sept. 1, 1790.

15. "On Benevolence," *Penn. Packet*, Aug. 17, 1787; "Delia," ibid., Feb.
28, 1787; *Indep. Gazetteer*, Jan. 20, 1787; "Effects of Misfortune,"
The Minerva, April 22, 1797; Thomas Scott, *A Sermon Preached at
St. Peter's Church, on Sunday the 26th of August, 1792* (Philadelphia: Stewart & Cochran, 1792).

16. "Humanity," Jan. 2, 1796, and "Pity," Jan. 27, 1798, in *The Minerva;*
"Monitor," *Indep. Gazetteer*, Nov. 9, 1793; *Indep. Gazeteer*, May 18,
1793, and cf. "On Benevolence," *Indep. Gazeteer*, Sept. 28, 1793;
"The Flower Girl," *The Minerva*, May 7, 1796; "The Beggars," *The
Federal Gazette, and Philadelphia Evening Post*, June 27, 1789 (here-
after, *Fed. Gazette*).

17. *Gaz. of U. S.*, April 7, 1796; *Penn. Journal*, March 17, 1790; *Indep.
Gazetteer*, Dec. 31, 1785, July 10, 1787, Jan. 8, 1791, and April 16,
1794; *Freeman's Journal*, June 25, 1783; *Penn. Packet*, Aug. 26,
1785; *Porcupine's Gazette*, Oct. 23, 1797, and Nov. 29, 1798; *Fed.
Gazette*, Sept. 6, 1791, and May 2, 1794; Powell, *Bring Out Your
Dead*, pp. 57–58.

18. PCA, "Guardians of the Poor: 'Daily Occurrences' at the Alms-house
March 26, 1792 to June 7, 1793." See entries for April 22, 1792,
and March 26, 1792. See also *Penn. Packet*, Nov. 9, 1786; *Penn.
Mercury*, June 21, 1788; *Aurora*, Nov. 1, 1790; *The Pennsylvania
Gazette, and Weekly Advertiser*, Oct. 1, 1788 (hereafter *Penn.
Gazette*).

19. *The Minerva*, Feb. 3, 1798; *Penn. Journal*, July 18, 1781; *Freeman's
Journal*, Sept. 24, 1788; *Indep. Gazetteer*, Feb. 28, 1789: *Am.
Daily Adv.*, Oct. 7, 1797; "On Generosity," *Penn. Packet*, Jan. 26,
1786; "On Frugality," *Penn. Packet*, Aug. 23, 1785; "On Charity,"
Penn. Mercury, Jan. 6, 1789; *Penn. Mercury*, Nov. 21, 1789; "The
Moralist," *The Minerva*, March 12, 1796. Some refused to accept
such a distinction and called for charity for all in need. See "Char-

ity," *The Minerva,* April 11, 1795; *Fed. Gazette,* June 13, 1789; "Benevolus," *Freeman's Journal,* Sept. 24, 1788.

20. The records of the House of Employment and Almshouse are remarkably complete. See PCA, various kinds of records listed under Guardians of the Poor and Managers of the Alms-House. The figures were normally printed in the newspapers each year. On the attitudes noted see PCA, "Minutes of the Overseers of the Poor of the City of Philadelphia MDCCLXXII [to September 27, 1787]," entries of Feb. 15, and Aug. 18, 1785; "Managers of the Alms-House Minutes May 1788 to March 1796," pp. 422–23.

21. On the lower classes being excluded from directories, see the good short comment by Stuart Blumin in *Nineteenth-Century Cities,* Stephan Thernstrom and Richard Sennett, eds. (New Haven: Yale Univ. Press, 1969), pp. 170–71.

22. *Aurora,* Nov. 19, 1790; "The Druid, No. V," *Penn. Journal,* May 9, 1781, and Weld, *Travels,* p. 72; "An American," *Indep. Gazetteer,* Aug. 14, 1787, and cf. "The Discontented Villager," *The Minerva,* Jan. 28, 1797.

23. "To the Public," *Penn. Packet,* March 11, 1784. The ratio of one in seven is based on the assumption that Philadelphia's population in 1783 was 33,870. See *A Century of Population Growth,* pp. 11 and 13. During that winter the public charity alone relieved 117 out pensioners and an average of 230 in the almshouse and this total does not include the "great" number of beggars and "vagrants" who were in the city. See PCA, "Managers of the Alms-House Minutes May 1780 to May 1788," entry of March 3, 1784.

24. While the number of taxables was declining in the city, the number of taxables in Philadelphia county was increasing. See "Return of Taxable Inhabitants," *Aurora,* Dec. 31, 1800, and Hazard, *Register,* 2: 352.

25. Cf. Jackson T. Main, *The Social Structure of Revolutionary America* (Princeton: Princeton Univ. Press, 1965), pp. 194–95, 194–95n, 286–87. See also Jesse Lemisch's cogent analysis of Main in *Towards a New Past,* Barton J. Bernstein, ed. (New York: Pantheon Books, 1968), pp. 7–8, 18–22, 32–33.

26. "Communication," *Aurora,* Oct. 28, 1796; *Penn. Mercury,* June 29, 1787; "Thoughts on Good Times," *Freeman's Journal,* July 9, 1788; Jacob C. Parsons, ed., *Extracts from the Diary of Jacob Hiltzheimer of Philadelphia, 1765–1798* (Philadelphia: Wm. F. Roll & Co., 1893), p. 204; "On American Manufacture," *Penn. Packet,* Aug. 26, 1785; "The American Cotton Manufactory," *Penn. Packet,* Nov. 12, 1788; Historical Society of Pennsylvania, Pennsylvania Society for the Encouragement of Manufactures and the Useful Arts, entry of Dec. 21, 1787 (hereinafter, the Historical Society will be abbreviated HSP). "An Old Whig," *Indep. Gazetteer,* Oct. 10, 1785; *Penn. Herald,* Jan. 18, 1786, and July 22, 1786; *Fed. Gazette,* March 9, 1792; *Aurora,* Sept. 29, 1797. Charles S. Olton, who has made a detailed study of Philadelphia artisans, believes the mechanics were

more of an "entrepreneurial" than a "dependent" class. (See his "Philadelphia Artisans and the American Revolution," unpublished Ph.D. dissertation University of California at Berkeley, 1967, pp. 3, 15–16. I am less sanguine about the place of mechanics in the social structure.)

27. "Oeconomy," *Penn. Herald,* May 30, 1787, and "C", *Fed. Gazette,* Sept. 6, 1791.

28. *Penn. Gazette,* Feb. 2, 1780.

29. *Indep. Gazetteer,* May 15, 1784, and Jan. 15, 1785; *Aurora,* March 16, 1793; *Penn. Packet,* April 27, 1785; *The New World,* Jan. 6, 1797. John F. Watson, *Annals of Philadelphia and Pennsylvania in the Older Time . . .,* 3 vols. (Philadelphia: Edwin S. Stuart, 1905), 1:189, 191–92.

30. Warner, *The Private City,* pp. 13–14, but cf. p. 17. And, for example, in 1780 West Mulberry ward had 527 taxables, of whom 104 were laborers. In 1781 Southwark had 723 taxables, of whom 101 were laborers. In centrally located wards in 1780, the figures run: Chestnut ward, 103 taxables, of whom one was a laborer; Lower Delaware ward, 104 taxables, of whom three were laborers; High Street ward, 175 taxables, of whom 4 were laborers. (I am responsible for all of the above figures, which were obtained from the Constable's tax returns in PCA where the returns are listed by ward and date.) When the federal census was taken in 1790, the occupations of 827 residents of Southwark were listed; 200 of the 827 were "laborers, porters, helpers," or held other menial jobs. In the more centrally located area between South and Race Streets, there were 2,758 residents with their occupations listed, but only 239 residents of this area were "laborers, porters, helpers, etc." Considering only people whose occupations were listed, the ratio of residents of the more central area to Southwark is about 3.5 to 1. But the ratio of doctors is 12 to 1, the ratio of merchants and dealers is 13 to 1, and the ratio of lawyers is 12 to 1. (All ratios approximate.) Southwark obviously had much less than its share of professional people. (*A Century of Population Growth,* pp. 142–43). In 1800 in the eastern Northern Liberties, 378 of 1,734 taxables (approximately 22 percent) were laborers. In the western Northern Liberties, 469 of 1,788 taxables (approximately 26 percent) were laborers. In eastern Southwark the percentage of laborers was only about 10 percent. This is due to the fact that eastern Southwark had a high concentration of sailors, seamen, and mariners (approximately 26 percent), many of whom were members of the lower class. In the western area of Southwark, over 10 percent of the taxables were laborers. (HSP, "Enumeration of the Taxable Inhabitants within the County of Philadelphia 1800." I am responsible for the listing of total number of laborers and for the percentages.) Cf. also Norman J. Johnson, "The Caste and Class of the Urban Form of Historic Philadelphia," *Journal of the American Institute of Planners,* 32 (Nov. 1966):334–50, especially pp. 340–41.

31. See entry of Feb. 5, 1798, in HSP, "Philadelphia Poor House 1765–68," in the Edward Wanton Smith Collection, and PCA, "Managers of the Alms-House Minutes May 1788 to March 1796," pp. 82–83.

32. For example, three of the four laborers who lived in High Street ward in 1780 lived together or next to each other. See PCA, Constable's tax returns for 1780, p. 120 and cf. to pp. 116–22 *passim.* Warner claims that "variety best characterizes the occupational structure of the [Middle] ward as it did all the other wards of the first Philadelphia" (*The Private City,* p. 17), yet in the Middle ward Warner was studying, almost 50 percent of the laborers lived in Elbow Alley or in the extreme western part of the ward. (See PCA, Constables Returns of the City of Philadelphia for 1775.)

33. See Powell, *Bring Out Your Dead.* There were twenty-four householders, but in all records Peter Mercer is merely listed as "Negroe." (See PCA, Constables Returns for South Mulberry ward, 1791, pp. 36–37.) The census listed fourteen heads of households, of whom three were laborers. (See *Heads of Families at the First Census of the United States Taken in the Year 1790 Pennsylvania* [Washington, D.C.: Government Printing Office, 1908], p. 232.)

34. "Truth," *Fed. Gazette,* July 10, 1799; *Fed. Gazette,* Feb. 5, 1796, and June 5, 1799; *Penn. Packet,* May 24, 1787; *Carey's United States' Recorder,* Feb. 17, 1798 (hereafter, *U.S. Recorder*).

35. Mathew Carey, *A Short Account of the Malignant Fever . . .,* 2d. ed. (Philadelphia: Mathew Carey, 1793), p. 74; *Porcupines' Gazette* Aug. 9, 1798; HSP, Ebenezer Hazard to Robert Ralston, Sept. 13, 1797, in Gratz Collection; HSP, "Ann Parrish Visitations to the Sick, 1796," p. 7 in Parrish Collection; HSP, Samuel Duffield to Alexander Dalles, July 27, 1794 in Gratz Collection.

36. "Tents," *Porcupine's Gazette,* Sept. 25, 1798; PCA, "Minutes of the Board of Health beginning 26th July 1796 and ending the 3d of May 1798" entry for Sept. 21, 1797; HSP, St. George's Society Minutes for April 23, 1772 to Dec. 17, 1812, *passim.*

37. HSP, "Penn. Abolition Society Committee for Improving Condition of Free Blacks, Minutes, 1790–1803," entry of April 10, 1790 (hereafter, "Penn. Abo. Soc.").

38. Mathew Carey, *Short Account of the Malignant Fevers Lately Prevalent in Philadelphia,* 4th ed. (Philadelphia: M. Carey, 1794), p. 17.

39. HSP, "Penn Abo. Soc.," p. 35 and cf. pp. 59–60. See also W. E. B. DuBois, *The Philadelphia Negro* (New York: Schocken Books, 1967 [original 1899]), pp. 83–84.

40. For the quotations see "Honestus," *Penn. Packet,* Sept. 3, 1785; *Porcupine's Gazette,* Jan. 16, 1798; "The Picture," *Penn. Packet,* Aug. 20, 1785. See also Hazard, *Register,* vol. 2, p. 326; "A.B.," *Indep. Gazetteer,* Nov. 8, 1783; "M," Dec. 23, 1788, and Oct. 16, 1790, in *Fed. Gazette; Penn. Journal,* Aug. 10, 1798; *Penn. Gazette,* Aug. 17, 1791; *Am. Daily Adv.,* Dec. 17, 1790, To the Orderly; *Aurora,* Aug. 24, 1795; "An Enquiry," *Penn. Packet,* June 11, 1787. Riotous people were not necessarily poor, but the link was often made.

41. *Penn. Herald,* Nov. 11, 1786; *Indep. Gazette,* Nov. 12, 1785; *Penn. Journal,* Feb. 8, 1780, and Aug. 10, 1791; *Porcupine's Gazette,* Sept. 15, 1797; *Gale's Independent Gazetteer,* Dec. 23, 1796; *Am. Daily Adv.,* Jan. 17, 1797; *The New World,* Jan. 6, 1797; "A Citizen," *Penn. Packet,* Nov. 28, 1789.

42. The sources for the construction of these figures are in PCA, Sentence Docket, 1794–1804; Philadelphia County Inspectors of the Jail and Penitentiary House Prisoners for Trial Docket 1790–97 (hereafter, Trial Docket, 1790–97); Philadelphia County Inspectors of the Jail and Penitentiary House Prisoners for Trial Docket 1798–1802 (hereafter, Trial Docket, 1798–1802). These sources list a convict's place of birth, race, and, on occasion, occupation. The percentages are based on 320 prisoners convicted in the Mayor's Court of Philadelphia from 1794 through 1800. (We have no similar sentence dockets from earlier periods for Philadelphia). Twenty-eight criminals who were repeat offenders were counted only once. The percentages given are a very conservative estimate of the percentage of immigrant and black crime because the figures only reflect place of birth. Also, when a person was not specifically described as a black, he was put in the white category. Thus three convicts born in Guinea and one man described as being "a yellowish man" were not included in the totals for blacks. However, using a list of convictions may somewhat overstate the degree of crime by the poorer element. It is quite possible that the more prosperous Philadelphians, even if engaged in crimes, avoided conviction.

43. See Dubois, *The Philadelphia Negro,* pp. 17, 22–23; Wausey, *Journal,* p. 184; HSP, "Penn. Abo. Soc.," pp. 112, 219–20; *Gale's Independent Gazetteer,* Jan. 3, 1797.

44. Only 63 of the 320 criminals had an occupation listed. (Note that the imprecise nature of the records allows for a possible variance in the listing of the total number of prisoners who had an occupation listed. But the possible variation is small and the basic proportions remain consistent.) See PCA, Sentence Docket, 1794–1804; Trial Docket, 1790–97, pp. 258, 260; Trial Docket, 1798–1802, p. 269.

45. January 3, 1797 and see also *Penn. Herald,* Sept. 18, 1787; *Porcupine's Gazette,* Sept. 15, 1797; *U. S. Recorder,* June 7, 1798.

46. Weld, *Travels,* p. 17. And see also *The Philadelphia Monthly Magazine, or Universal Repository of Knowledge and Entertainment,* 2 (July, 1798): 22, and *The Minerva,* April 11, 1795.

47. Benjamin Rush, "To the Citizens of Philadelphia," dated March 28, 1787 in Butterfield, *Letters,* 1: 412–15 *passim.*

48. *Penn. Herald.,* July 18, 1787; *Indep. Gazetteer,* Aug. 28, 1789; *Penn. Journal,* Jan. 27, 1790; *Penn. Packet,* Jan. 21, 1790.

49. *Am. Daily Adv.,* Feb. 9, 1796; *Gaz. of U. S.,* Jan. 9, 1796; "Z," *Fed. Gazette,* Nov. 20, 1788.

50. DuBois, *The Philadelphia Negro,* pp. 83–84; *Penn. Mercury,* Nov. 22, 1788; James Mease, *The Picture of Philadelphia* (Philadelphia: B. & T. Kite, 1811), pp. 251, 261, 262–63; *Fed. Gazette,* Dec. 2, 1793: *Aurora,* Feb. 12, 1791 and May 17, 1796; James Hardie, *The Phila-*

delphia Directory and Register, 2d. ed. (Philadelphia: Jacob Johnson and Company, 1794), p. 212; *Gaz. of U. S.,* July 18, 1787, and Aug. 27, 1796; *Gale's Independent Gazetteer* April 21, 1797.

51. *Gaz. of U. S.,* Aug. 2, 1796; *Penn. Packet,* May 21, 1787; *Aurora,* Dec. 15, 1791.

52. *Freeman's Journal,* Aug. 8, 1781, Oct. 23, 1782, Sept. 29, 1784, and Jan. 28, 1789: *Indep. Gazetteer,* Sept. 16, 1786, May 5, 1789, and Jan. 30, 1790; *Fed. Gazette,* April 8, 1789 and Oct. 7, 1799; *The New World,* Nov. 1, 1796.

53. "A.B.," *Penn. Packet,* April 30, 1786 and *Penn. Journal,* Sept. 10, 1783; cf. *Indep. Gazetteer,* Jan. 13, 1786, and *Penn. Herald,* Nov. 30, 1785.

54. Edward P. Allinson and Boies Penrose, *Philadelphia 1681–1887* (Philadelphia: Allen, Lane and Scott Publishers, 1887), pp. 9, 19, 60–62.

55. "No Freeholder," *Indep. Gazetteer,* March 26, 1789; "An Old Mechanic," March 28, 1789, and Dec. 1, 1792, *Fed. Gazette; Aurora,* March 26, 1794, March 28, 1794, July 8, 1794, Oct. 5, 1795, and Jan. 30, 1796.

56. Quote from "Justitia," *Aurora,* Oct. 5, 1795. See also *Aurora,* March 21, 1795; *Indep. Gazetteer,* Dec. 14, 1793; *Fed. Gazette,* Oct. 26, 1793, and Dec. 19, 1793; *Penn. Gazette,* May 15, 1793, and May 7, 1794.

57. *Porcupine's Gazette,* Oct. 10, 1797, Nov. 13, 1797, Feb. 7, 1798; *Gaz. of U. S.,* Feb. 21, 1798, Oct. 9, 1797; *Fed. Gazette,* Oct. 9, 1797; *Am. Daily Adv.,* Oct. 10, 1797; *Aurora,* Feb. 24, 1798.

58. *Porcupine's Gazette,* Oct. 13, 1798. And see nn. 66 to 68 below.

59. *Aurora,* Oct. 9, 1797, and cf. "Humanitus," *Fed. Gazette,* Oct. 24, 1797.

60. The pro-Morgan argument also included the claim that the election in Southwark was not held at the legally designated polling place. See *Fed. Gazette,* Jan. 23, 1798; Jan. 25 1798; *Aurora,* Jan. 26, 1798, Feb. 8, 1798; *Am. Daily Adv.,* Jan. 27, 1798.

61. "A Republican," *U. S. Recorder,* Feb. 17, 1798; "A Democrat," *U. S. Recorder,* Feb. 20, 1798; "Truth," *Gaz. of U. S.,* Feb. 20, 1798.

62. Quotes from *Fed. Gazette,* Feb. 13, 1798, and *U. S. Recorder,* Feb. 17, 1798. See also *Fed. Gazette,* Feb. 17, 1798; *Aurora,* Jan. 18, 1798; *Am. Daily Adv.,* Feb. 19, 20, 21, 1798.

63. Quotes from "Foresight," *Gaz. of U. S.,* Feb. 21, 1798; *Penn. Gazette,* Feb. 21, 1798; *Gaz. of U. S.,* Feb. 16, 1798. See also *Gaz. of U. S.,* Feb. 17 and 21, 1798; *Penn. Gazette,* Feb. 21, 1798.

64. *U. S. Recorder,* Feb. 24, 1798; *Aurora,* Feb. 26, 1798.

65. *Porcupine's Gazette,* Feb. 24, 1798.

66. Ibid., and Feb. 26, 1798.

67. *Aurora,* February 24 and 26, 1798.

68. Israel was elected Sheriff of Philadelphia County in 1800.

69. "Contentment," *Penn. Mercury,* Aug. 24, 1787; See also *Penn. Packet,* Nov. 24, 1785.

70. Quotes in *The Mail: or Claypoole's Daily Advertiser,* April 1, 1793, June 17, 1793 (hereafter, *The Mail*). See also *Penn. Packet,* July 23, 1789, July 28, 1789, July 17, 1790; *Penn. Mercury,* Aug. 26,

1785, Aug. 24, 1787; *U. S. Recorder,* March 13, 1798; *The Minerva,* Jan. 9, 1796.

71. *The Minerva,* Feb. 20, 1796, Oct. 7, 1797, April 15, 1797. I have found only one item in the press that calls the idea of the rich being less happy or having more misery absurd. See "Reflections," *Freeman's Journal,* Feb. 8, 1786.

72. Quotes from *Penn. Packet,* Jan. 16, 1790; *Penn. Mercury,* Aug. 29, 1785; *Penn. Packet,* Sept. 4, 1790; *Penn. Mercury,* Aug. 28, 1787. See also *The Minerva,* Feb. 28, 1795 and Oct. 29, 1796; *Am. Daily Adv.,* Dec. 29, 1800; *The Mail,* Feb. 25, 1792; *Freeman's Journal,* Oct. 26, 1785, March 7, 1787, and Oct. 6, 1790; *Penn. Packet,* Nov. 24, 1785, Jan. 11, 1786, June 21, 1787, July 5, 1788, and Oct. 13, 1789; *Aurora,* March 3, 1795.

73. *Am. Daily Adv.,* Oct. 7, 1797; *Aurora,* Sept. 14, 1791; *Indep. Gazette,* Jan. 7, 1788; *The Minerva,* Jan. 16, 1796; *The Merchant's Daily Advertiser,* July 19, 1797.

74. John Higham, "The Cult of the 'American Consensus' Homogenizing Our History," *Commentary* 27 (Feb. 1959): 93–100 and his "Beyond Consensus: The Historian as Moral Critic," *American Historical Review* 67 (April 1962): 609–25.

Stuart M. Blumin

2

Residential Mobility Within the Nineteenth-Century City

The study of the physical movements of nineteenth-century Americans has taken a new turn in recent years with the appearance of what has been called "the new urban history." Interested primarily in the social mobility of the male residents of selected cities and utilizing such sources as city directories and the population schedules of the United States Census, a number of historians have found that a large proportion of men whose names are drawn from one directory or census cannot be successfully traced in subsequent editions. Overlooked at first, then treated as a problem affecting the interpretation of those cases which *can* be traced, these "missing cases" have been recognized as indicators of a very high turnover of local populations.

Taking their cue from the consistency of these indicators, Stephan Thernstrom and Peter R. Knights have thoroughly and effectively pursued the question of population movement in one city, late nineteenth-century Boston.[1] Their results are staggering, even in the context of old clichés about the mobility of Americans. Between 1880 and 1890, according to Thernstrom and Knights' elaborate calculations, almost 1,500,000 persons migrated into or out of the city of Boston, which even at the end of the decade could claim only 488,000 inhabitants.[2] Truly, Boston in the 1880s was more process than place.

But what is most interesting about these findings is not their magnitude but their urban and Eastern context. Traditionally, high population turnover (as distinct from mere in-migration) has been associated primarily with the settlement of the West, even to the point of being part of the whole package of traits which supposedly distinguishes East from West and city from frontier. But now it appears that an extraordinary impermanence of place was a general fact of American life. Any attempt to understand the nineteenth-century American city must incorporate this physical transiency.

Indeed, the large cities of the East were even more fluid than the above figures suggest for, as Thernstrom and Knights indicate, "it was possible to move a great deal and still remain within their boundaries." [3] This local movement has been almost entirely neglected by students of population mobility, who have traditionally conceived of migration only in more dramatic terms—Europe to America, East to West, farm to city, city to suburb—and only as movement between politically distinct areas. If we think of migration as a significant and enduring change in human and physical environments, and not merely as distance covered or political boundaries crossed, we can appreciate the possible significance of residential mobility within the large city. But why bother? First, there is a real difference between out-migration and local residential mobility in terms of their significance to the city. Out-migrants are lost to the city, and presumably have no further impact upon it, except perhaps to affect further out-migration by their successes and failures. Local movers are still part of the city. If their changes of address are significant to them personally, they may well be, in the aggregate, significant to the communal life of the city itself.

A second reason for examining residential mobility has as much to do with methodological convenience as with nineteenth-century America. In most if not all studies of out-migration, the mover is lost to the historian. It is virtually impossible to make useful estimates of where all the migrants resettled and, more importantly, of what other changes occurred during or after migration. Did the migrant assume his old occupation in his new home? How did his new home and neighborhood compare with his old home and neighborhood? Did he prosper, fail, or continue at his old level of income? Although we cannot assume that movements within the city are typical or in any way representative of moves beyond the city, at least they permit observations at both ends of the move.

The purpose of this paper is to analyze the magnitude and pattern of local residential mobility in Philadelphia in the four decades before the Civil War, and to speculate upon its significance for those who moved and for the city as a whole. My basic method has been to select four large samples of male names (along with their listed addresses and occupations) from the city directories of 1820, 1830, 1840, and 1850, and to trace these names through each of the next ten annual directories. This procedure produced ten-year residential and occupational histories of approximately five thousand individuals arranged into groups representing each of the four decades preceding the Civil War.

Specifically, I have divided Philadelphia (including the settled districts beyond the political boundaries of the city), according to criteria and evidence described later, into three broad zones of residence. These, in turn, were arbitrarily subdivided into thirteen districts which are intended to represent meaningful boundaries. For example, we will observe later that the upper section of the Northern Liberties, along with Kensington and the upper wards of Spring Garden, comprised a working-class district. But this is a large area which, even leaving aside well-known ethnic hostilities, cannot realistically be considered a neighborhood. In particular, the wharves and maritime trades of Kensington and the eastern wards of Northern Liberties set the eastern part of this broad belt of wage-earners and small tradesmen off from the western wards bordering on open farmland. Accordingly, I have divided this northern zone into two districts or "neighborhoods," one representing the eastern portion and one the western portion. The rest of the city was similarly divided into eastern and western portions of broader residential zones, with the addition of unique neighborhoods on the eastern bank of the Schuylkill River, in West Philadelphia and in Germantown, the latter two emerging as parts of the city only at the very end of the period. Observing moves between these thirteen districts results in a somewhat arbitrary picture of overall residential mobility, but one which is effectively similar, I believe, to one which might be based on a more careful delineation of real neighborhoods.[4]

Table 2.1 summarizes the movements of sampled Philadelphians from one district to another during the four decades before the Civil War. Perhaps the most striking aspect of this table is the increase in total mobility each decade, from 26.8 percent in the 1820's to 37.6 percent in the 1850s. But a prior point, perhaps, is the high rate sustained throughout the period. It must be remembered that the individuals we are looking at are those who remained in the city over the decade. In the context of the usual discussions of geographic mobility these are the immobiles, those who stayed behind when countless others left the city entirely. What Table 2.1 reveals, in other words, is that these "immobiles"

TABLE 2.1 Interdistrict Residential Mobility, 1820–60, Philadelphia

	1820–30	Percentage	1830–40	Percentage	1840–50	Percentage	1850–60	Percentage
To contiguous districts	140	14.7	177	16.2	185	19.2	198	18.2
To diagonal districts	44	4.7	92	8.4	273	6.8	58	5.3
To non-contiguous districts	71	7.4	98	9.0	195	9.6	153	14.1
Total mobility	255	26.8	367	33.6	653	35.6	409	37.6
Total sample	953	100.0	1092	100.0	1835	100.0	1088	100.0

Total Mobility	Percentage 1820–30	Percentage 1830–40	Percentage 1840–50	Percentage 1850–60
Contiguous	54.9	48.2	53.9	48.4
Diagonal	17.3	25.1	19.0	14.2
Non-contiguous	27.8	26.7	27.1	37.4
Total	100.0	100.0	100.0	100.0

SOURCE: from Stuart Blumin, "Mobility and Change in Ante-Bellum Philadelphia," in *Nineteenth-Century Cities*, Stephan Thernstrom and Richard Sennett, eds. (New Haven, Conn.: Yale Univ. Press, 1969). Reprinted by permission.

were not so sedentary after all. From one-fourth to three-eighths of them experienced a form of mobility themselves, and even this estimate purposely excludes those who moved into a new home in the immediate vicinity of their old one.[5] Put another way, the unknown residual of the truly immobile, those who remained in the same homes throughout the decade, was considerably smaller than even the most enthusiastic students of American migration would have us believe.[6]

On the other hand, our own enthusiasm must be contained by the realization that approximately half of the intra-city mobility observed each decade involved mobility between contiguous districts, and that another 14 percent to 25 percent involved districts which were diagonal to one another. In the period 1820–50, moves to noncontiguous districts comprised a stable 27 percent of all moves, a figure which increased to 37 percent in the 1850s, largely because of the development of the "suburbs" of West Philadelphia and Germantown. In the final analysis, the distance of residential mobility within the city was a good deal less dramatic than its frequency.

Yet the fact remains that antebellum Philadelphians moved around a great deal. The real question, however, is not the magnitude of residential mobility, but its significance for understanding the urban social system. The remainder of this paper will be devoted to a discussion of three significant issues which may be illuminated by a knowledge of the magnitude and pattern of residential mobility. By no means does this exhaust the possible uses of these data. For example, this paper ignores questions which might be raised about urban values, hits only obliquely on questions concerning urban tensions and family life, and gives only a passing glance toward ethnically- and racially-based group life in the city. Conceivably, each of these matters could have been decisively influenced by or have shaped residential mobility.

The first issue suggested by the concept of residential mobility is the relationship of residential change to vertical mobility. Indeed, the work from which this essay is derived is a study of the vertical mobility of antebellum Philadelphians. That study began, quite naturally, as an examination of occupational mobility, but it became evident as the research progressed that occupations told only part of the story of success and failure, that neighborhoods based on differential wealth and status existed, and that Philadelphians moved around the city even more than they moved up and down its occupational structure. In fact, residential mobility seemed to constitute an equivalent or even better index of social or economic mobility than occupational mobility.

Furthermore, specifying the vertical dimension of residential mobility on the city's map proved, if anything, easier than ranking occupations. In figure 2.1, for example, each of the city's wards and politically defined "liberties" or districts is assigned its average property tax assessment in 1820. The striking and consistent pattern of these averages is their direct relationship with proximity to

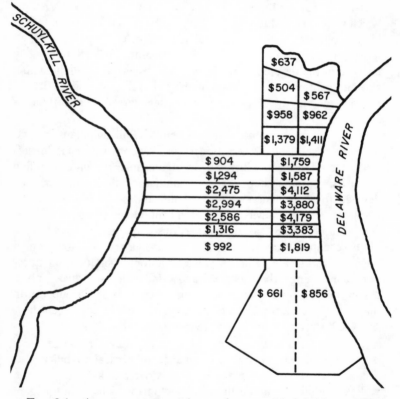

FIG. 2.1 Average assessment by ward per taxable inhabitant, 1820. Source: Stuart Blumin, "Mobility and Change in Ante-Bellum Philadelphia," in *Nineteenth-Century Cities,* Stephan Thernstrom and Richard Sennett, eds. (New Haven, Conn.: Yale Univ. Press, 1969). Reprinted by permission.

the city's center. The innermost wards have by far the highest average assessments. Next highest are those which immediately surround the center, including the two southernmost wards of Northern Liberties. Finally, there are a number of wards, forming the periphery of the urban population, which display the lowest average assessments of all.[7] From this map, therefore, were established three broad zones of residence radiating outward from the city's center. Maps prepared for subsequent decades indicated the need for occasional shifting of boundaries, but each reaffirmed the overall pattern. The single exception to this rule was the appearance of the suburb of Germantown by 1860, where wealthy Philadelphians lived on a year-'round basis, commuting daily to the center of the city. Subsequent decades would intensify this new pattern and, in effect, turn the city inside-out. But by 1860 this was a minor pattern in comparison with the persistence of the one described above, and is, in any case, easily incorporated into the analysis which follows.

First, however, it should be made clear that this seemingly arbitrary and mechanical dissection of Philadelphia produced results which were far from original. Historians and contemporary commentators alike bear out this scheme with few if any differences.[8] For example, in 1848 and 1849, a *New York Tribune* reporter named George G. Foster published a series of short descriptive pieces collectively entitled "Philadelphia in Slices," dealing for the most part with the more spectacular features of urban life.[9] Interestingly, the second zone is entirely ignored in favor of the first and the third. The only area discussed specifically as a residential district is Chestnut Street:

> The upper part of Chestnut-street [*sic*] is occupied almost exclusively by dwelling-houses, all plain and unostentatious, but many of them very rich and substantial, furnished with marble steps and plate-glass windows. The side walks, which are punctually subjected to a tri-weekly scouring that rubs the skin off the face of the bricks and lays bare their crimson integuments, are frequently ornamented with young vigorous trees, rich with verdure and scattering an incense of shady coolness around. Their whispering branches are responded to by innumerable garden-yards, filled with a luxuriant growth of grape-vines, clematis and seringos, which keep the atmosphere pure and sweet, embalmed in previous odors.[10]

It must be admitted that Foster goes on to say that this Keatsian foliage "is common throughout the city," but it is clear that he does not mean to include the outer districts. He does imply at least some continuity between the first and second zones, but when he finally selects a neighborhood which combines all of the character-istics of elegant living, it is Chestnut Street that he chooses.

The outer districts receive most of Foster's attention:

> Beyond the city on the North are the immense suburbs or 'dis-tricts' of Spring Garden, Northern Liberties, Kensington and Penn Township, and on the South, Southwark and Moyamensing. . . . These districts . . . have become infested with a set of the most graceless vagabonds and unmitigated ruffians. . . . The districts, especially of Southwark and Moyamensing, swarm with these loafers, who, brave only in gangs, herd together in squads in clubs, ornamented with such outlandish titles as 'Killers,' 'Bouncers,' 'Rats,' 'Stingers,' 'Nighthawks,' 'Buffers,' 'Skinners,' 'Gumballs,' 'Smashers,' 'Whelps,' 'Flayers,' and other appropriate and verminous designations, which may be seen in any of the suburbs written in chalk or charcoal on every dead-wall, fence and stable-door.[11]

The gangs of the districts are well-known, and may represent little more than the erosion of the apprentice system in the city. But Foster's description of Dandy Hall, a place of evening amuse-ment in Southwark, provides a specific characterization of the dis-trict itself:

> Dandy Hall is the core of the rottenest and most villainous neighborhood ever peopled by human beings. It is the Five Points of Philadelphia, a moral Golgotha of civilization. . . . To constitute a house of nuisance under the laws of Pennsyl-vania it is requisite that the neighbors should testify to being regularly disturbed by what takes place in it. Now, as the neighbors, without exception, are exactly as bad as the inmates of Dandy Hall, and as most of them are in the constant practice of mingling in the disgraceful proceedings carried on in it, who is to complain? [12]

Even gambling houses varied according to prediction. In the center of the city were three such establishments, "very handsomely got up and conducted with the most perfect quiet and politeness. A free supper stands ever ready for the guests in a side room, and wines and liquors are furnished gratis and of the best quality." [13]

Far more numerous were the gambling houses of Spring Garden, Southwark and Moyamensing. "They are, however, of an inferior class, generally kept in the back room or garret of some low groggery." [14]

Table 2.2 describes residential mobility over the four decades between the three zones.[15] Briefly, the picture obtained is one of stable upward mobility and dramatically increasing downward mobility. While both figures stood at approximately 14 percent in the 1820s, downward mobility was almost three times as frequent as upward mobility in the 1850s. Of course, it may be argued that I have simply been too conservative in adjusting the zonal boundaries each decade to reflect the city's growth, and that this automatically produced the pattern just described. To some extent this is probably true, particularly in the last decade studied, but to a much greater extent the increase in downward mobility must be explained in terms of what actually was occurring in Philadelphia. In particular, the increase in downward mobility seems to reflect a very real shift in the social structure toward a large wage-earning, poor and near-poor, unskilled and semi-skilled, native and immigrant work force.[16] The increase in the size of the third zone, in proportion to the other zones, is an accurate reflection of the increase in this urban proletariat. What is interesting in this context is that the poorer sections of the city were not peopled strictly by new arrivals from Ireland and Germany, nor even by them in conjunction with older residents of these sections. To a significant and increasing degree, the industrialization of Philadelphia sent residents of middle-class and even upper-class neighborhoods into the poorer sections to find new homes.

Of course, "downward" residential mobility is not necessarily equivalent to downward social or economic mobility. Residence, like occupation, is but one dimension of social life and one of several correlates of wealth and income. It would make little sense to express reservations over the validity of inferring social or economic mobility from occupational change and then proceed to make the same inferences from residential change. What is clearly needed, in the absence of direct measures of changes in wealth, income, and prestige, is an analysis which would incorporate all or nearly all of the relevant variables. What table 2.2 indicates, therefore, is not the pattern of social or economic mobility in antebellum Philadelphia, but the probable influence of one important dimension of mobility on the overall pattern.

TABLE 2.2 Summary of Residential Mobility, 1820–60, Philadelphia

	Percentage Upward (Converging) Mobility				Percentage Downward (Radiating) Mobility			
	1820–30	1830–40	1840–50	1850–60	1820–30	1830–40	1840–50	1850–60
Zone 1								
To Zone 2					14.3	19.0	19.4	24.1
To Zone 3					4.2	9.2	9.7	11.8
Total					18.5	28.2	29.1	35.9
Zone 2								
To Zone 3					10.3	14.4	21.7	28.3
Average downward mobility					14.2	21.4	24.7	31.8
Zone 2								
To Zone 1	11.0	11.3	11.1	9.6				
Zone 3								
To Zone 2	12.4	11.0	12.3	7.8				
To Zone 1	3.7	5.5	3.2	3.8				
Total	16.1	16.5	15.5	11.6				
Average upward mobility	13.7	13.9	13.4	10.9				

But even if we experience some difficulty in specifying the significance of individual moves to individual careers, we can at least assume that the overall pattern of residential mobility reflects to a large degree the shifting pattern of economic opportunity in the city. This leads us into a second and entirely different area of inquiry, namely, the temporal and spatial dynamics of the city's economic development. The point is that, by and large, men follow jobs. Thus, by tracing specific occupational groups to specific places at specific times, it is possible to catalog not only the temporal but also the spatial distribution of economic changes.[17] The value of such information is obvious where there is no other information available concerning, say, the timing and location of factory construction or the shift within specific factories from journeyman to machine production. But even where such information is available, residential mobility provides unique insights. To what extent is each increase in the demand for labor met by the immediate neighborhood, or, conversely, to what extent do responses to labor demand create the residential fluidity we have already described? Do specific changes draw men from specific areas of the city? What, in turn, does this tell us about the city as a communications network, or, indeed, as a community?

This last question implies yet a third area of inquiry, namely, the nature of group life in the city. How did the pattern and magnitude of residential mobility shape the ways in which Philadelphians interacted with one another? Because my own data deal only with mobility and not with interactions, I cannot begin to probe this question empirically. But the sheer magnitude of mobility does suggest some things about the possibilities of group life, particularly within the neighborhood itself. The outstanding feature of Philadelphia in the Age of Jackson was its size. Excepting New York City, which had passed Philadelphia in size in the first quarter of the century, nothing like it had ever been seen on the American landscape. The cities of the eighteenth century, and the new western cities of the nineteenth century, were "walking cities" of twenty or fifty thousand. Philadelphia in 1820 exceeded 100,000 (including the districts) and by 1860 was a city of more than a half-million. It is obvious that no extant notion of community could apply to a collection of that many people spread over so many square miles. And as Sam Bass Warner notes in *The Private City,* none did. On the contrary, Philadelphia in this period passed

"the communitarian limits of a city of private money makers." [18]
New definitions of community would have to be created if residents
of the city were to maintain any sense of localized identity beyond
the family, and new organizations would be needed to give these
new communities effective power over themselves and in the
increasingly remote city government. Perhaps the most obvious
choice would have been to redefine the community in traditionally
spatial terms, to substitute the neighborhood for the town. But,
as Warner notes, this is precisely what did not happen:

> By 1860 the combined effects of Philadelphia's rapid growth
> . . . contributed to the thorough destruction of the informal
> neighborhood street life which had characterized the small-scale
> community of the eighteenth-century town. In response to these
> new conditions all Philadelphians, of every class and back-
> ground, reacted in the same way to the loss of the old patterns
> of sociability and informal community. They rushed into clubs
> and associations.[19]

It is inaccurate to associate the astonishing rise of voluntary
associations in mid-nineteenth century America solely with urban
growth. Tocqueville, after all, found the same phenomenon in the
small towns of America. But, whatever its function in the towns,[20]
club life in the city offered "a replacement for the old street, shop
and neighborhood life of eighteenth-century town conditions." [21]
More to the point, "clubs, lodges, parishes, and gangs were not
media which could nourish effective and inclusive community
growth." [22] Voluntary associations were, ultimately, imperfect
means for redefining community in a large city. They were exclusive of too many intimates such as wives and children, and inclusive of near-strangers often known only through the association
itself. They were specialized in function, recent in development,
and had little day-to-day reality. Certainly, they did not pervade
the lives of their members. Some could but others could not exert
an effective political voice. But if clubs were ineffective, why did
neighborhoods fail to fill the apparent void? Warner suggests a
complex answer, consisting of the newness and facelessness of many
neighborhoods in the outer regions of the city and of changes in
the daily pattern of work and informal association brought about
by early industrialization. I would add high rates of residential
mobility as another critical factor. We have already seen that the
city's neighborhoods experienced extremely rapid turnovers of

population. Only about one-third of the members of the directory samples described earlier could be traced through the next ten annual directories, and of this group an average of another one-third were located in different sections of the city. Assuming these figures to be roughly congruent with reality, they indicate that, on the average, only one out of every four or five adult male inhabitants (and probably their families) remained in a given neighborhood as long as ten years. If the creation of a meaningful community, consisting of informal as well as formal interaction networks, depends in large part upon a substantial continuity of personnel, then it is reasonable to suggest on this basis alone that Philadelphia's neighborhoods could not have become communities, except for a very small proportion of the city's population. There was simply too much movement for individuals, even friendly ones, to create significant numbers of enduring personal relationships which could be related to a specific locality within the city. Relationships could be made through formal organizations as long as these were not based upon residence in a specific neighborhood. This is Warner's point—that formal groups were a *substitute* for the formal and informal life of the neighborhood.[23] What I am suggesting is that this substitution was made necessary by the physical transiency of the city's population.[24]

Whatever its significance may be, the fact of residential mobility cannot be denied. Antebellum Philadelphia must be seen as a highly fluid environment in which only a small proportion of individuals sank permanent neighborhood roots. Many moved beyond Philadelphia, some to Norristown, some to California. But even those who stayed behind were not entirely immobile. To the extent that the district, neighborhood, street or dwelling constituted a significant and unique locality, the migration of Philadelphians, consisting of their movements both beyond *and within* the city, was truly immense in its proportions. It may thus turn out that the real significance of this inquiry and those like it lies in their reaffirmation of the old idea of America as a mobile society.

NOTES

1. Stephan Thernstrom and Peter R. Knights, "Men in Motion: Some Data and Speculation about Urban Population Mobility in Nine-

teenth-Century America," *Journal of Interdisciplinary History* 1 (Autumn 1970): 7–35.

2. Ibid., p. 19.

3. Ibid., p. 32.

4. A definitive analysis of both neighborhoods and mobility will soon be possible, owing to the remarkable efforts of Theodore Hershberg, whose research is described elsewhere in this volume.

5. One of the special provisions of the research design was the elimination of short moves over the boundary between two districts. Individuals who moved only a block or two, but who crossed a district boundary, were coded in the same district throughout the decade. This was done to assure that the mobility rates would apply only to moves of some significance.

6. Except, of course, Thernstrom and Knights. See "Men in Motion," p. 23.

7. The assessments actually apply to all property, residential and commercial alike, but an examination of four widely dispersed wards, whose original (and more informative) tax lists survive, indicates that fig. 2.1 actually understates the differences between the average residential assessments of the various wards. Fig. 2.1 and a slightly different discussion of it appear in Stuart Blumin, "Mobility and Change in Ante-Bellum Philadelphia," in *Nineteenth-Century Cities*, Stephan Thernstrom and Richard Sennett, eds. (New Haven: Yale Univ. Press, 1969), pp. 165–208.

8. See, for example, Ellis Paxson Oberholtzer, *Philadelphia: A History of the City and Its People*, vol. 2 (Philadelphia: S. J. Clark, 1911); E. Digby Baltzell, *An American Business Aristocracy* (New York, 1962); Norman J. Johnston, "The Caste and Class of the Urban Form of Historic Philadelphia," *Journal of the American Institute of Planners* (November 1966): 334–50; Charles J. Cohen, *Rittenhouse Square: Past and Present* (Philadelphia, 1922).

9. George Rogers Taylor, " 'Philadelphia in Slices' by George G. Foster," *Pennsylvania Magazine of History and Biography* 93 (January 1969):23–72.

10. Ibid., pp. 58–59.

11. Ibid., p. 35.

12. Ibid., p. 39.

13. Ibid., p. 47.

14. Ibid., p. 48.

15. Table 2.2 appeared previously in Blumin, "Mobility and Change," p. 191.

16. Blumin, "Mobility and Change," pp. 197–206.

17. Two problems should be noted here. First, the emergence of an urban transit system in this period was beginning to make it possible to travel a considerable distance to work and, therefore, to pursue job opportunities without changing homes. On the other hand, I doubt that many factory workers commuted before 1860. Secondly, much of the labor force consisted of women and children, whose names

and occupations would appear in the Census (after 1840) but seldom in city directories.

18. Sam Bass Warner, Jr., *The Private City* (Philadelphia: Univ. of Pennsylvania Press, 1968), p. xi.
19. Ibid., p. 61.
20. For a statement that it played exactly the same role in small towns, see Page Smith, *As a City Upon a Hill* (New York: Knopf, 1966), p. 174.
21. Warner, *The Private City,* p. 62.
22. Ibid.
23. For a similar thought concerning trans-local migration, see Thernstrom and Knights, "Men in Motion," p. 35.
24. Of course, the loss of community may also be viewed as personal liberation from narrow confines. According to this view, the substitution of formal organizations for informal neighborhoods would have been made not frantically but eagerly, and residential mobility would have been an element facilitating the development of a freer urban life rather than one necessitating a painful accommodation.

Michael Feldberg

3

Urbanization as a Cause of Violence: Philadelphia as a Test Case

The ghetto riots which swept through American cities in the 1960s made scholars, politicians, and the general public aware that America was suffering an acute "urban crisis." The destructiveness of collective violence since 1965 has moved historians to reexamine the record of American urban development in order to gain insight into the sources of municipal upheaval.[1] As America's first great nineteenth-century manufacturing city, Philadelphia offers a good test case for many generalizations about urban historical development and its relationship to violence.

Historians often use the concept of "urbanization" to account for human behavior.[2] They have argued that over the centuries, as large numbers of persons flocked to urban settings, they engaged in such positive activities as experimenting with new technologies or evolving new political forms, while, on the negative side, urban migrants abandoned older communal peasant values and faced each other hostilely across revolutionary barricades or ghetto walls.[3] This chapter will examine some examples of violence in Jacksonian Philadelphia to test the usefulness of the hypothesis that urbanization leads to increasing levels of collective violence.

In studying New York, Boston, and Philadelphia in the Jackson period, several historians have found a direct correlation between violence and urbanization.[4] Sometime between 1830 and 1850 these northeastern cities developed into America's first metropolitan areas. The historians have provided a model for this growth: ragged immigrants and rural natives crowded into rapidly expanding cities and suburbs which had but a few years earlier been large but well-integrated eighteenth-century towns. Philadelphia as late as 1830, Sam Bass Warner, Jr., tells us, "had been a booming town, but still a place whose manners followed the familiar paths of English and American provincial towns." [5] Until the 1820s, Boston was a "community," "still relatively homogeneous, small, and able to govern itself by the traditional town meeting." [6] Even in bustling New York, social behavior prior to 1830 was controlled less by formal law enforcement than by informal deference patterns.[7]

According to the conventional accounts, this congenial pattern of civic harmony simply broke down. "After 1820, [Boston] grew in area, population, and complexity, and was transformed by immigration and industrialization." [8] In New York, the 1830s and 1840s were "decades of rapid population growth with sharp increases in immigration, heightened distinctions between class, ethnic, and religious groups with consequent social strain, and a dizzying cycle of economic boom and bust." [9] "Respectable" native-born middle- and upper-class citizens segregated themselves residentially and politically from the "turbulent" and "degraded" foreigners and lower classes. A description of New York's social structure summarizes the conventional view of Boston and Philadelphia as well:

> No longer was the city a homogeneous community with a common culture and a shared system of values and moral standards. Rather, the city was becoming a mosaic of subcommunities, separated from one another by barriers of class and culture and by attitudes and behavior derived from different traditions, or in the case of many immigrants, by the destruction of tradition.[10]

Local government, long accustomed to serving as few functions as possible, proved unable to exercise adequate social control when community deference patterns dissolved.

Liberated from the constraining consensus of eighteenth-century town or rural values, our model tells us, new groups in Jacksonian cities retrogressed into increasing amounts of collective violence. With their sense of community gone, and professional police forces not yet established, the native and immigrant working classes acted out their "frustration, prejudice, and anger" through "fragmentary outbursts" in the streets.[11] According to Warner, Philadelphia's "successive riots from 1834 to 1849 show in a series of brief dramatic episodes the interaction of the most important elements of the big-city era: industrialization, immigration, mixed patterns of settlement, changing styles of leadership, weakness of municipal institutions, and shifting orientations of politics." [12] Ethnic politics especially helped to replant those "uprooted" from the European

sod and integrate them into the peaceable processes which supposedly characterize American politics.[13]

In sum, the conventional model attempts to explain urban collective violence by stressing broken traditions, uprooted cultures,
overcrowding, and economic deprivation. The emphasis is on discontinuity: torn out of familiar settings and placed under hardship
in their new urban environment, various groups acted out their
hostilities by turning on each other. We must beware, however, of
swallowing whole the "frustration" theory of urban violence.[14]
Disorientation and misfortune often lead as easily to apathy and
isolation as to energetic collective action such as rioting or looting.
By stressing disruption and discontinuity, the conventional historical model overlooks the ongoing political and cultural cohesion
which are necessary for collective action by all but the most random
crowd.[15]

The conventional model for collective violence has other short-
comings, particularly when applied to Jacksonian Philadelphia.
First, by stressing only the confrontations among newly displaced
groups, the standard historical model becomes somewhat ahistori-
cal. John Alexander's chapter in the present volume, for example,
points out that Philadelphia had probably never been the peaceable eighteenth-century town which Warner envisaged. Similar
evidence has now come to light about the violent nature of other
major eighteenth-century European and American cities.[16] Secondly, the model fails to account for the ways in which collective
violence was an integral and "legitimate" part of the city's political
system, a tool in the "social bargaining" process by which classes
and interest groups tested each other's strength.[17] Finally, while
rapid population expansion and the arrival of immigrants (mostly
Irish) did make Philadelphia a battleground for new groups (see
Bruce Laurie's chapter on the increasing number of firemen's
fights caused by ethnic hostility), violence had long been an
integral part of the city's native-born artisans' cultural heritage, a
heritage which antedated the mass arrival of Irishmen.

Thus no simple explanation can account for all the forms of
collective violence in Jacksonian Philadelphia. And there was
much collective violence to explain: in 1834 an anti-Negro riot
broke out in the southside ghetto; in 1842 fighting between blacks
and whites erupted again; in 1835 a crowd threw abolitionist
literature into the Delaware River and in 1837 a similar group

burned abolitionist-built Pennsylvania Hall; on the labor front, the city's handloom weavers fought violent battles with their employers and the sheriff's posse in a series of strikes between 1842 and 1844. This train of violence was capped by the massive and prolonged Native American riots of May and July of 1844 in which thousands of native-born Protestants, mostly from the artisan class, battled first immigrant Irish Catholics and then the state militia. The Native American Riots took at least thirty lives. By any measure, the period from 1835 to 1850 was the most violent in Philadelphia's history.[18]

But collective violence had long been an expected and even tolerated aspect of Philadelphia life. In the eighteenth century, combative sailors were hired by patrician politicians to keep opposition voters from the polls, women tore down fences to permit their pigs to graze on private property, and Market Street residents destroyed a partially completed market house whose construction in their neighborhood they opposed.[19] Sociologists have labeled this form of violence "instrumental," that is, well-defined, clearly limited, goal-oriented behavior. Especially for the "lower orders," whose economic and political power was relatively weak, violence was an effective means for obtaining desired ends.[20] While illegal, such goal-oriented violence was considered legitimate by its users.

A large part of Philadelphia's "bargaining" through violence was directed toward economic issues. Major cities on both sides of the Atlantic in the late eighteenth and early nineteenth centuries proved highly sensitive to economic fluctuations, especially price rises and food shortages. The urban working classes often responded to national trends by trying to control local prices and wages through coercion. In Philadelphia especially, skilled craftsmen were in the forefront of these efforts. Violent strikes were the most effective means of persuading employers to accede to wage demands. Violence had other uses as well. The "Wilson Riot" during the Revolutionary War, for example, was a classic eighteenth-century food riot in which the rioters attempted to reestablish what they considered just market prices for food and punish "forestallers." [21] Even the anti-Irish Native American riots of 1844, so intimately related to religious differences between Protestants and Catholics, had economic overtones. Part of the hostility between the natives and Irish stemmed from the threat which the unskilled immigrants posed to native-born craftsmen.[22] The riots served for a while to discourage Irishmen from migrating to Philadelphia and providing additional labor for the city's early factories, or a cut-rate work force for the handloom weaving industry.

But it would be an oversimplification to "reduce" working-class violence in Philadelphia to purely economic causes. Violence was central to the city's artisan culture. While little evidence about artisan life has survived to sit on archive shelves, what evidence we do have about artisan life tells us that their culture was a vibrant and belligerent one.[23] In the 1830s and 1840s, Philadelphia still led the nation in manufactures (New York would soon surpass her). The city's predominance was built less on the volume of invested capital than on the high number of skilled workers in her population. Most craftsmen were native-born Protestants who traced their American lineage to the Colonial period. Traditionally, the city's artisans were fiercely proud of their standing as skilled craftsmen. They gloried in the fact that "the name PHILADELPHIA MECHANIC [had] become synonymous with skill and superiority in workmanship." [24] They enjoyed the "highest incomes and status of any wage earners and were psychologically the most firmly wedded to the social values and practices of the traditional artisan." [25] Among Philadelphia journeymen, in fact, allegiance to the customs and practices of individual crafts far outweighed class consciousness, so that city-wide labor unions had only one brief period of success before the Civil War.[26]

Aside from the shared values and camaraderie which artisans developed in their workshops, craft cohesion was reinforced by such factors as occupational clustering in neighborhoods,[27] socializing in taverns, and the many violent strikes which punctuated labor relations in such industries as shoemaking and weaving. Journeymen within a craft found their ties drawn more closely together by fights against the sheriff's posse or groups of scabbing workers. Even in the city's first nativist riot in 1828, the natives attacked not random Irish victims but Irish weavers who congregated at a Kensington tavern. The nativists' fury was redoubled when the weavers hung their banner from the tavern's second-floor window.[28]

The native artisans gave philosophical legitimacy to their violent defense of social values or economic interests by propounding their own version of American political and social theory. The artisan claimed equality and individual rights as the result of

American victory in the War for Independence.[29] Discussing this
legacy, David Montgomery asserts that "the mechanics proudly
preserved an intellectual heritage blended of Ben Franklin's maxims
and Tom Paine's 'Rights of Man.' "[30] Referring to the artisan
districts of Southwark and Moyamensing (scene of the Native
American riots in July 1844), Warner has described them as
"intensely patriotic, white-equalitarian, anti-Negro, anti-foreigner,
in short, strong followers of the old radical Revolutionary tradition."[31] Drawing on this heritage, the craftsman argued that he
need never take a back seat to men from any class in society. The
butchers' guild, for example, liked to think of itself as a "fraternity
of men" which no less than merchants or bankers was "essential
and indispensable to the body politic."[32] On the Fourth of July,
orators praised the craftsmen as the city's backbone, and on election day middle-class candidates vied for the title "workingman's
friend."[33]

Violence fit neatly into the artisans' version of their Revolutionary heritage. In the Jacksonian era, the Philadelphia artisan still
clung to his "right of resistance" to governmental abuse or unjust
market relationships, and he understood the notion of "popular
sovereignty" to mean that the rights of minorities had to be sub-
servient to the will of the majority.[34] When government failed to
act, such as in enforcing the assize of bread [35] or protecting the
community from disruptive ideas, the working classes considered
it legitimate to take limited though violent action on their own
behalf. Such a formulation helps explain the Wilson riot, the
burning of Pennsylvania Hall, or the Kensington anti-railroad riots
described below. Pauline Maier expressed it well when she defined
American majoritarian forms of collective violence as "extralegal"
defense of "community interest."[36] In all these cases, action was
motivated, or at least rationalized, by appeals to natural justice,
constitutional rights, and the notion that community interest super-
seded private rights.

Such a struggle between community and private rights precipitated one of the era's little known but most characteristic "instrumental" riots, the Kensington anti-railroad riot of 1840. Kensington's struggle against the railroad lasted for two years. Early in
1840, the Pennsylvania state legislature granted the Philadelphia
and Trenton Railroad a right of way down Kensington's busy
Front Street, despite protests from the entire Philadelphia delega-

tion. Because they ran right on the street, spewing hot coals from their smokestacks, railroads were then considered a dangerous innovation. Their roadbeds tended to block local wagon traffic, and Kensington's draymen were among those most actively opposed to the grant. Front Street property owners opposed the trains because they posed a threat to their wooden homes and shops. Their hostility was further increased by the legislature's failure to include any financial compensation for the disruption during construction or the decline in property values. The district's tenants, mostly weavers, opposed the railroad for the nuisance and dangers it posed to pedestrians and children playing in the street. When the legislature refused to reverse its grant to the railroad and the courts upheld the grant's legality, the various factions in Third Ward Kensington united to take limited but direct action on their own.

The weavers and draymen entered into coalition with their middle-class landlords and employers, as well as professional politicians, to resist the railroad. Their diverse interests were reconciled under the umbrella of appeals to natural and constitutional rights and resistance to legislative tyranny, rhetorical formulas with roots in radical Revolutionary ideology. Today we would label the issue one of community control. The railroad's opponents argued that "a *public* highway . . . could not be legally or properly chartered out to a *private* corporation," especially since the local community opposed that charter. A strongly Locofoco neighborhood, Third Ward Kensington called for "No Monopoly! Free Passage to All!" "We ask nothing but what is Right, and Submit to nothing Wrong. . . . The Constitution protects the People in the Use of their Highways." [37] To protect these constitutional guarantees, both respectable property owners and turbulent weavers used their right of resistance to unjust laws.

The neighborhood's struggle against the company shifted tactically from violent confrontation to legal action to political organization and back to violence. The force employed in these instances was clearly limited in its goals: the crowd destroyed railroad ties and diverted shipments of rails. No one was seriously injured, much less killed. Violence was used only in conjunction with political organization to persuade the company to give up its grant. Violence was no more than an extension of the bargaining process.[38]

Space does not permit more than a cursory summary of the

struggle. In all, the anti-railroad fight lasted from March 1840 through June 1842, when the legislature was finally persuaded to repeal the charter. For two years, whenever work gangs came to dig up Front Street and lay ties, neighborhood men, women, and children used the upturned paving stones ("ground apples," as they were known) to drive the work gangs off. They then burned the ties. This scene recurred at least four different times between March 2, 1840, and February 3, 1841. In mid-March 1840, the county sheriff obtained an injunction deputizing all Kensington citizens into his posse and making those who opposed his efforts to guard the workmen subject to prosecution for treason. Despite the severe penalty, the railroad thought it best to suspend work rather than risk any further loss of supplies and willing laborers.[39] On another occasion, the sheriff arrived in Kensington with a posse intent on guarding the workers, but even this group, armed with maces, was driven off by weavers using their dye-sticks and paving stones as weapons. That evening, a crowd attacked and burned Emery's Tavern, Front and Phoenix Streets, which had served as the posse's headquarters. While Emery was temporarily out of business, the real loser was Joseph Naglee, president of the Philadelphia and Trenton, who rented the tavern to Emery.[40]

While the Third Ward crowd held up construction, Philadelphia's Democratic party leadership was busily making political capital out of this David and Goliath confrontation between popular rights and monopoly capitalism. Among the politicos prominent in the agitation were William English, one of the original founders of the Philadelphia Workingmen's Party and a perennial foe of corporate charters; Edward Penniman, a Democratic "workingman's friend" then sitting in the state legislature; ex-Congressman and Southwark tavern keeper Lemuel Paynter, later a leading nativist; and renegade patrician Charles Jared Ingersoll, lone Democrat in an old-line Whig family. These politicians persuaded Democratic governor David R. Porter to pardon all those convicted of burning Emery's tavern. They also led a Kensington rally which called on the district commissioners to refrain from reimbursing the sheriff for his efforts to maintain order. The meeting also urged the commissioners to confiscate as a public nuisance any railroad property left in the streets.[41]

In this manner the struggle dragged on sporadically for two years: violence, political rallies, new court appeals to overthrow the railroad's charter, a dropping-off of interest in the subject, renewed attempts in the dead of winter to start construction again (apparently the long, hot summer was a factor in Philadelphia in 1840 as well as today), another violent response by the Third Ward's residents, and further lobbying in the state legislature by both sides in the dispute.[42] In May 1841 the state legislature even offered to pay reparations to Front Street's property owners, but at that late date such a gesture was not enough to win the acquiescence of owners or their tenants. Finally, in June 1842, the *Ledger* reported the end of hostilities between the railroad directors and the people. After several "investigations and enactments" by the state legislature, Kensington representative Thomas M. Scott finally persuaded that body to repeal the railroad's grant. His achievement made him a local hero, and the neighborhood celebrated the repeal with two days of illuminations and street parties. Even the *Ledger,* which in so many other cases condemned the city's propensity to "mob rule," blamed this instance of "discord and contention" on the legislature's "misdirected legislation." [43] Thus even Philadelphia's most law-and-order press vindicated the neighborhood's belief in its right of resistance to unjust laws. The railroad was never built.

The Third Ward's handloom weavers were centrally involved in other violent episodes during this era. Some, as Irish Catholics, defended their homes and churches in the Native American riots of 1844, and almost all handloom weavers, regardless of ethnicity or religion, defended their occupation from extinction throughout the 1840s.[44] In this latter instance, the handloom weavers were struggling against their absorption into the industrial factory system.[45] They resisted by forming craft associations, making political appeals to public sympathy, and by using violence—much the same variety of tactics with which they had fought the Philadelphia and Trenton. The narrative of their struggle against both power looms and the industrial work discipline which the looms demanded is too long to permit complete retelling. What interests us here is the role which characteristically goal-oriented violence played in the weavers' struggle for survival.

While handloom weaving was not a highly skilled occupation— in fact it suffered from a constant influx of unskilled workers, many of them immigrants, who were able to learn the trade in a short period of time—the handloom weavers apparently had a high degree of craft cohesion built on a long and violent history in Philadelphia.[46] Like several of the more skilled occupations, hand-loom weavers were victims of the "Transportation Revolution." Due to the reorganization of the national market and the introduction of merchant jobbers,[47] Philadelphia's wool weaving industry was, by the 1840s, concentrated in the hands of eighteen employers. Banded together in the Philadelphia Handloom Manufacturers Association, these bosses employed most of the city's 4,000 hand-loom weavers. Because power looms had not yet infiltrated the Philadelphia wool industry, wool weavers, unlike their counter-parts in the cotton industry, did not work in factories. But more efficient power looms located elsewhere in the country were able to keep handloom wages at or below subsistence levels, and the economic recovery of 1843–44 had little impact on the wool weavers. A journeyman, assisted by his wife and children and working a six- or seven-day week for sixteen hours per day, could earn little more than three dollars per week. Furthermore, the concentration of employment opportunities in relatively few hands meant that employers could begin to exercise the kind of dis-cipline which was used in Manayunk's cotton mills or the mills of New England. Although the handloom weavers worked in small shops or at home and could not be as intensely overseen as the mill hands, they were constrained by other forms of industrial discipline. Employers started demanding that, unless an entire batch of work given out at the start of a month was completed when returned at the end of the month, a weaver would get no pay at all, even for the finished portion. Some employers paid their weavers in store orders, forcing them to shop at the boss's own shop or one of his choosing. Such practices often meant that the weavers had to pay inflated prices for their purchases, an addi-tional 10 per cent being the figure most often cited.[48]

In short, the handloom weavers found themselves part of an increasingly marginal occupation. They were losing control not only over their wage rates but over conditions of their labor as well. Squeezed by their employers, who in turn claimed that the national market was squeezing them, the weavers turned to strikes to defend themselves from increased discipline and further wage cuts. When failure threatened their efforts, they turned to violence and intimidation to keep their strikes and hopes alive.

The handloom weavers had a continuing history of rioting and striking. Although the period from 1842 through 1844 was the most violent, the struggle to defend their wage rates began with the Depression of 1837 and continued until the Civil War, when the last weavers were replaced by power looms.[49] Industry-wide bargaining between the employers' association and the weavers was reopened every season (approximately half-yearly), but occasionally the employers unilaterally announced a wage decrease. Claiming that the market would not bear the current wages, they announced one such cut in August 1842. The Moyamensing weavers immediately turned out, called a meeting in Wharton Market, and appointed a committee to negotiate with the employers. The journeymen's delegation persuaded fifteen of the eighteen manufacturers to restore the old rates, but three would not relent. Their resistance made it impossible for the other fifteen to honor the old rate, since weavers could always be found to work for the other three at the new rate. The weavers therefore decided to keep everyone from working at the new, lower rate.[50]

August 1842 was still a period of depression, and many weavers preferred to "scab" rather than sustain the hardship of a strike. The Moyamensing weavers felt compelled to use violence, intimidation, loom smashing, and especially the technique of pouring acid on any scab-woven cloth. Having shut down all production in Moyamensing using these tactics, the district's weavers in early September decided to extend the strike to Kensington. Marching north in a body, they entered houses, destroyed goods, and threw scabbing workers' looms in the street. They entered two "factories" —probably no more than large workshops—belonging to Messrs. Floyd and Baird and forced or persuaded all hands to turn out. The weaving industry was kept more or less at a standstill in this manner until the spring of 1843.[51]

The strike continued along these lines until May of 1844. In that month, the strike was upstaged by the Native American riots which swept through Kensington's weaving district. Until then, however, the strike pattern remained unchanged: scabs would occasionally attempt to resume work at the reduced rates offered by some manufacturers; a strike vigilance committee would march, sometimes with fife and drum, to the offender's house, pour acid on his goods, break his loom or furniture, and explain to his neighbors the necessity and justice of their deeds.[52] We do not know how the strikers managed to support themselves for nearly

two years without work. Perhaps some of the employers continued
to pay the old, higher rate; perhaps some men took other jobs
while maintaining their vigilance. In any event, for two years
certain manufacturers found their goods under constant attack.[53]
No one was ever seriously injured or killed, however, and with one
exception only the intransigent employers ever used guns. Two
notable incidents of the long struggle further illustrated the characteristically limited nature of Jacksonian labor violence: the
attack on Kempton's cotton mill and the battle of Nanny Goat
Market.

The attack on Kempton's mill in Manayunk was one of the
weavers' few attempts (perhaps the only one, in fact) to destroy
the power looms which were the cause of their low wages and
unemployment. Although power looms had not yet replaced the
wool weavers, apparently Kempton's power looms "manufactured,
by a much cheaper process, an article of cotton goods . . .
hitherto . . . made by the handloom weavers." On September 23,
1842, Sheriff Henry Morris heard a rumor that some Kensington
weavers planned to attack the mill. Morris roused Kempton and
encouraged him to arm his friends in defense of his property.
Manayunk's constables and additional volunteers patrolled all roads
leading to the town. Around 1:30 a. m., a band of seven constables
encountered a group of thirty to fifty men north of Manayunk.
After the strangers offered them a friendly greeting the constables
turned to go. Shots rang out and two constables fell wounded.
Hearing the sound of gunfire, lookouts began ringing the factory
bells, obviously a prearranged signal in case of trouble. The
sounding of the bells must have carried the same meaning to the
band of strangers, and, fearing that Kempton's mill would be
heavily protected, they disappeared in the direction of Kensington.[54]

The strikers' most brazen encounter with authority occurred on
January 11, 1843, about six months after the strike first began.
On the ninth, approximately 300 Moyamensing strikers turned out
for a solidarity march through the district. Following the usual
pattern, they broke into scab weavers' homes and destroyed their
goods. When they reached the South Street border of the Old City,
the mayor and his deputies turned them back. Determined to
march in Kensington, the weavers gathered there two days later.
Marching and entering homes again, the weavers were met by
Kensington aldermen Potts and Lukens who tried to arrest one

Thomas Lynch for rioting. The weavers severely beat Lukens for his efforts. That afternoon, the weavers vowed to punish any other peace officers who interfered with the strike. Sheriff William Porter, the governor's brother and successor to the late Sheriff Morris, arrived soon afterwards in hopes of addressing the meeting. When his pleas for peaceable behavior were hooted down, Porter decided to raise a posse and disperse the strikers.

Returning from the city in late afternoon, Porter and his men were given a rousing reception at the Nanny Goat Market, Master and Washington streets in the heart of the Third Ward.[55] A volley of stones and occasional bullets dispersed the unarmed lawmen. Only Porter and three others stood to confront the weavers, and they were quickly overwhelmed. Knocked down and badly bruised by stones, Porter was allowed to escape before he was seriously injured. The strikers' victory was dulled somewhat the next day when eight individuals were arrested for assault.[56]

We must piece together our information on how the strike turned out. There were two more periods of violence between the Nanny Goat Market battle and May of 1844: in Moyamensing from August 11 to September 2, 1843, and in both Kensington and Moyamensing in November 1843. The *Ledger* reported a weavers' rally on May 1, 1844, in Kensington, less than a week before the great Native American riots broke out. Until that time, apparently, the strike had met with some small success, for the paper reported that the weavers were earning $4.25 per week, no great sum but better than the $3.00 of 1842. When the Native American riots tore through Kensington, however, destroying homes and looms, the Irish weavers were in no position to resist their employers. The manufacturers reduced wage rates and had no trouble finding weavers willing to work.[57] The strike resumed in the winter of 1846, and periodic strikes occurred right into the Civil War period, until finally the wool weavers disappeared into factories or other occupations.

The anti-railroad and weavers' riots are far from a complete sample of the many varieties of violence which marked Jacksonian Philadelphia. But they do demonstrate certain of the general tendencies which characterized much of the violence in that period. They clearly display a goal-oriented, purposive nature—in the sociologist's language they were "instrumental." The riots were limited in extent, rarely bloodthirsty or brutal, and often aimed at property rather than persons. They also point up the cohesiveness of occupational groups within Philadelphia's "turbulent" classes. To illustrate their self-confidence and collective strength, the Kensington weavers warned all law enforcement officials not to intervene in their strike. One can easily imagine the weavers or the anti-railroad rioters gathered at local pubs, reliving the day's exploits against the posse. Above all, these riots reveal the complex interaction between the rioters' traditional definition of their rights, their willingness to fight for clearly discernable self-interests, and the ineffectiveness of public authority to control their behavior. The crowd's interpretation of the doctrine of resistance to oppression legitimated its violence; the struggle to protect property, livelihood or values made that violence appear essential to each of the groups which used it.

All of which is to say that violence in Jacksonian Philadelphia was conditioned by the complex interaction of many factors beyond "urbanization" or "industrialization." It is true that both phenomena threw together more diverse and larger groups than ever before in a city environment and that the institutions of government and community regulation were put under unprecedented strain. But the role of the crowd in Jacksonian Philadelphia cannot be explained simply as a result of dislocation and crowding. We must define more precisely than we have done so far the traditional, ideological nature of urban violence in the Jacksonian culture.[58] We must further define the ways in which violence was part of, rather than distinct from, the normal processes of the Jacksonian political and economic bargaining system. We might also try to establish more concretely the relationships between traditional culture and other nineteenth-century transformations such as industrialization, economic growth, bureaucratization, and the other grand hypotheses which are used to explain the entire range of historical development in modernizing societies.

NOTES

1. See especially Sam Bass Warner, Jr., *The Private City: Philadelphia in Three Periods of its Growth* (Philadelphia: Univ. of Pennsylvania Press, 1968).
2. The definition of urbanization used here is the simplest one agreed on by social scientists: the in-migration of population to cities.

3. For a review of urban historiography see Lewis Mumford, *The City in History* (New York: Harcourt, Brace, and World, 1961).

4. This chapter is particularly concerned with Warner's *The Private City;* Roger Lane, *Policing the City: Boston, 1822–1887* (Cambridge, Mass.: Harvard Univ. Press, 1967); James F. Richardson, *History of the New York Police* (New York: Oxford Univ. Press, 1970).

5. Warner, *Private City,* p. 49.

6. Oscar Handlin, in Lane, *Policing the City,* p. vii.

7. Richardson, *New York Police,* p. 25. Cf. Lane, *Policing the City,* p. 2.

8. Handlin, in Lane, *Policing the City,* p. viii.

9. Richardson, *New York Police,* p. 25.

10. Ibid.

11. Warner, *Private City,* p. 125.

12. Ibid.

13. Ibid., p. 156.

14. H. L. Nieburg, *Political Violence* (New York: St. Martin's Press, 1969), p. 39.

15. Random crowds are those which are "casually drawn together" at events like baseball games or sidewalk speeches. Most significant crowd violence does not stem from this type of group. See George Rudé's distinction between "direct contact," "face-to-face," "aggressive" crowds which have had the greatest historical impact and random crowds in *The Crowd in History* (New York: Wiley, 1964), pp. 3–4.

16. The growing bibliography now includes Pauline Maier, "Popular Uprisings and Civil Authority in Eighteenth-Century America," *William and Mary Quarterly* 27 (Jan. 1970): 3–35; Leonard Richards, *Gentlemen of Property and Standing* (New York: Oxford Univ. Press, 1970); Jesse Lemisch, "Jack Tar in the Street, Merchant Seamen in the Politics of Revolutionary America," *William and Mary Quarterly* 25 (1968): 371–401; Gordon S. Wood, "A Note on Mobs in the American Revolution," *William and Mary Quarterly* 23 (1966): 635–42.

17. Nieburg, *Political Violence,* p. 5.

18. For good discussion of these riots see Warner, *Private City,* chap. 7.

19. William T. Parsons. "The Bloody Election of 1742," *Pennsylvania History* 36 (July 1969); Elizabeth M. Geffen, "Violence in Philadelphia in the 1840's and 1850's," *Pennsylvania History* 36 (Oct. 1969):382.

20. The use of violence has never been a fully accepted part of the American political process as it was in eighteenth-century Europe because the white American male has had the vote since the Revolution. Supposedly, all differences in America could be solved at the ballot box. But, as this chapter will demonstrate, economic inequalities between the upper classes and the artisan and lower classes gave disproportionate power to the upper classes, an imbalance which the lower orders tried to redress through violence and coercion when the ballot box proved inadequate.

21. Warner, *Private City,* pp. 45–46.

22. For a discussion of the Native American riots of 1844 in relation to the economic strains on native-born artisans, see Michael Feldberg,

"The Philadelphia Riots of 1844: A Social History" (unpublished diss., Univ. of Rochester, 1970), chap. 2. Fully 75 percent of the nativist participants in the Native American riots were skilled artisans. Their preoccupation with the threat of unskilled immigrants is reflected in their formation of the United Order of American Mechanics.

23. Beginnings towards the history of pre-industrial American artisans have been made by David Montgomery. "The Working Classes of the Pre-Industrial American City, 1780–1830," *Labor History* 9 (Winter 1968):3–22.

24. Edwin Freedley, *Philadelphia and Its Manufactures* (Philadelphia: E. Young, 1857), pp. 72–73.

25. Montgomery, "Working Classes," pp. 7–9.

26. For Philadelphia labor unions in the period 1827–37, see John R. Commons, ed., *History of Labor in the United States* (New York: Macmillan, 1921), vol. 1.

27. For a discussion of artisan neighborhood clustering, see Sam Bass Warner, "If All the World Were Philadelphia," *American Historical Review* 74 (Oct. 1969):38.

28. Scharf and Westcott, *History of Philadelphia* (Philadelphia: L. H. Everts, 1887), vol. 1, p. 623.

29. Alfred Young, "After Carl Becker: The Mechanics and New York City Politics, 1774–1801," *Labor History* 5 (Fall 1964):215–24.

30. Montgomery, "Working Classes," p. 13.

31. Warner, *Private City,* p. 88.

32. *Public Ledger,* July 19, 1836.

33. Ibid., Oct. 2, 1842.

34. For a discussion of "popular sovereignty" in the context of collective violence, see Richard Maxwell Brown, "The History of Extralegal Violence in Support of Community Values," *Violence in America,* Thomas Rose, ed. (New York: Vintage Books, 1969), p. 90.

35. *Public Ledger,* Jan. 4, 1837.

36. Pauline Maier, "Popular Uprisings," p. 5.

37. *Public Ledger,* June 22, 1842.

38. Nieburg, *Political Violence,* p. 5.

39. *Public Ledger,* March 3, 13, and 14, 1840.

40. Ibid., July 28, 1840.

41. Ibid., Aug. 4, 1840.

42. Ibid., Feb. 17; December 16, 1841; June 22, 1842.

43. Ibid., June 22, 1842.

44. Unfortunately, it is impossible to know the percentage of Irish and native handloom weavers or the length of residence in America for the Irish weavers. Scattered evidence suggests, however, that many of the Irish weavers were long-term residents rather than recent arrivals (possibly Protestant rather than Catholics), and they might easily have adopted the native artisan sense of craft cohesion despite their Irish nativity.

45. See William A. Sullivan, *The Industrial Worker in Pennsylvania* (Har-

risburg: Pennsylvania Historical and Museum Commission, 1955), for a fuller discussion of this struggle.

46. See Scharf and Westcott, *History of Philadelphia,* 1:623.

47. Stuart Blumin, "Social Mobility in a Nineteenth-Century City: Philadelphia, 1820–1860" (unpublished diss., Univ. of Pennsylvania, 1968), chap. 1.

48. *Public Ledger,* September 2, 1842.

49. For a discussion of Philadelphia's handloom weaving industry, see Sam Bass Warner, Jr., "Innovation and the Industrialization of Philadelphia, 1800–1850," in *The Historian and the City,* Burchard and Handlin, eds. (Cambridge, Mass.: MIT Press, 1963), pp. 67–69.

50. *Public Ledger,* Sept. 2, 1842.

51. Ibid., Aug. 29; Sept. 3, 8; Oct. 27, 1842.

52. See, for example, the account of the attack on Joseph Reimy in the *Public Ledger,* Oct. 27, 1842.

53. Ibid., Aug. 21, 26, 28, 29; Sept. 2, 22; Nov. 22, 1843; Jan. 20, 22; Feb. 7, 28; March 22; April 30; May 1, 1844.

54. Ibid., Sept. 26, 1842.

55. The Nanny Goat Market was a social center for the Third Ward's population. When, in the 1844 Native American riots, the American Republican party attempted to adjourn its May 6th rally to the market house, the local Irish responded with the cry, "Keep the damned natives out of *our* market," and the great riots were underway (emphasis added).

56. *Public Ledger,* Jan. 12, 13, 1843.

57. *Spirit of the Times,* Sept. 13, 1848.

58. David Grimsted, "Rioting in Its Jacksonian Setting," *American Historical Review* 77:361–77, makes a beginning towards this end. His admirable essay appeared too late to be included in this chapter's central argument.

4

Fire Companies and Gangs in Southwark: The 1840s

A recent history of Philadelphia characterized the second quarter of the nineteenth century as *"par excellence* the era of the urban parish church, the lodge, the benefit association, the social and athletic club, the political club, the fire company, and the gang." These institutions attracted Philadelphians who sought to compensate for the "loss of the old patterns of sociability and informal community." [1] As John Alexander suggests in his chapter on late eighteenth-century Philadelphia, however, such a mystical sense of community may never have existed. It is clear, nevertheless, that private associations did multiply dramatically during the second quarter of the nineteenth century. Gangs were all but unknown before that time, and of some seventy fire companies functioning in 1857, sixty-four of them were formed after 1825. [2] This chapter will examine the rise of gangs and changes in the social composition, roles, and functions of fire companies in the suburban district of Southwark in the 1840s.

Southwark was bordered by the city proper to its north, the Delaware River to its east, and Moyamensing to its west. With roots in the eighteenth century, it was a thriving community of 20,000 people in 1830. Although the population nearly doubled over the next twenty years, the increase for the 1840s (38 percent) lagged far behind the combined growth rate (83 percent) of the other suburban districts. [3] Prior to 1850 most of the residents were native-born Americans, but by that year, as table 4.1 indicates, immigrants dominated the Third Ward and had sizable minorities in the First and Sixth Wards. [4]

While some of these people toiled in industries as traditional as Moyamensing's handloom weaving establishments, others were found in works as modern as the textile mills of Manayunk. Wards Two and Three housed large concentrations of tailors and shoe-

TABLE 4.1 Southwark Population, 1850

			PERCENTAGES			
WARD	Native	Irish	German	English	Black	Other
1	51.1	19.1	17.0	7.7	0.3	4.7
2	75.8	8.0	7.1	4.8	0.8	3.5
3	40.0	34.4	12.0	3.9	5.4	4.2
4	66.0	16.8	4.0	5.5	3.6	4.1
5	72.7	14.0	4.8	5.1	1.5	1.9
6	58.6	20.0	6.8	8.6	1.5	4.5

makers, who, like handloom weavers, either worked at home or boarded and labored with masters in small shops.[5] Hundreds of ship carpenters and joiners, caulkers, riggers, and other artisans involved in shipbuilding plied their trades in a number of private and government-owned shipyards, and legions of sailors, mariners, and laborers serviced the ships they constructed. Southwark's famous iron foundries and machine shops were manned by black-smiths and machinists using some of the most advanced equipment in the world and were owned by the city's most prominent indus-trialists, such as Samuel Merrick and Matthias Baldwin. Merrick's Southwark Foundry provided work for 375 men and cast upwards of 15 tons of pig iron daily in 1852.[6]

The 1830s marked an extraordinary period in the history of this rich matrix of ethnic and occupational groups. Galvanized by trade-union activists espousing a blend of Ricardian socialism and Painite radicalism, wage earners forged an impressive alliance under the aegis of the General Trades' Union of the City and County of Philadelphia.[7] The Trades' Union orchestrated disparate occupa-tional groups by providing a common ground for all of them and mediating jurisdictional disputes. It financed nearly every strike in the county from 1833 to 1844, including the successful general strike for a ten-hour day in June of 1835.[8] Unions of artisans affiliated with the Trades' Union made unprecedented efforts to recruit foreign-born and specialized workers into their ranks.[9] The Union Beneficial Society of Journeymen Cordwainers, Ladies Branch, organized female shoe binders and corders, circulated German translations of broadsides, and elected immigrants to leadership positions.[10] The Association of Journeymen House Carpenters dispatched teams of organizers to the suburban districts, where most of the foreign-born practitioners of their trade resided.[11] Not traditionally concerned with the plight of unskilled laborers and the lower rungs of the working class, artisans about-faced and showed unparalleled compassion for them. The Trades' Union not only subsidized massive strikes of Irish handloom weavers, but also arranged for the legal defense of Irish day laborers on trial for conspiracy in 1836.[12]

Just as trade unions encompassed native-born and foreign-born workers in the 1830s, so did Philadelphia's Democratic party. The Democrats won the respect of most aliens, especially Catholics, by defending their cultural integrity against the nativist cant and schemes of the Whigs. Native-born wage earners admired the party's economic radicalism, and Democrats who violated the prescriptions of economic radicalism jeopardized their position in the party. One such Democrat was Joel Sutherland, the First Congressional District's Representative in Congress from 1828 to 1836. In 1836 he made the fatal mistake of defending state Senator Jesse Burden, who had voted in favor of granting Nicholas Biddle a state charter for his Bank of the United States. The reaction in Southwark was nothing short of devastating. The Democrats split into "bank" and "anti-bank" factions, and each supported candidates in the April elections. Master mechanics Lemuel Paynter and Thomas Grover headed the "anti-bank" ticket, which swept every ward with the aid and blessing of the district's working-men.[13] Maintaining their momentum through the summer and fall with rallies and meetings, the radicals drove Sutherland and Burden from the party at the nominating convention and named Paynter to run for Sutherland's Congressional seat. Sutherland ran as a Whig in the election, but the radical Paynter defeated him soundly.[14]

In the depression of 1837, however, the mood and temperament of Southwark's middle-class and working-class radicals changed markedly. Economic distress depleted the ranks of trade unions and collapsed the General Trades' Union. Unable to combat drastic wage reductions imposed by their employers, native-born workers found scapegoats in immigrants, charging that they under-mined the earnings of Americans by working for pittance. Nativist diatribes replaced the equal rights rhetoric of the 1830s, and when native-born wage earners revitalized their trade unions in the early 1840s, they barred immigrants.[15]

The emergence of cultural issues during the same period nourished the growing ethnic polarization. Demoralized Protestants in need of moral uplift flocked to temperance societies following 1837. Total abstinence had unique appeal among native-born artisans, who either formed temperance-beneficial societies or organized temperance clubs along craft lines.[16] By rallying to temperance and then to prohibition, American Protestants implicitly attacked Catholics, who were so easily identified with the liquor interests.[17]

Subsequent events strained the Democratic party's coalition of native-born Americans and Catholic immigrants to the breaking point. A smouldering dispute over the use of the King James Bible in the public schools came to a head in 1842 when Southwark's school directors summarily dismissed a Catholic teacher for refusing to read the King James Bible. The incident inspired Bishop Francis Patrick Kenrick, the city's leading Catholic prelate, to write to the county school board in protest. Kenrick used the occasion to air a number of affronts to Catholic children in the schools, namely Protestant religious exercises and the use of anti-Catholic textbooks. Kenrick requested permission for Catholic children to have separate religious services using their Bible, the Douay edition. The concluding chapters in this episode have been recorded elsewhere and need not be repeated here.[18]

The Bible question converged with the temperance crusade to breathe new life into nativist American Republican Associations, which had been operating without much success since 1837. By resisting temperance and rejecting the eternal truths contained in the King James Bible, Catholics lent credence to the claims of American Republicans that they were at best unfit for the responsibilities of democratic government and were at worst plotting to overthrow it. American Republicans demanded, therefore, that immigrants not be permitted to vote until they had been in the United States for twenty-one years and that they be barred from holding public office.[19] Southwark was one of the first Democratic strongholds to succumb to nativism. In the local elections in the fall of 1843 Southwarkians returned a slate of American Republicans, which included Paynter and Grover, and kept the district in the American Republican camp for another decade.[20]

Demographic change and the evolving pattern of ethnic politics account for the proliferation of Southwark's fire companies. Population spread southward and westward from a core centered north

of Catharine Street and east of Third Street, creating new neighborhoods and generating more need for firefighting services. Between
1827 and 1846 five companies appeared, making a total of seven,
and four of them were located in the newly-settled areas.[21] Two of
the companies rose in response to the cultural conflict of the
1840s.

Dissidents within the Weccacoe Engine Company formed the
Weccacoe Hose Company following a tiff over temperance. A
faction of budding American Republicans proposed in January
of 1842 that, in order to maintain a "high tone of moral
character," the company "be organized and its affairs conducted
on the principle of total abstinence from intoxicating drinks." [22]
This regulation so alienated non-temperate Americans and Irishmen that they bolted and formed a new company, the Weccacoe
Hose. Their headquarters was situated on Front Street below
Catharine, just two blocks from the parent company. Members
of the Weccacoe Hose Company allied with the Democrats; their
adversaries supported the American Republicans.[23]

Four years later American Republicans living on the border
of the Fifth and Sixth Wards established the Shiffler Hose Company. Their namesake was George Shiffler, the first native American fatality in the anti-Catholic riots of 1844.[24] Most of the
other companies also developed stable political allegiances in the
1840s. Like the Weccacoe Hose Company, the Southwark Fire
and Franklin Fire Companies endorsed the Democratic party.[25]

Of Southwark's seven companies, four were hose companies
and three were fire (or engine) companies. Hose companies
battled fires by connecting fire plugs to pumps carried by the
engine companies. Engine companies had as many as seventy
or as few as forty members, with the average lying somewhere in
between. Hose company memberships were ordinarily half the
size of engine companies. New members gained admission by a
majority vote of the members. Directors, elected from and by the
members, carried speaking horns and spanners (wrenches which
opened the water plugs) and supervised the fighting of fires.[26] The
dues ($1.00 to $5.00 annually) of contributing members, dona-
tions of friends and neighbors, and appropriations of public funds
($300 a year in 1845) supplied operating expenses.[27]

It is probable that the social composition of fire companies
changed in the early part of the century. Prior to the early 1830s

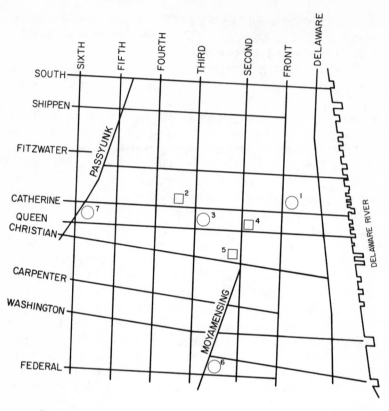

FIG. 4.1   Location of Southwark's fire companies, 1850. 1 = Wec-cacoe Hose, 2 = Franklin Fire, 3 = Niagara Hose, 4 = Weccacoe Engine, 5 = Southwark Fire, 6 = Shiffler Hose, 7 = Marion Hose.

political and social elites provided the leadership and middling social strata the manpower. Thereafter, less prestigious social classes supplanted these rather respectable elements.[28] By the 1840s the companies contained only sprinklings of middle-class occupational groups, namely master craftsmen, small shopkeepers, and clerks. Most of the officers and nearly all of the firefighters were skilled journeymen who owned no real property.[29]

By the 1830s fire companies no longer qualified as genteel dinner clubs, which met in rented inns or halls. Instead, firemen employed public funds to erect engine and hose houses, which successfully competed with local pubs and workshops for their members' attention and devotion. As a critic of the volunteers lamented in 1853: "The engine or hose house is the place where their heart is set upon, their accoutrements and highly embellished carriages their pride and joy." [30] Competition for alertness and efficiency, coupled with the desire for camaraderie, prompted many firemen to "bunk" in their houses. Bunkers passed many an evening socializing over tankards of ale or playing cards while taking turns watching for fires from the house tower. Fire alarms were the occasion for races, as rival companies pulled their tenders and carriages through Southwark's narrow streets. Racing was so ritualistic in the 1840s that the victor was awarded the coveted *"fox's tail*, a cockade formed of red, white and blue ribbons, which . . . [was] transferred from one to the other, as they [were] successful in the contest." [31]

Fire companies also provided status and recognition that the increasingly complex and impersonal urban society denied to artisans and to the marginal middle class. Being elected into a company was a sure sign of a man's acceptance by his neighbors. Executive offices were within reach of the more popular and ambitious firemen, and members bestowed no greater honor than electing one of their number to a directorship. An eyewitness tells us that achieving that office was the "summit of the hopes and wishes of one-half the clerks, counter hoppers, and quill drivers in the city. A trumpet in one hand, a spanner in the other and a lantern affixed to leathern belt around his waist, and a director is in the zenith of his glory. . . ." [32]

Fighting was a time-honored tradition among firemen. Most of the disputes flowed from functional differences. Hose companies fought for water plugs nearest a fire, and engine companies then did battle for prime hose locations. Being first to a fire engendered a great deal of pride, but the honor of extinguishing it was often achieved by fighting off later arrivals. Getting to a fire involved battling enthusiastic rivals who cut tow ropes and jammed carriage spokes with spanners to win the race.[33] Fire companies were thus grass-roots institutions of the first order and competing units in every sense.

Companies formed in the 1840s were especially competitive. Their members lived in circumscribed areas or neighborhoods.

A study of the residences of the adherents of four companies between the years 1846 and 1852 reveals that the newer the company, the greater the tendency of its members to cluster. With few exceptions the followers of the Weccacoe Hose Company (1842) lived within five square blocks of their hose house. No member of the Shiffler Hose Company (1845) resided north of Washington Street or west of Passyunk Avenue.[34] But high rates of intracity geographic mobility, reported in another chapter by Stuart Blumin, accumulated over time and destroyed the neighborhood cohesion of the members of the older companies. The followers of the Franklin Fire (1800) and the Niagara Hose (1827) companies were dispersed throughout Southwark, and some of them lived in the city proper.[35]

Additional competitive elements were introduced in the 1840s with the emergence of street gangs. Groups of young adults and teenagers bearing such names as the Rats, the Bouncers, and the Skinners defaced walls, fences, and buildings with their graffiti, much as they do today in Philadelphia. The *Public Ledger* described them as "armed to the teeth with slug shots, pistols and knives." [36] Nothing provoked them more than intrusions of rival gangs or imagined enemies into their turfs. For example, the Rats and Bouncers constantly feuded because each claimed a part of Southwark as its "place of nativity." [37]

Turf and neighborhood loyalties of the gangs coincided with those of the fire companies. A contemporary wrote that the "toughest" fireman was "gazed upon and followed with awe and reverence by the gangs." [38] Gangs "ran" with their favorite companies, and gang members shifted in and out of them, blurring the distinction between the two institutions. Nothing as drastic occurred in Southwark as in Moyamensing, where the Killers infiltrated and then took over the Moyamensing Hose Company,[39] but the development of Southwark's newer companies paralleled that of the Moyamensing Hose. They were far more receptive to gang members and absorbed them more readily than did the older companies. The Shiffler Hose Company established an alliance with the Shifflers, a gang which shared its turf and which had terrorized the southern portion of the district a year before the hose company appeared.[40] The Weccacoe Hose Company ran to and from fires escorted by the Bouncers, a number of whom held membership in the company.[41]

Fights involving these companies were not brief scuffles, but riots replete with arson, shooting, and murder. Their devotees fought regardless of fires, frequently assaulting Southwarkians who were not necessarily members of either gangs or fire companies. Contemporaries attributed this perceptible escalation in violence to numerous causes, including the lower-class nature of the companies, lax law enforcement, or simply the firemen's love of a fight.[42] All of these explanations contain grains of truth, but the viciousness of the fighting and the identities of the participants suggest that the violence was far more purposive than its observers believed.

In the main, geographic, ethnic, and political factors animated the battles between the Weccacoe and Shiffler Hose companies and their enemies. With resourceful neighborhood followings and passionate, recently-cultivated political allegiances, they focused their anger on neighboring political and/or ethnic groups and fire companies. They fought to regulate who lived near them, who socialized at their pubs and taverns, and which companies serviced their people. The fighting was more intense than in the past because more was at stake than just competing claims to fire plugs and hoses. These firemen waged battles in order to control their neighborhoods.[43]

Located at the intersection of Catharine and Front Streets, the Weccacoe Hose Company ran west on Catharine to answer fires in western Southwark. The route took the Weccacoes past the Franklin Fire Company's house on Catharine between Third and Fourth Streets. Depending on their mood, the Franklins greeted the intruders with either brickbats or epithets, and the companies fought whenever their paths crossed.[44] On one occasion, in June of 1845, a contingent of watchmen aborted the Weccacoes' attempt to storm their rival's house with the aid of a musket.[45] But since both companies were Democratic, they were amenable to compromise. After the Weccacoes captured and destroyed the Franklin's tender in May of 1847, the disputants arranged a meeting so that "good feelings might be restored and a breach of the peace prevented." [46] The parley produced an agreement whose details are unknown, but which created a lasting peace.

The Weccacoes harbored an uncompromising hostility toward their neighboring political enemy, however, the American Republican Weccacoe Engine Company, from which they had

seceded in 1842. The Weccacoes provoked most of the street
fights which characterized this rivalry.[47] In late June of 1844,
they resolved to deliver a coup de grâce and marched to the engine
house under the cover of darkness. Expecting the visitors, the
engine men fired muskets from the upper floor of their house and
scattered the mob. The Weccacoes carried their wounded to
Diehl's Tavern opposite their hose house and prepared for another
assault with a musket of their own. This assault also failed when
watchmen, aroused by the musket fire of the first encounter,
followed the mob to the tavern, ordered it to disperse, and con-
fiscated the weapon. The engine company's president then requested assistance from Alderman Charles Hortz, an American
Republican himself. On his orders a posse of sixty plus the Wayne
Artillery guarded the engine house for the next few nights. The
show of force prevented further incidents.[48]

The companies clashed a number of times in the following
years, but on the night of February 4, 1850, the Weccacoes finally
achieved their goal of putting the engine company out of commission. Four of them, including Levi Fort, a shoemaker and
secretary of the company, were completing the last leg of a
weekend excursion to the neighborhood taverns. The drunken
quartet first considered mounting an attack on the Shiffler Hose
house, but settled on burning out the Weccacoe Engine Company.
Masterminded by Carson, the plan was executed flawlessly. The
arsonists divided into two groups. One broke into the engine
house, tied the tender to a post to insure its being conflagrated,
ignited a pile of wood shavings, and fled. The other stole the
spanner of the Southwark Fire Company, which arrived to
extinguish the blaze. Unable to open a fire plug, the Southwark
had to wait for another company, and by the time one arrived
the fire had consumed the first floor of the newly-erected, three-
story building, causing over $2,000 in damages.[49]

The American Republican Shiffler Hose Company protected its
turf as belligerently as did the Weccacoes. Incomplete membership lists prevent determining if its members attacked a gathering
of Germans in 1849, but a year later they were clearly the
culprits in a similar incident.[50] On September 3 a group of
Germans celebrated in the upper floor of a tavern on Front Street
below Hazel in the native-American-dominated Fifth Ward. Their
noisy merriment attracted a mob of Shifflers, whose hose house

stood less than two blocks away. Forcing its way into the tavern, the mob stabbed one German and severely beat three more. The Shifflers then wrecked the inside of the building to warn the proprietor that he should exercise more discretion in renting his facilities.[51]

The Shifflers' principal opponent was the Irish Catholic and Democratic Moyamensing Hose Company. Although each company fought to control its neighborhood, an alliance with the Killers made the Moyamensings far more aggressive than the Shifflers. Most of Southwark's gangs and volunteer firemen recognized the Killers' "perfect supremacy" of eastern Moyamensing and rarely ventured there after 1846.[52] So the Killers and the Moyamensings carried the fight to Southwark and to the Shifflers in particular. Driven by an intense hatred of Catholics, the Shifflers willingly accepted the challenge.

The Killers' favorite tactic was to ignite a fire in Southwark, retreat to the alleys lining the Shifflers' rout, ambush them, and abscond with their carriage. They launched four ambushes in the summer of 1849 before they successfully wrestled away the Shifflers' carriage.[53] Fighting intensified with each encounter, and before long neither side left for a fire without carrying muskets and duck guns.

Firearms were standard weapons in January of 1850 when the Killers set fire to a carpenter shop on Fifth Street north of Wharton in Southwark's Sixth Ward and hid in a nearby valley formed by a gravel heap. As soon as the Shifflers approached, the Killers rose to the hill, pelting them with musket fire and brickbats before descending to fight hand-to-hand. But later arrivals armed with muskets reinforced the Shifflers. Their rain of fire sent the Killers fleeing toward home, leaving at least six of them wounded.[54]

Four months later another battle occurred. Again the Killers ignited a fire, this one in a rope factory on Fifth Street near the railroad. Instead of surprise, they based their strategy on the power of numbers. Returning to Moyamensing, they gathered a mob—overestimated by one newspaper at 400 to 500, but probably large, nonetheless—and ran to the fire, but the time lost permitted the Shifflers to arrive first. The Shifflers took cover one block from the blaze, primed their muskets, and fired as the mob appeared, wounding four Killers (and two innocent bystanders) and convincing the rest to retreat.[55]

By the summer, the Shifflers organized what amounted to vigilance committees, one of which spied Dick Manly, a notorious criminal and a Killer, not far from their hose house. Armed with a musket, four Shifflers stalked Manly as he emerged from a tavern. Realizing he was in a "bad neighborhood," Manly began to run. John Andrews, the musketeer, hurried his shot, which missed Manly and killed a youngster playing in the street. Andrews was arrested, tried for murder, but acquitted.[56]

Southwark's fire companies were barometers of demographic, political, and social changes. They proliferated with the rapid population increase in the late 1820s and with the rise of ethnic politics in the 1840s. They became social centers for propertyless wage earners by the 1840s, and most of them were held together by political allegiances and ethnic identities. Companies formed in the 1840s drew their members from the surrounding neighborhood, attracting gangs and neighborhood sympathizers in the process. An intensification in the kind and scope of violence accompanied this hardening of local loyalties. Indeed, ethnic identities were so ascendent that firemen and their devotees attacked political and ethnic rivals who were not members of gangs or fire companies.

For these reasons fire companies provide fertile, virgin ground for historical investigation. Their records can be used in a variety of ways to help solve problems which have vexed urban and labor historians. In the absence of adequate source materials, for example, scholars have been unable to distinguish Irish Catholic from Irish Protestant neighborhoods, institutions, and political loyalties. Fire company records and membership lists can be used to isolate each group. Once the religious preferences of the Irish companies are learned—as in the case of the Protestant Franklin Hose Company and the Catholic Moyamensing Hose Company, both of Moyamensing—membership lists can be collected and employed to determine Irish Protestant and Irish Catholic wards and neighborhoods.[57] Political preferences may then be determined. Tracing the names of the members to other institutions, such as temperance societies and labor unions, will reveal additional information about the values of each group. Were Irish Protestants temperance advocates? Did their values parallel those of native-born Americans, and did they identify with American Republicanism in opposition to Catholics? Did Irish Protestants cooperate with their Catholic countrymen in labor unions?

Historians interested in crime and law enforcement will also find fire company records useful. To take one example, the evidence presented here suggests that most of the street crime which plagued Southwark in the 1840s came from well-organized groups with fairly distinct values. Can the same be said of those who participated in the numerous riots of the period? Were anti-abolitionist, anti-black, or anti-Catholic rioters simply random gatherings of disgruntled men or were they composed of gang members and firemen drawn together in defense of their common values? Furthermore, law enforcement and its absence are clearly related to the political power of the fire companies. Southwark's American Republican firemen were influential enough to get some of their members appointed to the district watch and elected to the constabulary. Such men did not exercise much authority against American Republican lawbreakers, but assiduously arrested Democratic and immigrant rioters and unruly firemen.[58] Does this pattern hold true in other areas? Did a professional police force alter it?

Finally, studies of fire companies can reveal valuable information about the life-styles and leisure-time activities of various sectors of the working class. The minute books of two of Southwark's companies suggest that drinking and competetive sport were primary pastimes of the members. Most of these volunteers came from traditional crafts, such as tailoring, shoe-making, and construction, rather than from more innovative, discipline-oriented enterprises carried on in factories. This configuration probably stems from the fact that factory work generally demanded greater regimen and attention from the wage earner than did less advanced branches of industry. Relics of a pre-industrial age, fire companies did not respect the industrial time clock, for firemen who dashed to fires at all hours of the day did not make ideal factory workers. Factory owners may have forbade their employees to join fire companies, or these workers may have eschewed them voluntarily. Where fire companies persisted, one might expect the persistence of leisurely work habits.

NOTES

1. Sam Bass Warner, Jr., *The Private City: Philadelphia in Three Periods of its Growth* (Philadelphia: Univ. of Pennsylvania Press, 1968), p. 61.

2. Elizabeth M. Geffen, "Violence in Philadelphia in the 1840's and 1850's," *Pennsylvania History* 36 (Oct. 1969):406.

3. *Public Ledger,* Dec. 21, 1850.

4. United States Census Office, *Population Schedules of the Seventh Census of the United States, Philadelphia County,* mss. (Washington, 1850, microcopy). These figures include male heads of families only.

5. Ibid. These wards contained nearly 450 shoemakers and tailors, one of the largest concentrations of these tradesmen in the county.

6. *Public Ledger,* Jan. 17, 1852. See also ibid., May 10, 1849, Dec. 6, 1850, Sept. 19, 1851.

7. See Bruce Laurie, "The Working People of Philadelphia, 1827–1853" (diss. Univ. of Pittsburgh, 1971), chaps. 2, 3, and app. A.

8. Ibid., chap. 3. On the general strike, see Leonard Bernstein, "The Working People of Philadelphia from Colonial Times to the General Strike of 1835," *Pennsylvania Magazine of History and Biography* 74 (July 1950):336–39.

9. The Mechanics' Union of Trade Associations of the previous decade consisted of unions of artisans only, and they were limited to most honorable workers. See Laurie, "Working People," pp. 6–9.

10. *Pennsylvanian,* Apr. 25, Dec. 31, 1835, Mar. 28, 1836. James Ryan, an Irish immigrant, became president of this union in 1836. Solomon Demars, who migrated to Philadelphia from Lower Canada, was the Union Beneficial's delegate to the Trades' Union.

11. *United States Gazette,* June 4, 1835.

12. John R. Commons, et al., *A Documentary History of American Industrial Society,* 10 vols. (Cleveland: Arthur H. Clark Co., 1910–11), 5:377, 384. See also letter signed "J.C.," *Pennsylvanian,* Sept. 1, 1836.

13. *Pennsylvanian,* April 7, 12, 28, 1836.

14. Ibid., July 23, 26, Aug. 22, Sept. 21, 24, 1835. Warner, *Private City,* pp. 85–91 gives the erroneous impression that Sutherland left the party voluntarily.

15. Laurie, "Working People," chap. 8.

16. See, for example, *Public Ledger,* Jan. 20, 1838, Mar. 12, 1841, June 10, 1842. For notices of temperance societies formed by shoemakers, printers and tailors, see ibid., Feb. 21, 1842, Jan. 25, 1839, and Aug. 14, 1841.

17. For an excellent discussion of temperance, prohibition, and nativism, see Joseph R. Gusfield, *Symbolic Crusade: Status Politics and the American Temperance Movement* (Urbana: Univ. of Illinois Press, 1966), esp. pp. 36–86.

18. Vincent P. Lannie and Bernard C. Diethorn, "For the Honor and Glory of God: The Philadelphia Bible Riots of 1844," *History of Education Quarterly* 8 (1968):44–106.

19. See John H. Lee, *History of the American Party in Politics* (Philadelphia: Elliott, 1855).

20. *Public Ledger,* Oct. 11, 1843. Prior to this election, the Democrats received between 55 percent and 60 percent of Southwark's vote. See also Laurie, "Working People," app. B.

21. The two original companies were the Franklin Fire Company (1792) and the Weccacoe Engine Company (1800). The new companies were the Niagara Hose Company (1827), the Southwark Fire Company (1827), the Marion Hose Company (1833), the Weccacoe Hose Company (1842), and the Shiffler Hose Company (1846). For their locations, see fig. 4.1.

22. *Public Ledger,* Jan. 21, 1842.

23. The political allegiance of the companies was determined by tracing the members' names to lists of Democrats and American Republicans collected from the newspapers. The Democratic members of the Weccacoe Hose include James Eastwick, Samuel Erwin, and Levi Fort, all of whom ran for public offices. Nativists attached to the engine company were Thomas Grover, John Siddons, and Hiram Bunker, who served on the district Commission.

24. Frank H. Schell, "Old Volunteer Fire Laddies, the Famous, Fast, Faithful, Fistic, Fire Fighters of Bygone Days," (unpublished manuscript, n.d.), chap. 2, p. 4 in Frank H. Schell Papers, Historical Society of Pennsylvania.

25. The Franklin contained numerous Democrats. Charles Cathall, Edward Conway, George Brusstar, and Henry Peckle were ward leaders. John W. Ryan and Robert Lister ran for local offices. The most prominent Democratic member of the Southwark Fire Company was Henry Peckle, a perennial candidate for the Commission. The Niagara Hose Company alone had members who belonged to both political parties. The lack of membership lists prevents determining the political affiliations of the members of the Marion Hose Company.

26. See Schell, "Vounteer Fire Laddies," *passim; Public Ledger,* Sept. 13, 1903; Andrew Neilly, "The Violent Volunteers: A History of the Volunteer Fire Department of Philadelphia, 1736–1871" (diss., Univ. of Pennsylvania, 1959), chap. 3. See also *Statistics of Philadelphia: Comprehending a Concise View of all the Public Institutions and Fire Engine and Hose Companies of the City and County of Philadelphia on the First of January, 1842* (Philadelphia: n.p., 1842).

27. *Public Ledger,* Aug. 4 and Aug. 10, 1845.

28. See, for example, Nicholas B. Wainwright, ed., *Diary of Sidney George Fisher, 1834–1871* (Philadelphia: Historical Society of Pennsylvania, 1967), p. 122; Ellis P. Oberholtzer, *Philadelphia: A History of the City and its People,* 4 vols. (Philadelphia: S. J. Clark Publishing Co., 1911), 2:89–90; and report of the fire department reformers, *Public Ledger,* Jan. 14, 1853.

29. A list of names was collected from the *Minute Book of the Niagara Hose Company, 1833–1848 and 1848–1864,* which are available in the H.S.P., and traced to city directories and to the *Seventh Census* MSS. Of 102 names, 43, or just under 41 percent were found in the directories. Twenty of these names were located in the census, and only four of them owned real property. Two of the four were officers. In all, seven of the firemen had middle-class occupations, such as "grocer" and "tavern owner." Eighty-five percent of the members were skilled journeymen. Names of the members of the

Franklin Fire Company were collected from the *Minute Book of the Franklin Fire Company, 1838–1854,* and the adherents of the Weccacoe Hose and Shiffler Hose Companies were collected from lists in the newspapers. Tracing the names to the directories and to the census reveals occupational configurations approximating that of the Niagara Hose. See Laurie, "Working People," chap. 7, n. 22.

30. *Public Ledger,* Jan. 14, 1853.
31. Ibid., June 2, 1845.
32. Quoted in Oberholtzer, *Philadelphia,* 2:89.
33. See, for example, *Public Ledger,* Sept. 13, 1903; Schell, "Volunteer Fire Laddies," *passim.*
34. The addresses of eighteen members of the Weccacoe Hose Company and twelve members of the Shiffler Hose Company, about one-half the active memberships of both companies, were found in the city directories and traced to a street map of Southwark in Samuel Smedley, *Atlas of Philadelphia* (Philadelphia: Lippincott, 1862), pl. 3. Prof. Theodore Hershberg provided me with a photocopy of the plate, and George Alter of the University of Pennsylvania helped to locate the firemen on the map. See also, Oberholtzer, *Philadelphia,* 2:306.
35. The procedure described in n. 34 was employed here. The residences of about one-third (sixteen) of the members of the Franklin Fire Company and the residences of about two-thirds (twenty-two) of the members of the Niagara Hose Company were located on the street map.
36. *Public Ledger,* Aug. 13, 1846. See also report of a grand jury investigation of the gangs in ibid., Sept. 3, 1850.
37. Ibid.
38. Schell, "Volunteer Fire Laddies," chap. 2, p. 3.
39. Neilly, "Violent Volunteers," pp. 70–72. See also, Oberholtzer, *Philadelphia,* 2:307.
40. *Public Ledger,* May 28, 1845.
41. Nicholas Carson, John Diehl, and James Sipple, whom the *Public Ledger* identified as Bouncers, were members of the Weccacoe Hose Company. See ibid., Apr. 21, 22, 1845, Mar. 16, 20, 1846.
42. Cf. ibid., Jan. 14, 1853; Wainwright, *Fisher,* p. 122; Committee of Citizens of Philadelphia, *Paid Fire Department. Letters of the Judge of the Court of Quarter Sessions, and the Marshal of Police and Report of the Board of Trade* (Philadelphia: n.p., 1853).
43. Oberholtzer, *Philadelphia,* 2:303–4, offers an analysis similar to the one presented here. He contends that gangs, allied with fire companies, "did not conceal their objects under cover of protecting their community from fires or Abolitionists, of anti-Catholic sentiments, or of their love for Jackson or Clay." See also letter of Russell Jarvis in *Public Ledger,* July 26, 1844, and ibid., Sept. 13, 1903.
44. Cf. *Public Ledger,* Oct. 14, Dec. 9, 1844, June 18, 20, 1845.
45. Ibid., June 18, 21, 22, 1845.
46. *Minute Book of the Franklin Fire Company, 1838–1854,* May 14, 1847.

47. See, for example, *Public Ledger,* June 27, 1844, Jan. 1, 1845.
48. Ibid., June 25–29, July 1, 4, 1844.
49. Ibid., Feb. 5, 8, 9, 16, 1850. See also *Daily Sun,* Feb. 5, 8, 15, 23, Mar. 1, 2, 1850.
50. Ibid., Sept. 19, 1849.
51. Ibid., Sept. 3, 1850. A number of the assailants were members of the Shiffler Hose Company.
52. Ibid., Aug. 13, 1846. See also, ibid., Apr. 25, 1850.
53. *Daily Sun,* Sept. 29, 1849.
54. Ibid., Jan. 28, 1850.
55. Ibid., April 19–20, 1850.
56. Ibid., Aug. 7, 22, 1850. See also *Public Ledger,* Aug. 7, 8, 12, 22, Oct. 2, 1850.
57. Schell, "Volunteer Fire Laddies," chap. 2, p. 4.
58. Laurie, "Working People," pp. 152, 179–80.

5

Crime Patterns in Philadelphia, 1840–70

Thomas Welsh, down on his luck, was about to stumble onto a fortune. A clerk in the offices of Jay Cooke and Company, at Third and Chestnut, had spilled the contents of a bag of gold coins he had been counting. While he and the other clerks scurried about on the floor retrieving the money, a shabbily dressed man walked in. Everyone assumed he had business in the rear of the office; but the stranger departed hastily and someone noticed another bag containing $5,000 had disappeared with him. When pursuit proved useless, the clerks notified the police. Headquarters sent officers to watch all the railroad depots and other exit points in the city, and began a fruitless search. Several hours later a prosperous looking fellow walked into a jewelry store only five blocks from the scene of the crime. He bought a ring, paying for it with a $20 gold piece. Another customer, having heard of the robbery, became suspicious because of the mode of payment. He took the liberty of hefting the gentleman's valise, and thinking it rather heavy, called for the police. After his arrest, Welsh made no attempt to deny the theft, "but said he thought that he needed the money as much as Cooke & Co.." [1]

This robbery typified crime in Philadelphia during the years from 1840 to 1870. Opportunity and inclination proved time and again to be the combination which resulted in thefts and assaults. This does not mean that each criminal incident had no larger context. Some thieves, such as Welsh, stole because they either needed or wanted money. For others larceny constituted part of a life style—a group of rowdies might deprive a passing stranger of his cash in order to buy themselves liquor or amusement. Those of a more deliberate turn of mind might plan and execute a burglary of a store or home. [2] Physical violence often derived from racial prejudice. Rivalries between various gangs also accounted for a large number of assault cases. And deep hostilities among volunteer fire companies prcduced a long series of riots and minor battles which enlivened urban life. Crime was therefore both rational and random: rational because individuals had sufficient reasons (at least in their own minds) to commit these acts; and random because cpportunities to steal or to assault someone depended upon time and circumstance.

Crime patterns in the mid-nineteenth century conformed to Philadelphia's demographic changes. In 1840 the Delaware and Schuylkill rivers, and Vine and South streets formed the city's political boundaries. The business section, lying along the Delaware River from Walnut to Arch, had penetrated only as far west as Second street. This concentration was only relative. Many merchants maintained warehouses and stores outside this area. Because Philadelphia was still a walking city, her upper classes resided close to their places of work. Few wealthy citizens lived west of Broad or in the various districts surrounding the city. Because of the mixture of residences and businesses, then, there was no commercial nexus in the modern sense. Most Industries were located beyond the political confines of Philadelphia, especially in Spring Garden, Kensington, and Southwark. The working classes lived in housing clustered around the factories. A small slum existed along South street, from the Delaware to Seventh, and from Pine (within the city limits) to Fitzwater (in Southwark). This area served as the entry point for immigrants and as the home of Philadelphia's blacks. These spatial arrangements meant that the low-income groups, as well as the least desirable housing, were on the fringe of the city.[3]

During the next three decades the residential patterns underwent drastic changes. With the advent of the omnibus, the upper classes began to leave the central city for the suburbs. Sidney George Fisher, a local Philadelphian, noted in 1847 that "the taste for country life is increasing here very rapidly. New & tasteful houses are built every year. The neighborhood of Germantown is most desirable."[4] Led by the wealthier citizens, people began moving in large numbers toward the northwest and across the Schuylkill into West Philadelphia. The main thrust of this migration was up Ridge Avenue, though many residents also bought new houses within the city, west of Broad. The slum district along South street remained the worst section of the city and expanded slowly toward Broad Street. By 1870 these population movements had reversed the character of the suburbs and city. The outlying districts now contained the best, not the worst, housing.[5]

Philadelphia's downtown grew steadily as the well-to-do citizens moved outward. Shopkeepers either took over abandoned houses or demolished them to make room for imposing new commercial buildings. These conversions occurred most rapidly on Chestnut street, but the other major east-west avenues (Walnut, Market, and Arch) were not far behind. Some of the north-south streets also developed major concentrations of businesses. Third, from Walnut to Willow, and Eighth and Ninth from Walnut to Vine were especially noteworthy for their fine stores. By the mid-1860s the area bounded by Third, Eighth, Market, and Walnut had emerged as the center of the downtown district. The merchants on these streets served the upper and middle classes.

South street became the major shopping thoroughfare for low-income families. A miscellaneous collection of stores, offering a vast assortment of cheap wares, lined this artery running through the heart of the slums. The division of the city's two business districts along socioeconomic lines also occurred in the types of entertainment located near each. While the streets adjacent to Walnut, Chestnut, and Market offered such diversions as theaters and museums, the avenues surrounding South (especially Bedford and Spafford) enticed the passerby with numerous houses of prostitution.[6]

Philadelphia's property crime patterns closely followed residential and business shifts.[7] The accompanying maps (figs. 5.1–5.4) show that throughout the period under study the emerging downtown area from the Delaware to Broad, and from Vine to South (wards 5 and 6 after 1854) had a persistent concentration of this type of offense. Sneak thieves, till-tappers, and window smashers victimized merchants in that district.[8] Shopowners sometimes aided the thieves by placing merchandise on the sidewalk fronting their stores during business hours. Daring sneak thieves simply walked off with whatever they could carry. In the days before cash registers, the merchant kept his money in a till (a drawer under the counter). A group of boys could send the smallest of their number around the counter to raid the till while they occupied the owner's attention. Or a customer might ask for something which he knew was in the back of the store, and,

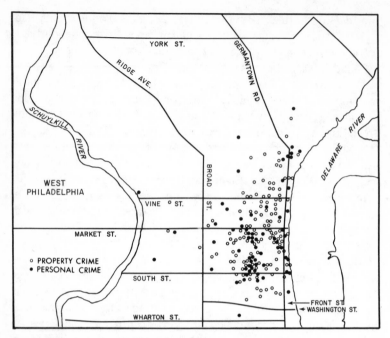

FIG. 5.1 Crime pattern, 1840. Source: Philadelphia *Public Ledger*. Base map, 1869, Historical Society of Pennsylvania.

while the clerk searched for it, the thief reached over the counter and emptied the cash drawer. There were many variations of till-tapping, which seems to have been a favorite endeavor among juveniles.

Thieves also took advantage of improvements in displaying goods. In the 1820s merchants began to replace their old, small shop windows with large bulk windows.[9] A handy brick or stone and nimble hands combined to make window smashing a prevalent form of larceny by 1840, and the offense continued to plague store keepers throughout the period. Because of the noise involved in this particular crime, its practitioners soon turned to various glass cutting instruments to reduce the possibilities of attracting attention (and perhaps to reduce the chances of getting cut on jagged glass fragments).

As the residential pattern of Philadelphia spread, so did the incidence of thefts from houses. A comparison of the 1840 map

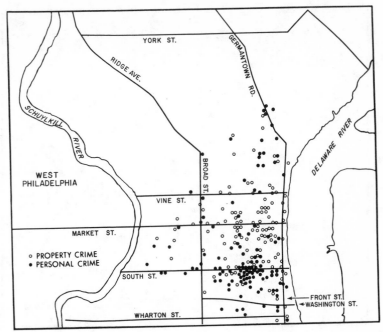

Fig. 5.2 Crime pattern, 1850. Source: Philadelphia *Public Ledger*. Base map, 1869, Historical Society of Pennsylvania.

(fig. 5.1) with that for 1870 (fig. 5.4) demonstrates this trend. The heaviest concentration of these property losses occurred in those areas where the upper- and middle-income groups settled, especially in the western and northwestern parts of the metropolis. The sneak, or entry-way thief, was very prevalent. His victims contributed to his success by habitually leaving coats, hats, umbrellas, boots, and similar wearing apparel hanging on a rack just inside the doorway of a home. The criminal had only to step inside briefly, grab whatever was within reach, and depart. Bolder sneak thieves, posing as service or repairmen, entered homes and stole any watches, jewelry, and clothing that was lying loose. Juveniles were especially persistent depredators. Among their favorite targets were new houses which had not yet been occupied. They broke into many such residences and stripped away the plumbing fixtures to secure the brass and lead. When elaborate door knobs and knockers became popular, youthful thieves devel-

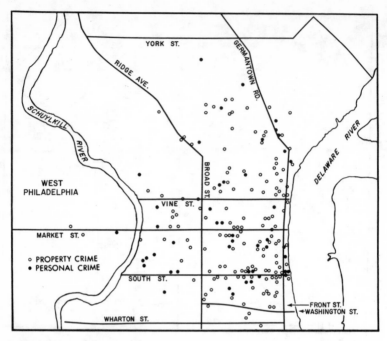

Fig. 5.3   Crime pattern, 1860. Source: Philadelphia *Public Ledger*. Base map, 1869, Historical Society of Pennsylvania.

oped the ability to quickly rip those objects from their fastenings without undue noise. Even the family wash disappeared frequently, as did any miscellaneous household items carelessly left in view. The cash loss in most of these thefts was low, but these incidents were extremely annoying to the victims.

And finally there was a special class of property crimes, highway robberies, which often shaded into violent attacks on persons. This form of theft occurred anywhere in the city or suburbs, though its perpetrators seem to have favored either side streets or the less densely settled areas. Juveniles and young men, especially those wandering about in small groups, committed many of these offenses. Two social customs aided the thieves. First, most victims usually had enough money in their possession to make the robbery worthwhile. In the days before checking accounts and credit systems, people normally carried their cash with them when conducting business or while engaged in shopping. In one variation

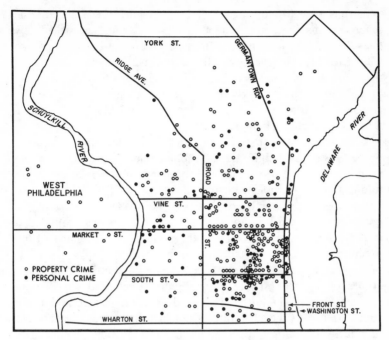

F<small>IG</small>. 5.4   Crime pattern, 1870.   Source: Philadelphia *Public Ledger*.   Base map, 1869, Historical Society of Pennsylvania.

on this practice, merchants employed messenger boys who conveyed large sums from their employers to the banks.   This arrangement made robberies even easier, since a juvenile could offer only minimal resistance.   Secondly, watches (a favorite target with thieves) were scarce before the Civil War because few people could afford them.   Due to their relative rarity, it became customary to ask strangers for the time of day.   Thieves used this habit to their advantage.   When a pedestrian pulled out his watch in order to answer a query as to the time, the criminal grabbed it and ran.   Or, if the watch happened to be attached to a chain, he pulled the victim off balance by jerking the watch toward him, at the same time quieting the owner with a blow on the head.   Either method usually proved successful.

Philadelphia's thieves stole everything from washtubs to diamonds.   They took anything which might have some cash value because a market existed for these goods.   The city's numerous pawnbrokers and junk dealers purchased most of the pilfered items for a fraction of their value, and they asked few questions about ownership. Because those merchants were so willing to buy whatever was offered, the petty thieves (and even the more serious offenders such as burglars) always had a way to convert their day's work into ready cash. A part of the commercial structure of the city therefore provided the incentive for these particular offenses.[10]

Crimes against property, then, tended to concentrate where the property was available: in the commercial district and in the rapidly expanding residential neighborhoods of the relatively well-to-do. Crimes of violence against persons, in contrast, tended to occur where the poor lived. Because the residential areas of the poor remained fairly stable, crimes against persons exhibited a rather stable pattern throughout the period. As the maps (1860 excepted) indicate, the center of assaults was located in the heart of the Negro section, around Seventh and Lombard. From there, crimes of violence spread along South Street, and from South to near Market via Fifth, Sixth, and Seventh. Water and Front streets (close to the Delaware river) also had recurring episodes of attacks on various people. In the old districts, Southwark's residents from South to Wharton consistently experienced a number of these incidents in varying forms. The working-class areas of Northern Liberties and Kensington, with Germantown Road forming an apparent axis, also had a persistent pattern of these offenses.

Customs of a different sort from those involving property crimes produced the opportunities for violence. The city's streets were centers of social life in the nineteenth century. Every evening, and especially on the weekends, the avenues teemed with people seeking relief from the day's tasks. The street corners performed a special function as the focal point for crowds of youths. Numerous citizens throughout the period complained about corner loungers, and the *Public Ledger's* frequent attacks on the practice led one such "lounger" to write a defense of that habit. He justified his companions' behavior by claiming young men had nowhere else to go, and he asserted it was only natural for them to gather and talk among themselves. Furthermore, he argued that corner loungers had redeeming social values: they helped pull fire engines and were the first to volunteer in wartime. He suggested that, if the citizens of Philadelphia wanted to stop the practice of congregating on the corners, they should provide places for juveniles to go "where we could talk ourselves and not have an orator or preacher to do the talking." [11]

This champion of the corner lounger had a point. Urban society provided few places for recreation, and proper society tended to feel that leisure time should be spent listening to informative lectures or in other educational pursuits. But the weight of the evidence favors the critics of the corner loungers. Unfortunately for many citizens, those youths did a great deal more than talk among themselves. Their amusements also included loud, obscene verbal abuse of other pedestrians. They pelted the passing citizenry with snowballs, rocks, or bricks, and anyone who objected to this treatment faced the prospect of a beating. The loungers' defender correctly noted their eagerness to pull fire engines. Men had to haul these primitive mechanisms to a fire. Long ropes attached to the engine enabled many people to join the regular crew and somewhat increased the speed with which the apparatus arrived at a fire. But the prospect of a good fight probably had much to do with the readiness to help. After a fire, and sometimes while getting to it, the followers of an engine often clashed in battles ranging from a brief fist fight to a full-scale riot.

The corner loungers also swelled the ranks of Philadelphia's gangs. Although no one knows how many of these bands existed, a survey of a single newspaper from 1836 to 1878 uncovered fifty-two gangs which were identified by name.[12] Whatever the total might have been, the pre-Civil War era was one of the most gang-plagued periods in urban history. These associations concentrated their activities along South street and in Southwark and Moyamensing. Although a few were located in the northern working-class districts, newspaper coverage suggests these were neither as numerous nor as dangerous as their brethren on the south side of town.[13]

The distribution of violent gangs was due in part to the age composition within the city's wards. In 1840, just before the height of juvenile gang activity, those ages which tended to form these associations (ten to fourteen and fifteen to nineteen) comprised 3.6 and 4.4 percent of the total city population. Cedar Ward (bounded by Seventh, Spruce, the Schuylkill River, and South street) had 12.9 and 9.6 percent, respectively, in those age categories. Among the ten- to fourteen-year-olds that was the highest density in the entire city. Other wards had percentages higher than the average, but none had so many violent gangs operating within its borders.[14]

Newspaper accounts said little about the internal structure of these bands. The author of a fictional romance dealing with an actual gang, the Killers, left the only contemporary description of that group's composition: [15]

> They were divided into three classes—beardless apprentice boys who after a hard day's work were turned loose upon the street at night, by their masters or bosses. Young men of nineteen and twenty, who fond of excitement, had assumed the name and joined the gang for the mere fun of the thing, and who would either fight for a man or knock him down, just to keep their hand in; and fellows with countenances that reminded of the brute and devil well intermingled. These last were the smallest in number, but the most ferocious of the three.

The Killers, according to this account, used an abandoned building as their headquarters. Other gangs also had clubhouses, but most had only a street corner which they reserved for themselves. The vast majority of these groups had very short lives of three years or less. But a few persisted for much longer periods. The Schuylkill Rangers held the record (at least twenty-six years). Others, like the Buffers (ten years), the Forty Thieves (nine), and the Snakers (seven), provided additional exceptions to the general rule of a short, violent life.[16]

Street warfare between rival gangs formed one of the basic themes of city life during the middle years of the nineteenth century. These clashes generally occurred in the evenings and lasted as long as the participants felt like fighting. Any law officer who appeared on the scene did so at his peril. The weaponry ranged from fists to pistols. Since the newspapers usually listed only fatalities, not more minor injuries, it is difficult to judge how deadly this behavior became. Battles erupted so frequently, however, that the fighting developed some semiformal aspects. By 1850 there was an area of ground known as the "Battlefield" where opposing bands met regularly for combat. The place even attracted spectators who watched the fun and offered encouragement to their favorites.[17]

Gangs provided one type of organized violence. As the previous chapter makes clear, the volunteer fire companies supplied a related, and in some ways more serious, form of disruption. The volunteer system had been a product of necessity in the eighteenth century when fire posed one of the greatest hazards to urban life. That danger persisted throughout the nineteenth century as well, but while the problem remained, the nature of the fire fighters changed. Initially composed of the "best citizens," the membership in many companies shifted by the 1830s to include some of the worst elements in society.[18]

The conflicts between these rival associations became the major source of organized violence before the Civil War. Though fires were too frequent to suit most city residents, the volunteers' brawls had reached the point by the 1840s where many blazes were set deliberately to provoke a riot. As a company charged along a street in the direction of the fire, its opponent either collided with it, or lay in ambush. The engine was the supreme prize in these affairs, and several valuable pieces of equipment received severe damage or were totally destroyed in the battles. Any fire, incendiary or otherwise, became an excuse to fight. Whenever two companies met, the encounter usually ended in some form of combat. Most of these engagements were brief, but some went on for hours, covered several city blocks, and occasionally continued the next day or evening.[19]

One source of this conflict derived from the circumstances surrounding fire fighting. In the early nineteenth century good-natured contests to be first to a blaze, and first to a hydrant, slowly altered into determined battles between claimants for those honors.[20] Once this change occurred, partisans of one or another organization began attempting to prevent competitors from arriving at all. Fights developed on the route to a conflagration. As rowdies infiltrated some companies, the crowds which usually followed the engines also changed. Corner loungers and gangs attached themselves to several fire associations. When rivals, reinforced by their supporters, met in the streets, the excitement of the moment combined with an eagerness for combat to produce an outbreak of violence.

Deeply rooted social conditions also accounted for this warfare. Religious differences provided one excuse for conflict. The Irish Catholics of the Moyamensing Hose hated the Irish Protestants belonging to the Franklin Hose. Their fights were among the most savage contests which occurred. Community loyalties formed another basis for trouble. Many volunteers came from the same neighborhood. This gave cohesion to an outfit, but it also made the company competitive with others formed along similar lines. The internal structure of these organizations also contributed to a combative nature. Firehouses were built to include living quarters or a meeting place for members. What had been public associations became private clubs for the city's young men who had few other places to spend their time. This social aspect of fire fighting bred the same sort of pride as that connected with neighborhoods. The sense of belonging expressed itself in such rituals as elaborate parades and in battles with rivals.[21]

Small groups of rowdies wandering through the streets constituted another form of violence. Unprovoked assaults occurred with distressing frequency on the city's south side and in the less densely settled areas to the north. The victim might be a rival gang member, a lonely stroller, a man (or woman) suddenly slashed by a knife as he brushed past a gathering of juveniles, or—especially along South street—a Negro. Racial antagonism kept the ghetto area in turmoil for years. Philadelphia experienced five major anti-Negro riots between 1829 and 1849. In the intervals between major battles, white and black youths constantly attacked one another. Raids and reprisals became commonplace and kept tensions high until the mid 1850s. Though the antagonism behind these assaults seems to have declined somewhat by 1860, it flared occasionally after that date, as in 1871 when a minor race riot erupted.[22]

Law officers were also frequent victims of assaults by bands of rowdies. Until the city and districts consolidated in 1854, the policing establishments in the metropolitan area suffered due to inadequate manpower and conflicting jurisdiction. A watchman pursuing an offender had to give up when the culprit crossed into another district. Roaming toughs took full advantage of this state of affairs. When a policeman interfered in an assault, they frequently turned upon him and beat him badly. Officers who attempted to disperse corner loungers also faced the prospect of an attack. If help arrived during these affairs, the rowdies simply headed for the nearest dividing line. In a refinement of this situation, some malefactors took to shooting at patrolmen of one district while standing in another. Under these circumstances, officers had great difficulty maintaining any semblance of public order.[23]

Toward Social Order

At the same time that crime, and particularly violence, seemed to be gaining momentum, other factors were at work to impose a higher degree of discipline on urban society. Philadelphia's more orderly citizens did not remain passive bystanders while the rowdy elements indulged themselves in a miscellaneous assortment of riots, assaults, and thefts. A reorganization of the police, the abolition of the volunteer fire companies, and the emergence of political bosses all contributed to the decline (though not the elimination) of crime.

Philadelphians reduced the amount of criminal violence by creating a more effective police force in the 1850s. The multiplicity of jurisdictions within the metropolitan area complicated the struggle to achieve this particular reform. As a result, the movement to establish an efficient police became one of the themes in the consolidation crusade which culminated successfully in 1854. The Marshall's Police (1850–54) served as a transitional force between the old watch system and the more modern organization which emerged in 1855.[24]

Though a temporary solution at best, the Marshall's Police did set a pattern regarding the recruitment of a particular type of man who did much to curtail crime in the nineteenth century. Since a law officer's life was not particularly pleasant, individuals in the middle and upper classes did not find the work very attractive. Policemen came, therefore, from the lower classes in urban society. They also came from the volunteer fire companies and other rowdy elements. These latter groups were among the best equipped to handle the people whom the respectable citizens regarded as threats to the stability of society. A precedent did exist for appointing some men to the police who belonged to the very organizations which needed regulation. In a particularly bitter riot caused by a Moyamensing gang in 1849, the authorities had imported a rival band to suppress the disorder. The example, which had succeeded, was not ignored when the time arrived to select officers for the Marshall's Police, and the practice continued after that organization dissolved. Samuel Ruggles, chief of police under Mayors Richard Vaux, Alexander Henry, and Morton McMichael (1856–69), belonged to the volunteer Columbia Hose Company. Ruggles was only the most prominent officer on the force who had connections with the violent fire-fighters.[25]

Appointing such men to the police in effect legitimized hitherto illegal violence. Because patrolmen refused to wear distinctive uniforms throughout most of the 1850s, they did not change their outward appearance or habits with their altered status. Animosities which had been built up through the 1840s continued unabated, and a man's new position did not confer immunity from the hatreds held by rivals in opposing companies and gangs. The level of violence, though impossible to measure precisely, does not appear to have declined following the creation of the Marshall's Police, or after the emergence of the consolidated force in 1855. Although the number of physical assaults declined between 1850 and 1860, the decrease probably resulted from a shift to "legal" police violence (which the newspapers would not have considered criminal). There were some criticisms of the amount of force the police employed, but such complaints did not reach a peak until after 1870. In the early years of creating discipline on the streets, "respectable" opinion generally supported the patrolmen's methods for suppressing disorder.[26]

Not every officer had connections among those whom he had to control. Assaults on policemen, and the prevalence of force in making arrests, also derived from the newness of policing. Individual patrolmen had to learn their jobs. No academies existed to teach a man how to become a good officer. Consequently, the city's streets became his school. The problems arising from improvising arrest procedures in a hostile environment help account for some of the violence perpetrated by these men. Force came easily because it seemed to settle so many disputes, at least temporarily. The policemen's authority also represented something new on the urban scene. For volunteer firemen and gang members who had never respected anything but superior physical prowess, a certain amount of muscle was necessary to convince them that an officer meant business. The habit of obeying orders which came from a patrolman had to develop over time; many rowdies learned that lesson with the aid of "legitimate" violence.[27]

Reorganizing the fire companies proved to be as difficult as the effort to consolidate the districts and city. This reform also took more time. Politics proved be the most stubborn roadblock in the way of reformers. The volunteers wielded considerable voting power at elections, and they were very effective at carrying on the daily chores of running a campaign. Any politician who dared suggest that the existing fire-fighting system should be abolished risked defeat. In 1855 the city council improved conditions slightly by creating a single fire department run by a chief engineer. That official could not exercise much control over the various companies because he was elected by the membership of those organizations. As a consequence, although service became somewhat more efficient, the old habits of disorder returned by 1859.

Technology drove a wedge into the volunteers' ranks which reformers eventually exploited to establish a paid fire department. The steam-powered engine proved to be the instrument of destruction. The first of these machines arrived in Philadelphia in 1855 when some public-spirited citizens, impressed by the capabilities of these devices, purchased one for the city. It proved to be a financial disaster because it weighed 20,000 pounds and could not be moved without breaking down. But the idea began to catch on. In 1857 the Philadelphia Hose Company bought one of these engines; others followed their example until the old-style, hand-drawn pumpers became rarities by the 1860s. The adoption of these machines fundamentally altered the nature of fire-fighting. Because of their weight, horses replaced men as the means of locomotion. This reduced the number of men required to put the engine into operation. Secondly, these were delicate monsters which needed skilled mechanics to keep them in running condition. The volunteers, who knew more about fighting than machinery, thus lost part of their rationale for existence. Finally, the cost of maintaining these machines rose far beyond the means of any one company, and the city began to assume the greater part of the burden of keeping the engines in repair.

The cost of the new technology gave reformers the opportunity they had been looking for. The idea of economy in city government was as powerful a force politically as were the volunteers. The combination of increasing expenses and continuous street fighting between firemen at last convinced Philadelphia's politicians to vote for reform. After protracted debate, the city councils created a paid fire deparment which commenced operations in

1871. The volunteers maintained their old organizations as social clubs, but their excuse for rioting had disappeared.[28]

Political developments also contributed to the decline in violent crimes. Following the uncertainties and shifting loyalties which characterized the 1840s, local leaders began to divide along ethnic lines during the 1850s. The latter decade also witnessed the emergence of the professional politician at the city and ward levels.

William McMullin became the boss of the Fourth Ward, the most violent section of Philadelphia. The Fourth's boundaries (The Delaware River, South Street, Broad Street, and Fitzwater Street) encompassed parts of the old districts of Southwark and Moyamensing, and it was in the latter that McMullin first rose to fame and power. He was born in 1824, the son of a grocer at Seventh and Bainbridge. The future boss held a variety of jobs before he settled into politics. Apprenticed first to a printer and then a carpenter, he returned to work in his father's store for a time before joining the navy. After his enlistment expired, he came back to Philadelphia in the mid-1840s. At this point McMullin's later career began to take shape.[29]

He became a member of a gang which used a market place in Moyamensing as its headquarters. In August 1845 this group assaulted several persons, and an officer arrested McMullin for his part in the affair. With his credentials as a rowdy established, McMullin enlisted in a local regiment and fought in the Mexican War. Afterwards he joined the Moyamensing Hose Company, one of the most notorious fire associations. The activities of the volunteers and the numerous gangs in the district made that area the most dangerous part of the metropolitan area. Their depredations, according to testimony before a grand jury in 1850, made ordinary citizens fear for their lives. One witness declared that the rowdies had formed political organizations, and had committed some of their violence under the pretext of campaigning for their favorite candidates.[30]

In response to the deteriorating situation in Moyamensing, the grand jury indicted several persons who kept disorderly houses where rowdies congregated and handed the police a list of more than 100 other individuals whose reputations as dangerous characters made them liable to arrest. The results of the investigation remained secret while the police completed their preparations for a massive raid. One of their targets was a tavern at

Fourth and Shippen where the Keystone Club, one of those political organizations which numbered rowdies among its members, had planned a meeting. The officers arrived at the saloon while the Club was in session in an upstairs room. At the door of the chamber "the officers were met by Wm. McMullin, who drawing a knife, made several blows" at the raiders. McMullin surrendered after a struggle and the patrolmen captured a few other Keystoners in a wild melee.[31]

Politics, as well as a desire to suppress violence, probably played a role in the raid on the Keystone Club. The fall elections, held in October, were approaching and the Club was campaigning for the election of Horn R. Kneass, Democratic candidate for district attorney. Kneass won (a recount and investigation later nullified his victory) and the Keystoners were among the celebrants whom Kneass specifically commended for their zeal and exertions.

The Club and its followers were in a transition stage, moving from gang members to respected (if not respectable) citizens. Kneass represented the better element. A prominent Democrat in the 1840s, his conservative credentials earned him a place on the committee which successfully opposed the initial consolidation movement. By accepting the aid of the Keystone Club, Kneass and other politicians helped it become an eminent and powerful organization by the late 1850s. Rising from obscure origins and partially composed of disreputable types, the Club represented its party in trips outside Philadelphia and participated in important national political campaigns.[32]

McMullin's power rose with that of the Keystoners. He became president of that group and opened a saloon in 1854 at Eighth and Emeline. After that date his power expanded considerably. He won election to the Board of Prison Inspectors and secured an appointment as Lieutenant on the Marshall's Police force. The Fourth Ward became a Democratic stronghold in the process. The ward's vote for Richard Vaux (Democratic candidate for mayor) in 1854 was one of the three largest in the city. When Vaux ran in 1856 and 1858 for the same office, McMullin's machine returned the greatest majorities of any ward for the mayoral aspirant.[33]

McMullin's stranglehold on the Fourth Ward did not entirely eliminate violence there. He and his followers were too accustomed to the use of force for that to happen. Moreover, he could not control some assaults which occurred along South Street and elsewhere. Personal quarrels continued, and racial tensions, though considerably restrained, provided another source of trouble. But McMullin's political influence could channel some conflict into legitimate avenues, as when he secured the appointment of at least six volunteer firemen from the Moyamensing Hose to the police force.[34] The presence of these men, and others like them, helps explain the paradoxical condemnation and praise of Mayor Vaux's policing policies. The *Public Ledger* complained that Vaux appointed disreputable men to the force; yet it complimented him for keeping "public order excellently preserved." [35] The officers may have had reputations as rowdies, but they knew how to deal with disorder.

The emergence of a single man in charge of the politics of a ward also reduced violence by limiting the number of persons and groups who were allowed to commit illegal acts. Influence brought immunity from prosecution or punishment, but only if the offender belonged to the ruling clique. Hugh Mara, a one-time member of McMullin's organization, testified in 1872 that The Squire, as McMullin had been nicknamed, was responsible for concealing the murder of a policeman by one of his henchmen. McMullin had also given the order which resulted in an attempt to assassinate a federal revenue detective in 1869. When the plot failed, he secured defense attorneys for his men and tampered with the witnesses. After the jury convicted the assailants, McMullin used his power to obtain a pardon for the men.[36]

In 1867 McMullin led his Moyamensing Hose followers in a riot involving the Hope Engine Company. The Common Council appointed a special committee to investigate because the Squire was an alderman. Although the testimony of several witnesses led the committee to conclude that McMullin was guilty of mob action, the city solicitor informed the Council that it had no power to impeach the alderman. A motion not to print the testimony passed, and McMullin escaped unscathed.[37]

While the Squire obviously continued some of his previous violent activities throughout the 1860s, the general pattern of assaults showed a relative decline during the same period. McMullin's machine certainly did not monopolize that type of offense, but his rise to dominance in the ward had reduced the number of contestants who sought power. Rival organizations could not successfully compete against him. The violence associated with political agitation therefore declined. The machine, under Mc-Mullin's direction, brought its own peculiar form of social order to the neighborhood.

Other factors certainly influenced crime patterns from 1840 to 1870. The age distribution of the city's population had a great deal to do with the level of gang activity, for example. If the general birth rate declined in the years between 1800 and 1860, as one study asserts, then the relative drop in gang incidents by the latter year may be partially attributed to that fact.[38] Business changes also altered the crime pattern. As South street developed into a low-income shopping district, the dominant type of offense in that area shifted from assault to theft.

Crime did not disappear during these three decades. Rather, it continued while certain trends laid the foundation for the basic discipline of a modern urban society. The achievements of these years were structural in nature; they concentrated on reforms of the way the city was organized. The creation of publicly paid police and fire departments helped to control the excesses of rowdies and destroyed their social roots. The rise of the ward boss, though not a welcome change in other ways, made a contribution to the decline in the violence which had racked the city for so many years. None of these innovations solved the crime problem; but they were important stepping-stones for the future.

NOTES

1. Philadelphia *Public Ledger*, Jan. 20, 1863.
2. This paper concentrates on non-professional crime. One did not have to be a professional criminal to plot a burglary. Disgruntled clerks, teenage gangs, and men like Welsh were perfectly capable of plundering businesses and homes.
3. Sam B. Warner, Jr., *The Private City: Philadelphia in Three Periods of its Growth* (Philadelphia: Univ. of Pennsylvania Press, 1968), chap. 3. Stuart Blumin, "Mobility and Change in Ante-Bellum Philadelphia," in *Nineteenth-Century Cities: Essays in the New Urban History*, Stephan Thernstrom and Richard Sennett, eds. (New Haven: Yale Univ. Press, 1969), pp. 187–90. W. E. B. DuBois, *The Philadelphia Negro: A Social Study* (New York: Schocken Books, 1967), pp. 302–3.

4. Nicholas B. Wainwright, ed., *A Philadelphia Perspective: the Diary of Sidney George Fisher covering the years from 1834 to 1871* (Philadelphia: Historical Society of Pennsylvania, 1967), p. 202.

5. Kenneth T. Jackson, "Urban Deconcentration and Suburbanization in the Nineteenth Century" (unpublished paper in the possession of the author). *North American and United States Gazette,* September 12, 1859.

6. The movement of the downtown has been traced through accounts in the *Public Ledger;* see, for example: Nov. 11, Dec. 15, 1847; March 29, 1848; Dec. 19, 1850; April 4, 1851; Jan. 13, Feb. 23, 27, 1855; June 17, 1856; Aug. 31, 1857; Jan. 14, Feb. 29, March 20, April 12, 14, 1860; July 26, 1864; Aug. 30, 1865; July 23, 1869; April 26 (supp.), April 30 (supp.), May 3 (supp.), 1873. With regard to the locations of respectable amusements and houses of prostitution, cf. *The Stranger's Guide in Philadelphia and its Environs* (Philadelphia: Lindsay and Blakiston, 1854), pp. 48–53, and the *Public Ledger,* June 10, December 19, 1840; November 30, 1852. See in addition George R. Taylor, ed., "Philadelphia in Slices: Slice IV: Dandy Hall," George C. Foster, *Pennsylvania Magazine of History and Biography* 93 (Jan. 1969): 39.

7. The discussion of crimes against both property and persons is based on a sample taken from the *Public Ledger* at ten-year intervals. In each year, every other day's catalogue of incidents was examined and the author recorded every crime story in which a geographic location was given. This method resulted in a record of the following number of incidents:

Year	Property	Personal
1840	122	68
1850	117	116
1860	143	47
1870	272	104

On the figs. 5.1–5.4, each dot therefore equals *one* crime. The sample is in all probability statistically insignificant, but it was impossible to record any offenses which were not located geographically by the *Ledger.*

8. Pickpockets and shoplifters also plagued storeowners, but by the 1840s they tended to be professional thieves and are therefore omitted from this discussion.

9. John F. Watson, *Annals of Philadelphia.* . . . (Philadelphia: E. L. Carey & A. Hart, 1830), p. 201.

10. Watson, *Annals,* pp. 218–19. *Public Ledger,* January 5, 1844; September 15, 1871; letter to editor signed "Honest Dealer," February 14, 1874 (supp.).

11. Letter to editor signed "A Corner Lounger," *Public Ledger,* July 25, 1856. Examples of complaints against loungers are: ibid., July 19, 1859; March 29, 1867; March 8, 1873 (supp.); June 16, 1877 (supp.).

12. The gangs, with the dates when they appeared in the *Public Ledger*, were: Bleeders, June 17, 1851; Blood Tubs, July 17, 1855; Blossoms, Feb. 1, 1848; Bouncers, Feb. 1, 1848; Buffers, May 5, 1845, June 4, 1845, July 17, 1855; Bugs, July 17, 1855; Bulldogs, Feb. 21, 1848; Centre Street Boys, May 2, 1872; Chesapeakes, March 7, 1845; Crockets, Oct. 6, 1845; Darts, Dec. 1, 1869; Deathfetchers, Feb. 1, 1848; Dogs, June 21, 1860; Dog-Towners, May 2, 1872; The Forty-Thieves, Sept. 21, 1868, Dec. 29, 1869, Jan. 24, 1870, July 15, 1871, Feb. 23, 1877; Garroters, Feb. 29, 1860; Gumballs, Oct. 29, 1844, April 1, 1845, Feb. 1, 1848; Hyenas, Dec. 19, 1844, Feb. 1, 1848; Jack of Clubs, Dec. 30, 1857; Jumpers, Oct. 29, 1844, Aug. 2, 1845, Feb. 1, 1848; Juniatta Club, Jan. 22, 1872; Keystone No. 2, Sept. 30, 1850; Killers, Aug. 2, 1847, Feb. 1, 1848; Lancers, Jan. 20, 1854; Molly Maguires, Aug. 7, 1878; Neckers, Aug. 10, 1848; Pickwick Club, Aug. 19, 1844; Pluckers, Feb. 1, 1848; Pots No. 2, Sept. 30, 1850; Privateer Club No. 1, Nov. 26, 1847, Jan. 22, 1850, March 18, 1850; Rats, May 28, 1845; Oct. 16, 1845, Nov. 23, 1847, Feb. 1, 1848; Rangers, March 7, 1845, Feb. 21, 1848; Reading Hose Club, Dec. 5, 1873; Sept. 4, 1876; Rebels, Dec. 11, 1845; Red Roses, July 18, 1860; Reed Birds, June 22, 1850; Schuylkill Rangers, Aug. 14, 1850, Oct. 16, 1854, July 23, 1860, March 6, July 26, 1876; Shifflers, May 28, 1845, June 4, 1845; Skinners, Dec. 9, 1844, March 7, 1845, Oct. 16, 1845; Smashers, June 22, 1850; Snakers, Feb. 1, 1848, Aug. 11, 1855; Snappers, Dec. 19, 1844, Feb. 1, 1848; Spiggots, Dec. 21, 1857, June 21, 1860; Sporters, Dec. 9, 1844; Springers, Jan. 3, 1855; Stockholders, May 12, 1854; Tormentors, Feb. 1, 1848, Feb. 8, 1850, June 17, 1851, Jan. 16, 1854; Turks, Aug. 15, 1850, Nov. 20, 1850; The Vesper Social, March 8, 1878; Weecys, Oct. 16, 1845; Wild Cats, May 28, 1845; Waynetowners, Oct. 24, 1850.

13. This summary is based on the author's examination of 134 incidents involving gangs which the *Public Ledger* reported between 1840 and 1878.

14. Calculated from the *Sixth Census or Enumeration of the Inhabitants of the United States, 1840*, p. 150.

15. Anon., *Life and Adventures of Charles Anderson Chester, the Notorious Leader of the Philadelphia "Killers"* (Philadelphia: Yates and Smith, 1850), pp. 27–28.

16. Determined from data given in n. 12.

17. *Public Ledger*, April 30, 1850.

18. J. Thomas Scharff and Thompson Westcott, *History of Philadelphia*, 3 vols. (Philadelphia: L. H. Everts, 1884), 3: 1883 ff. George R. Taylor, ed., "Philadelphia in Slices: Slice III: The Rowdy Clubs," by George C. Foster, *Pennsylvania Magazine of History and Biography* 93 (January, 1969): 35–36.

19. *Public Ledger*, Jan. 30, 1844; Jan. 25, 1848; April 19, 1850; July 1, 1850; Sept. 24, 1858; Nov. 7, 1865; Sept. 17, 1866. Scharf and Westcott, *History of Philadelphia*, 2:691–92.

20. Andrew J. Neilly, "The Violent Volunteers; a History of the Volunteer Fire Department of Philadelphia, 1736–1871" (unpublished diss., Univ. of Pennsylvania, 1959), p. 28.

21. *Public Ledger,* April 16, 1850. Scharf and Westcott, *History of Philadelphia,* 3:1887–88, 1899–1901, 1910. Neilly, "The Violent Volunteers," pp. 130, 143. I am indebted to Professor Bruce Laurie for pointing out the religious differences among the fire companies.

22. Leon F. Litwack, *North of Slavery; the Negro in the Free States, 1790–1860* (Chicago: Univ. of Chicago Press, 1961), p. 100. Scharf and Westcott, *History of Philadelphia,* 1:837.

23. The *Public Ledger* reported numerous assaults on policemen; see, for example, Feb. 2, 14, 1840; Feb. 27, 1845; July 23, 1850; March 20, Aug. 24, 1855; Aug. 27, Oct. 20, 1860; Jan. 17, 1865; Feb. 1, March 22, 1870.

24. Howard O. Sprogle, *The Philadelphia Police: Past and Present* (Philadelphia: n.p., 1887), pp. 93–94.

25. Ruggle's obituary, *Public Ledger,* April 22, 1874. The use of gangs to suppress riots was noted by Sidney George Fisher; see Wainwright, ed., *A Philadelphia Perspective,* p. 226.

26. David R. Johnson, "Police Arrest Practices in Nineteenth Century American Cities: Some Preliminary Observations" (a paper presented at the American Historical Association Convention, December 30, 1970), pp. 1–4.

27. Johnson, "Police Arrest Practices," pp. 8–9.

28. Scharf and Westcott, *History of Philadelphia,* 3:1908–9, 1912–13; Neilly, "The Violent Volunteers," pp. 55–58, 103–4, 189 ff.

29. The general background on McMullin came from the obituaries published at his death. See the *Public Ledger,* April 1, 1901, and the *Philadelphia Inquirer,* April 1, 1901. Ellis P. Oberholtzer, *Philadelphia: A History of the City and its People* (Philadelphia: S. J. Clarke, n.d.), 2:307 has a brief sketch.

30. *Public Ledger,* Aug. 1, 1845; Sept. 3, 1850.

31. Ibid., Sept. 2, 1850.

32. Scharf and Westcott, *History of Philadelphia,* 1:674n, 722–23.

33. Warner, *The Private City,* p. 154.

34. *Public Ledger,* August 8, 1856.

35. Ibid., May 4, 1858.

36. The affidavit recounting these events appeared in the *Philadelphia Inquirer,* Nov. 25, 1872.

37. *Public Ledger,* July 26, Sept. 13, 1867.

38. Yasukichi Yasuba, *Birth Rates of the White Population in the United States, 1800–1860: an Economic Study.* The Johns Hopkins University Studies in History and Political Science, series 79 (1961), no. 2

Theodore Hershberg

6

Free Blacks in Antebellum Philadelphia

Afro-American history in general has received a great deal of attention from historians in the past decade. The same cannot be said about the history of black Americans free before the Civil War. Studies published since Leon Litwack's *North of Slavery* have considered racial discrimination in the legal tradition, the relationship between race and politics, the establishment of black utopian communities, and the role of blacks in the abolitionist movement.[1] With a few exceptions, the literature lacks a solid empirical base, a sophisticated methodological and theoretical approach, and a focus on the black community itself.[2] There exists an important need for new studies of the family and social structure, of the development of community institutions such as the church, school and beneficial society, and of migration and social mobility.[3]

Antebellum Philadelphia offers the historian an important opportunity to study each of these topics. The free-black population of the city had its roots in the eighteenth century. The city's free-black population in 1860, upwards of 22,000, was the largest outside the Slave South and second only to Baltimore. All-black churches, schools, and voluntary societies were numerous. The National Negro Convention Movement met for the first time in Philadelphia in 1830, and the city hosted such meetings fre-

This chapter is a revised version of an article that appeared in the *Journal of Social History* 5 (Winter, 1971–72): 183–209. Those readers interested in fuller documentation are referred to the footnotes in that article.

A special note of thanks must go to the Metro Center of the National Institute of Mental Health. Their financial support (2ROI. MH. 16621), which began in April 1969, has made this research possible.

quently thereafter. Many of the leading black abolitionists such as James Forten, Robert Purvis, and William Still were Philadelphians. Most significantly for the historian, the data describing all facets of this history are extant. The black history collections and the papers of the Pennsylvania Abolition Society at the Historical Society of Pennsylvania and the Library Company of Philadelphia are even richer for the antebellum period than the Schomburg Collection of the New York Public Library.

This essay is a preliminary progress report.[4] It deals with three important themes which emerge in the study of nineteenth-century black Philadelphians: the socioeconomic deterioration of the antebellum black community, a comparison of the condition of ex-slaves and free-born blacks in the city, and a discussion of the value of understanding the urban experience in the study of black history.

A Context of Decline

The decision of the Pennsylvania Abolition Society in 1837 to take a census of Philadelphia's free-Negro population was made for both a specific and a general purpose. The specific purpose was to defeat the move, already underway in Harrisburg, to write into the new state constitution the complete disfranchisement of Pennsylvania blacks. The general purpose was "to repel" those who denounced "the whole of the free colored people as unworthy of any favor, asserting that they were nuisances in the community fit only to fill alms houses and jails." [5]

The strategy employed to accomplish these ends reveals a good deal about the faith which the abolitionists had in hard fact and reasoned argument. The data from the census were presented to the delegates at Harrisburg, and to the public at large, in the form of a forty-page pamphlet summarizing the data.[6]

The pamphlet argued that disfranchisement should be defeated because the free-Negro population made a worthy contribution to the well-being of the entire community. Blacks paid considerable taxes and rents, owned property, were not disproportionately paupers and criminals, cared for their own underprivileged, and, finally, put money as consumers into the income stream of the general economy. The facts contained in the published pamphlet, therefore, "gave great satisfaction affording the friends of the colored people strong and convincing arguments against those who were opposed to their enjoying the rights and privileges of freemen." [7]

Although unsuccessful in the specific purpose—blacks were disfranchised in Pennsylvania until 1870, when the 15th Amendment was adopted—the Abolitionists and Quakers undertook further censuses in 1847 and 1856.[8] As in 1838, these later censuses were followed by printed pamphlets which duly noted the discrimination and problems facing free Negroes and counseled patience to the "magnanimous sufferers," as they referred to their Negro brethren. The general tone of the pamphlets, however, was *optimistic* and pointed to important *gains* made in past decades. The overall optimism, however, proved unfounded when the actual manuscript censuses were submitted to computer analysis.

The "friends of the colored people," unfortunately, had been carried away by their admirable purpose. It was one thing to document that free Negroes were not worthless, that they could indeed survive outside of the structured environment of slavery, and even that they could create a community with their own churches, schools, and beneficial societies; but it was quite another thing to argue that the people and the institutions they created actually *prospered* in the face of overwhelming obstacles. It is not so much that the Abolitionists and Quakers were wrong, as that they went too far. And in so doing, they obscured a remarkable deterioration in the socioeconomic condition of blacks from 1830 to the Civil War.

Beginning in 1829 and continuing through the ensuing two decades, Philadelphia Negroes were the victims of half a dozen major anti-black riots and many more minor mob actions. Negro churches, schools, homes, and even an orphanage were set on fire. Some blacks were killed, many beaten, and others run out of town.[9] Contemporaries attributed the net loss in the Negro population between 1840 and 1850 in large part to riots.[10] In the same decade, the white population grew 63 percent. While it is important to maintain the perspective that the anti-black violence occurred within a larger context of anti-Catholic violence, this knowledge must have been small comfort to Philadelphia Negroes.

A victimized minority, one reasons, should organize to bring *political* pressure on local government officials. But black Philadelphians after 1838, as we have seen, were denied even this remedy. Disfranchisement of all Negroes, even of those citizens who owned sufficient property to vote in all elections during the previous twenty-three years, was all the more tragic and ironic because, at the same time, all white males in Pennsylvania over the age of twenty-one were specifically given the right to vote.

In addition to the larger, less measurable forces such as race riots, population decline,[11] and disfranchisement, after 1838 black Philadelphians suffered a turn for the worse in wealth, residential segregation, family structure and employment.

The antebellum black community was extremely poor. The total wealth—that is, the combined value of real and personal property holdings—for three out of every five households in both 1838 and 1847 amounted to $60 or less.[12] The distribution of wealth itself, moreover, was strikingly unequal within the black population. In both 1838 and 1847 the poorest half of the population owned only one-twentieth of the total wealth, while the wealthiest 10 percent of the population held 70 percent of the total wealth; at the very apex of the community, the wealthiest 1 percent accounted for fully 30 percent of the total wealth.[13]

Between 1838 and 1847, there was a 10 percent decrease in per capita value of personal property and a slight decrease in per capita total wealth among Philadelphia blacks. Although the number of households included in the 1847 census was 30 percent greater than in 1838, the number of real property holders fell from 294 to 280, and their respective percentages fell from 9 percent to 6 percent. There was, in other words, despite a considerable increase in the number of households, both an absolute and percentage decrease in the number of real property holders.

The decline in wealth was accompanied by a measurable rise in residential segregation over the decade. Disfranchisement, a decade of race riots, and a general backlash against abolitionist activities, all contributed to the creation of a social atmosphere in which it was considerably more difficult for even the wealthiest of Negroes to acquire real property. It is tempting to conclude quite simply that rising racism meant that a far higher price had to be paid in order to induce a white man to sell land to a black man. Stating such a conclusion with complete confidence, however, requires further *comparative* research in order to determine if instead this phenomenon applied equally to all ethnic groups. That is, was it a period of generally appreciating land values?

The actual measurement of residential segregation depends upon
the use of a "grid square"—an area roughly one and one quarter
blocks square—and is a vast improvement over far larger geographical entities such as districts or wards. For the period under
study, each Negro household was located on detailed maps and
its precise grid square recorded. All variables about each household, then, are observable and measurable in small, uniquely
defined units.

Residential segregation is measured in two dimensions: (1) the
distribution of the household population—that is, the number of
grid squares in which Negro households were located; and (2)
the *density* of the population—that is, the number of Negro
households per grid. Residential segregation was rising in the
decade before 1838 and it increased steadily to 1860. Between
1838 and 1847, average density of blacks increased 13 percent in
all grid squares inhabited by blacks; more important, however,
the percentage of households occupying the densest grid squares
(those with more than 100 black households) increased by almost
10 percent. Between 1850 and 1860 the average density changed
very little, but the trend toward settlement in the densest grids
continued. By 1860 the number of households occupying the
densest grid squares reached more than one in four, an increase of
11 percent over the previous decade and the high point between
1838 and 1880. During the Civil War decade, residential segregation fell off but rose again from 1870 to 1880 as migration from
the South swelled the Negro population of Philadelphia to 31,700,
an increase of 43 percent over both the 1860 and 1870 totals.

Data from the Abolitionist and Quaker censuses, the U. S.
Census of 1880 and W. E. B. DuBois' study of the Seventh
ward in 1896–97 indicate, in each instance, that two-parent households were characteristic of 78 percent of black families. That
statistical average, however, belies a grimmer reality for the poorest
blacks. There was a decline in the percentage of two-parent
households for the poorest fifth of the population from 70 percent in 1838 to 63 percent ten years later, and for the poorest
half of the black population the decline was from 73 percent to
68 percent. In other words, among the poorest half of the community at mid-century, roughly one family in three was headed
by a female.[14]

An unequal female-male sex ratio no doubt indirectly affected family building and stability. Between 1838 and 1860 the number of black females per 1,000 black males increased from 1,326 to 1,417. For whites in 1860, the corresponding figure was 1,088. Between 1860 and 1890 the sex ratio for blacks moved in the direction of parity: 1,360 in 1870, 1,263 in 1880 and 1,127 in 1890. The age and sex distribution throughout the period 1838–90 indicates that the movement away from, and after 1860 back toward, equal distribution of the sexes was due to a change in the number of young black males in the 20 to 44 age bracket. Changes in this age bracket usually result from two related factors: occupational opportunities and in- and out-migration rates. The remarkably high excess of females over males throughout the period probably reflects poor employment opportunities for black men (while the demand for black female domestics remained high) accompanied by net out-migration of young black males, and the gradual improvement of industrial opportunities for young black males after 1860 accompanied by net in-migration of increasing numbers of young black men. The sociological consequences of such an imbalance in the sex ratios are familiar: illegitimacy, delinquency, broken homes. In light of these statistics it is surprising that the percentage of two-parent households was as high as it was.

More important for our purposes, however, is another measure of the condition of the entire black population often obscured by the debate over the matrifocality of the black family, focusing as it does on narrow statistical analysis of traditional household units. How many blacks were living outside of black households? How many were inmates of public institutions? How many were forced not only to delay beginning families, but to make lives for themselves *outside* the black family unit, residing in boarding houses as transients, or living in white homes as domestic servants? [15]

The data indicate that there was a slow but steady rise in the percentage of black men and women who found themselves outside the black family. Between 1850 and 1880 their numbers nearly doubled. By 1880, 6,000 persons—slightly less than one-third of the adult population (inmates, transients and servants combined)—were living outside the normal family structures. One out of every five adults lived and worked in a white household as a domestic servant. That so many Negroes took positions outside their traditional family units is testimony to the strength and pervasiveness of the job discrimination which existed at large in the economy; that this occurred within a context of widening occupational opportunities for whites, a benefit of increasing industrialization and the factory system, makes it even more significant. In 1847 less than one-half of 1 percent of the black male work force was employed in factories. And this came at a time, it should be remembered, when thousands of Irish immigrants were engaged in factory work.

Blacks were not only denied access to new jobs in the expanding factory system; because of increasing job competition with the Irish they also lost their traditional predominance in many semi-skilled and unskilled occupations. The 1847 census identified 5 percent of the black male work force in the relatively well-paying occupations of hod-carrier and stevedore. A letter to a city newspaper written in 1849 by one "P. O." reported,

> that there may be, and undoubtedly is, a direct competition between them [the blacks and Irish] as to labor we all know. The wharves and new buildings attest this fact, in the person of our stevedores and hod-carriers as does all places of labor; and when a few years ago we saw none but blacks, we now see nothing but Irish.[16]

"P. O." proved perceptive indeed. According to the 1850 U.S. Census the percentage of black hod-carriers and stevedores in the black male work force fell in just three years from 5 percent to 1 percent. The 1850 Census, moreover, reported occupations for the entire county, and included 30 percent more black male occupations than the 1847 Census; nevertheless the absolute number of black hod-carriers fell sharply from 98 to 28 and stevedores from 58 to 27.

A similar pattern of increasing discrimination affected the ranks of the skilled. Blacks complained not only that it was "difficult for them to find places for their sons as apprentices to learn mechanical trades," [17] but also that those who had skills found it more difficult to practice them. The "Register of Trades of the Colored People," published in 1838 by the Pennsylvania Abolition Society to encourage white patronage of black artisans, noted that 23 percent of 656 skilled artisans did not practice their skills because of "prejudice against them." [18] The 1856 Census recorded considerable deterioration among the ranks of the skilled.

The percentage of skilled artisans not practicing their trades rose from 23 percent in 1838 to approximately 38 percent in 1856. Skilled black craftsmen were "compelled to abandon their trades on account of the unrelenting prejudice against their color." [19]

Job discrimination, then, was complete and growing: blacks were excluded from new areas of the economy, uprooted from many of their traditional unskilled jobs, denied apprenticeships for their sons, and prevented from practicing the skills they already possessed. All social indicators—race riots, population decrease, disfranchisement, residential segregation, per capita wealth, ownership of real property, family structure and occupational opportunities—pointed toward socioeconomic deterioration within Philadelphia's antebellum black community.

Ex-slave and Free-born

Among the 3,300 households and 12,000 persons included in the 1838 census, about one household in four contained at least one person who although free in 1838 had been born a slave. Living in these 806 households were some 1,141 ex-slaves (or 9 percent of the entire population).

What was the condition of the ex-slave relative to his free-born brother? Were ex-slaves in any way responsible for the socioeconomic deterioration just described? Contemporaries perceived two very different effects of direct contact with slavery. "Upon feeble and common minds," according to one view, the slave experience was "withering" and induced "a listlessness and an indifference to the future." Even if the slave somehow managed to gain his freedom "the vicious habits of slavery" remained "worked into the very grain of his character." But for others "who resisted . . . and bought their own freedom with the hard-earned fruits of their own industry," the struggle for "liberty" resulted in "a desire for improvement" which "invigorated all their powers and gave energy and dignity to their character as freemen." [20] An analysis of the data permits us to determine whether both groups were found equally in antebellum Philadelphia or whether one was more representative of all ex-slaves than the other.

The richness of detail in the census schedules allows us to make several important distinctions in the data describing the ex-slave households: we know which of the 806 households were headed by ex-slaves themselves—314—and how these 40 percent of all

ex-slave households were freed—if, for instance, they were "manumitted" or if, as they put it, they had "bought themselves."

We are dealing, then, with four ex-slave categories: (1) 493
households in which at least one ex-slave lived, but which had
a free-born household head; I shall refer to this group as free-
headed, ex-slave households; (2) 314 households in which at least
one ex-slave lived and which had an ex-slave household head; I
shall refer to this group as ex-slave headed households. In this
second group of ex-slave headed households, I have selected two
sub-groups for analysis: (3) 146 ex-slave household heads who
were manumitted, and (4) 96 ex-slave household heads who
bought their own freedom.[21]

Cutting across all four of these groups is the dimension of sex.
The census identified household heads as males, females, and
widows. There was a strong and direct relationship between
family size, wealth, and male sex, so that the largest families had
the most wealth and the greatest likelihood of being headed by a
male. Because there was also a strong and direct relationship
between sex and almost all other variables, with males enjoying
by far the more fortunate circumstances, it is important to dif-
ferentiate by sex in comparing the general condition of the four
ex-slave groups to that of the free-born population. Ex-slaves
differed from their free-born neighbors in a variety of significant
social indicators:

Family Size

The family size of all ex-slave households was 10 percent larger
than households all of whose members were free-born: 4.27
persons as compared to 3.88. Families of ex-slave households
headed by free-born males and those families headed by males
who bought their own freedom, were 20 percent larger: 4.70.
The instances in which free-born families were larger occurred
only where female, and to a lesser extent, widow ex-slave households were involved. (This, by the way, is the general pattern
in most variables; in other words, ex-slave females and widows
more closely resembled their free-born counterparts than ex-slave
males resembled free-born males.)

Two-Parent Household

The percentage of two-parent households was generally larger for
the ex-slaves. Taken together, two-parent households were found

80 percent of the time among ex-slaves, while the figure for the free-born was 77 percent. A significant difference, however, was found in the case of ex-slave household heads who bought their own freedom. In this group 90 percent were two-parent households.

Church

For two basic reasons the all-black church has long been recognized as the key institution of the Negro community: first, an oppressed and downtrodden people used religion for spiritual sustenance and for its promise of a better life in the next world; second, with the ability to participate in the political, social, and economic spheres of the larger white society sharply curtailed, Negroes turned to the church for fulfillment of their secular needs.

Important in the twentieth century, the church was vital to blacks in the nineteenth. Philadelphia Negroes were so closed off from the benefits of white society that church affiliation became a fundamental prerequisite to a decent and, indeed, bearable existence.[22] For this reason, non-church affiliation, rather than poverty, was the distinguishing characteristic of the most disadvantaged group in the community. Non-church goers must have enjoyed few of the benefits and services which accrued to those who were affiliated with a church in some manner. The socioeconomic profile of non-church goers is depressing. They fared considerably less well than their church-going neighbors in all significant social indicators; they had smaller families, fewer two-parent households, high residential density levels, and they were disproportionately poor; their ratios for membership in beneficial societies and for the number of school-age children in school was one-fourth and one-half, respectively, that of the larger community; occupationally, they were decidedly over-represented among the unskilled sectors of the work force.

In this sense, then, the percentage of households with no members attending church is a more valuable index of general social condition than any other. Eighteen percent of the free-born households had no members attending church; for all ex-slave households the figure was *half* as great. Ex-slave households were one in four in the community-at-large; they were less than one in ten among households with no members attending church. The ratios were even lower (one in twenty) for ex-slave headed households and lowest (one in thirty) for ex-slaves who bought themselves.

About 150 households, or 5 percent of the church-going population of the entire community, attended 23 predominately white churches. These churches had only "token" integration, allowing a few Negroes to worship in pews set apart from the rest of the congregation. Ex-slaves of all groups attended white churches in approximately the same ratio as did the free-born: one household in twenty.

The church-going population of the entire community consisted of 2,776 households distributed among five religious denominations: Methodists (73 percent), Baptists (9 percent), Presbyterians (7 percent), Episcopalians (7 percent), and Catholics (3 percent). Methodists worshipped in eight and Baptists in four all-black congregations scattered throughout the city and districts. Together they accounted for more than eight of every ten churchgoers. The various ex-slave groups were found an average of 11 percent more frequently among Methodists, and 30 percent more frequently among Baptists.

In any case, Methodists and Baptists differed little from each other and to describe them is to characterize the entire community: poor and unskilled. Within each denomination, however, a single church—Union Methodist and Union Baptist—served as the social base for their respective elites. And while ex-slaves attended all of the community's all-black churches, it was in these two churches where the ex-slaves were most frequently found. The ex-slave members of these two church shared the socio-economic and cultural characteristics of the community's elite denominations, the Episcopalians and the Presbyterians, and it should not be surprising, therefore, to find ex-slaves of all groups underrepresented in each of these last two denominations.

Beneficial Society

Next to the church in value to the community were the all-black beneficial societies. These important institutions functioned as rudimentary insurance groups which provided their members with relief in sickness, aid during extreme poverty, and burial expenses at death.

There were over 100 distinct societies in antebellum Philadelphia. They grew out of obvious need and were early manifestations of the philosophy of "self-help" which became so popular later in the nineteenth century. Almost always they were affiliated directly with one of the all-black churches. The first beneficial society, known as the "Free African Society," was founded in 1787. A dozen societies existed by 1815, 50 by 1830 and 106 by 1847.

Slightly more than 50 percent of free-born households were members of the various societies. Making good the philosophy of "self-help," half a century before Booker T. Washington, the societies found ex-slaves more eager to join their ranks than free-born blacks. Each group of ex-slaves had a higher percentage of members, especially ex-slave headed households (61 percent), ex-slaves who purchased their own freedom (65 percent), and the males among the latter group (70 percent).

Membership in beneficial societies varied significantly by wealth and status. Ranking the entire household population in thirty distinct wealth categories revealed that, beginning with the poorest, the percentage of membership rose with increasing wealth until the wealthiest six categories. For this top 11 percent of the population, however, membership in beneficial societies declined from 92 percent to 81 percent. Among the wealthiest, and this applied equally to ex-slaves, there was less need for membership in beneficial societies.

Education

One household in four among the free-born population sent children to school. For ex-slave households the corresponding figure was more than one in three. Ex-slave households had slightly fewer children, but sent a considerably greater percentage of their children to school. For free-born households the percentage was 55 percent; for all ex-slave households 67 percent; and for ex-slave headed households the figure rose to 72 percent. To the extent that education was valuable to blacks, the children of ex-slaves were better off.

Location and Density

Small groups of ex-slaves clustered disproportionately in the outlying districts of Kensington, Northern Liberties, and Spring Garden. Twenty-five percent of the entire black population of Philadelphia, they comprised about 35 percent of the black population in these areas. Most ex-slaves, however, lived in the same proportions and in the same blocks as did the free-born population.

More interesting than the pattern of their distribution throughout the city, however, was the level of population density in which they lived, that is, the number of black neighbors who lived close by. To calculate the number of black households in a grid square of approximately 1¼ blocks, three density levels were used: 1–20, 21–100, and in excess of 100 households per grid square.[23]

The less dense areas were characterized by larger families, greater presence of two-parent households, less imbalance between the sexes, and fewer families whose members were entirely not native to Pennsylvania. In these areas lived a disproportionately greater number of wealthy families, and among them, a correspondingly over-represented number of real property owners. Here white-collar and skilled workers lived in greater percentages than elsewhere in the city, and unskilled workers were decidedly few in both percentage and absolute number. The major exceptions to the distribution of wealth and skill came as the result of the necessity for shopkeepers and craftsmen to locate their homes and their businesses in the city's more densely populated sections.

Ex-slave households were more likely than free-born households to be found in the least dense areas (one in four as compared with one in five). Conversely, ex-slave households were less likely to be found in those areas with the greatest density of black population.

Wealth

The parameters of wealth for Negroes in antebellum Philadelphia have already been described. The community was impoverished. Poverty, nevertheless, did not touch all groups equally. In terms of average total wealth—including both real and personal property —free-headed ex-slave households differed little from the free-born population. In considering the ex-slave headed household, however, differences emerge. Average total wealth for this group was 20 percent greater; for males in this group, 53 percent greater; and for males who freed themselves, 63 percent greater.

The most significant differences in wealth by far occurred

in real property holding. One household in thirteen or slightly
less than 8 percent among the free-born owned real property. For
all ex-slave households the corresponding ratio was one in eight;
for ex-slave headed households, one in five; for males who were
in this group, one in four; and most dramatically, for males
who purchased their own freedom, one in three owned real property. To these ex-slaves, owning their own homes or a piece of
land must have provided something, perhaps a stake in society, of
peculiarly personal significance. Distribution of wealth, to view
the matter from a different perspective, was less unequal for ex-
slave households, particularly ex-slave household heads. The
poorest half of the free-born and ex-slave headed households
owned 5 and 7 percent respectively of the total wealth; for the
wealthiest quarter of each group the corresponding figure was 86
and 73 percent; for the wealthiest tenth, 67 and 56 percent; and
for the wealthiest one-hundredth, 30 and 21 percent. Overall
wealth distribution, in other words, while still skewed toward
pronounced inequality, was more equally distributed for ex-slave
household heads in the middle and upper wealth categories.

Occupation

The final area of comparison between the ex-slaves and the free-
born is occupation.[24] Analysis of the data using the same classification schema for Negroes as for white ethnic groups shows that,
although such schema are necessary in order to compare the
Negro to white ethnic groups, they are entirely unsatisfactory
tools of analysis for social stratification within the Negro community. Despite the fact that the Negroes who comprised the
labor force of antebellum Philadelphia described themselves as
engaged in 400 different occupations, a stark fact emerges from
the analysis: there was almost no occupational differentiation!

Five occupations accounted for 70 percent of the entire male
work force: laborers (38 percent), porters (11.5 percent), waiters
(11.5 percent), seamen (5 percent), and carters (4 percent);
another 10 percent were employed in miscellaneous laboring
capacities. Taken together, eight out of every ten working men
were unskilled laborers. Another 16 percent worked as skilled
artisans, but fully one-half of this fortunate group were barbers
and shoemakers; the other skilled craftsmen were scattered among
building-construction (3.2 percent), home-furnishing (1.3 per-

cent), leather goods (1.2 percent), and metal work (1.2 percent). Less than one-half of 1 percent of Negroes, as pointed out in another context, found employment in the developing factory system. The remaining 4 percent of the labor force was engaged in white-collar professions. They were largely proprietors who sold food or second-hand clothing from vending carts, and should not be considered as "storeowners."

The occupational structure for females was even less differentiated than for males. More than eight out of every ten women were employed in day-work capacities (as opposed to those who lived and worked in white households) as domestic servants: "washers" (52 percent), "day-workers" (22 percent), and miscellaneous domestics (6 percent). Fourteen percent worked as seamstresses, and they accounted for all the skilled workers among the female labor force. Finally, about 5 percent were engaged in white-collar work, which, like the males, meant vending clothing and food.

It should come, then, as no surprise that there are few distinctions of significance to make between the occupational structure of the ex-slaves and free-born work forces. The differences in vertical occupational categories find male ex-slave household heads more likely to be in white-collar positions (7 percent as opposed to 4 percent for the free-born), equally distributed in the skilled trades, and slightly less represented in the unskilled occupations (75 percent as opposed to 78 percent). Within the horizontal categories there were few important differences. Male ex-slave household heads were more likely than the free-born to be employed as porters, carpenters, blacksmiths, preachers, and clothes dealers.

In summary, then, we find the ex-slaves with larger families, greater likelihood of two-parent households, higher affiliation rates in church and beneficial society, sending more of their children to school, living more frequently in the least dense areas of the county, generally wealthier, owning considerably more real property and being slightly more fortunate in occupational differentiation. By almost every socioeconomic measure the ex-slave fared better than his free-born brother. While ex-slaves were distributed throughout the socioeconomic scale, they were more likely to be part of the community's small middle class, characterized more by their hard-working, conscientious, and God-fearing life style than by a concentration of wealth and power.

An Urban Perspective

On the basis of the data presented it is possible to state two conclusions, offer a working hypothesis, and argue for the necessity of an urban perspective. First, the relatively better condition of the ex-slave, especially the ex-slave who was both a male and who bought his own freedom, confirms the speculations of a few historians that the slave-born Negro freed before the Civil War was exceptional: a uniquely gifted individual who succeeded in internalizing the ethic of deferred gratification in the face of enormous difficulties.[25] More striking was the fact that the socioeconomic condition of the great majority of ex-slaves was not, as one would expect, markedly inferior to that of the free-born. That ex-slaves were generally better off than free-born blacks, however, should not suggest anything more than relative superiority; it does not imply prosperity and should not obscure the generally impoverished and deteriorating condition of the black community. Second, because the remaining 91 percent of Philadelphia's antebellum black population was free-born, the dismal and declining socioeconomic circumstances of that population cannot be attributed to direct contact with the "slave experience." Direct contact with slavery was undoubtedly a *sufficient* cause of low status and decay; it most certainly was not a *necessary* cause.[26]

This is not an argument that the impact of slavery was benign. Rather, it is an argument that the antebellum Northern city was destructive as well. Both slavery and the discrimination faced by free Negroes in the urban environment were aspects of the racism which pervaded the institutions and informed the values of the larger white society.

The comparison of the free-born and the ex-slave was undertaken in an effort to learn more about the question which students of the black experience want answered: What was the effect of slavery on the slaves? In the case of antebellum Philadelphia, the ex-slaves may not be representative of the slave experience. If they were, however, our insight would necessarily be limited to the effect of the mildest slavery system as it was practiced in Maryland, Delaware, and Virginia.[27]

De-emphasizing the direct impact of slavery does not imply that the institution of slavery, and the debasement and prejudice it generated, had no consequences. The indirect effect of slavery was pervasive. The pro-slavery propaganda provided a justification not only for slavery but for the widespread discriminatory treatment of the free Negro both before and after emancipation. Yet, despite an understanding of the pervasive impact of slavery and the historian's often overwhelming sense of moral outrage, the effects of the slave experience should not be treated monolithically. Although Stanley Elkins' interpretation of slavery may be in error, few historians doubt that his urging of scholars to end the morality debate and to employ new methods and different disciplines in the study of slavery was correct and long overdue.

There is no historically valid reason to treat the slave experience as entirely destructive or entirely benign; nor, for that matter, does historical reality necessarily fall mid-way between the two. It may be more useful to study the problems which blacks faced at different times and in different places in their history and make the attempt to trace their historical origins rather than to begin with slavery and assume that it represented in all instances the historical root. Some of the problems faced by blacks may more accurately be traced to the processes of urbanization, industrialization, and immigration, occurring in a setting of racial inequality rather than slavery.

A recent study presents data which suggest the post-slavery, and perhaps urban origins, of the matrifocal black family. In groundbreaking essays on the Negro family after the Civil War, Herbert Gutman has demonstrated convincingly that traditional interpretations of slavery and its effect on the black family are seriously misleading. Examining "the family patterns of those Negroes closest in time to actual chattel slavery," Gutman did not find "instability," "chaos," or "disorder." Instead, in fourteen varied Southern cities and counties between 1865 and 1880, he found viable two-parent households ranging from 70 percent to 90 percent.[28]

It is significant to note that of the areas studied by Gutman the four lowest percentages of two-parent households were found in cities: Natchez and Beaufort 70 percent, Richmond 73 percent, and Mobile 74 percent. The urban experience was in some way responsible for the weaker family structure, and for a whole set of other negative socioeconomic consequences, all of which are found in the Philadelphia data.

Yet the city is more than a locale. Slavery itself underwent major transformations in the urban setting.[29] Sustained advances in technology, transportation, and communication made the city the context for innovation, and the innovation, in turn, generated countless opportunities for upward mobility for those who could take advantage of them. And here was the rub. Blacks, alone among city dwellers, were excluded not only from their fair share, but from almost any chance for improvement generated by urban development. That the exclusion was not systematic, but, by and large, incidental, did not make it any less effective. The city provided an existence at once superior to and inferior to that of the countryside: for those who were free to pursue their fortunes, the city provided infinitely more opportunities and far greater rewards; for those who were denied access altogether (or for those who failed) the city provided few advantages and less comfort. There were few interstices between.

The data presented in this essay point to the destructiveness of the urban experience for blacks in nineteenth-century Philadelphia.[30] Although much research remains, it is possible to offer a hypothesis. The forces which shaped modern America—urbanization, industrialization, and immigration—operated for blacks within a context of institutional racism and structural inequality. In the antebellum context blacks were unable to compete on equal terms with either the native white American worker or the thousands of newly arrived Irish and German immigrants. Philadelphia Negroes suffered in the competition with the Irish and Germans and recovered somewhat during the Civil War and Reconstruction decades, only to suffer again, in much the same circumstances, in competition with the "new" immigrant groups—the Italians, Jews, Poles, and Slavs—who began arriving in the 1880s. Best characterized as a low-status economic group early in the century, Philadelphia's blacks found themselves a deprived and degraded caste at its close.

Students of black history have not adequately appreciated the impact of the urban experience. In part this is due to several general problems: to the larger neglect of urban history; to unequal educational opportunities which prevented many potential black scholars from study and other students from publication; to difficulties inherent in writing history "from-the-bottom-up"; and to present reward mechanisms which place a high premium on quickly publishable materials involving either no new research or shoddy and careless efforts.

There are, however, other and more important considerations involving no little irony. The moral revulsion to slavery prevented development of alternative explanations of low-status and decay. In the immediate post-slavery decades and throughout the twentieth century, blacks and their white allies took refuge in an explanation used by many abolitionists before them: namely, that slavery and not racial inferiority was responsible for the black condition. They were, of course, not wrong; it was rather that they did not go far enough. It was, and still is, much easier to lament the sins of one's forefathers than it is to confront the injustices in more contemporary socioeconomic systems.

The Philadelphia data from 1838 to 1880 enable one to examine this theme in minute detail. Although 90 percent of the nation's black population in 1880 was Southern and overwhelmingly rural, the key to the twentieth century lies in understanding the consequences of the migration from the farm to the city. The experience of Philadelphia Negroes in the nineteenth century foreshadowed the fate of millions of black migrants who, seeking a better life, found different miseries in, as E. Franklin Frazier put it, the "cities of destruction."

If we are to succeed in understanding the urban experience, we must dismiss simplistic explanations which attribute all present-day failings to "the legacy of slavery" or to "the problems of unacculturated rural migrants lacking the skills necessary to compete in an advanced technology." We must understand, instead, the social dynamics and consequences of competition and accomodation among different racial, ethnic, and religious groups, taking place in an urban context of racial discrimination and structural inequality.

NOTES

1. Leon Litwack, *North of Slavery* (Chicago, 1961); Arthur Zilversmit, *The First Emancipation* (Chicago, 1967); Eugene H. Berwanger, *The Frontier Against Slavery: Western Anti-Negro Prejudice and the Slavery Extension Controversy* (Urbana, 1967); V. Jacque Voegeli, *Free But Not Equal: The Midwest and the Negro During the Civil War* (Chicago, 1969); James A. Rawley, *Race and Politics,* (Philadelphia, 1969); Eric Foner, *Free Soil, Free Labor, Free Men* (New York, 1970); William and Jane Pease, *Black Utopia* (Wisconsin, 1963); Benjamin Quarles, *Black Abolitionists* (Oxford, 1969);

Carleton Mabee, *Black Freedom: The Non-Violent Abolitionists, 1830 to the Civil War* (New York, 1970).

2. Luther P. Jackson, *Free Negro and Property Holding in Virginia 1830–1860* (New York, 1942) and John Hope Franklin, *The Free Negro in North Carolina, 1790–1860* (North Carolina, 1943); there are, of course, many other state and local studies: W. E. B. DuBois, *The Philadelphia Negro* (Philadelphia, 1899); Edward R. Turner, *The Negro in Pennsylvania* (Washington, 1911); John Russell, *The Free Negro in Virginia, 1830–1860* (Baltimore, 1913); John Daniels, *In Freedom's Birthplace: A Study of Boston's Negroes* (Boston, 1914); James M. Wright, *The Free Negro in Maryland* (New York, 1921); Robert A. Warner, *New Haven Negroes* (New Haven, 1940); Emma Lou Thornbrough, *The Negro in Indiana* (Indianapolis, 1957). Especially valuable articles include Carter Woodson, "The Negroes of Cincinnati Prior to the Civil War," *Journal of Negro History* 1 (Jan. 1916); Charles S. Snydor, "The Free Negro in Mississippi before the Civil War," *American Historical Review* 32 (July 1927); E. Horace Fitchett "The Origin and Growth of the Free Negro Population of Charleston, South Carolina," *Journal of Negro History* 26 (Oct. 1941); J. Merton England, "The Free-Negro in Ante-Bellum Tennessee," *Journal of Southern History* 9 (Feb. 1943).

3. There are, of course, important beginnings. Among them are E. Franklin Frazier's *The Free Negro Family* (Nashville, 1932) and Carter G. Woodson's *The Education of the Negro Prior to 1861* (Washington, 1915), *The History of Negro Church* (Washington, 1921), and *Free Negro Heads of Families in the United States* (Washington, 1925).

4. The research, known informally as the Philadelphia Social History Project, is a study of comparative social mobility in nineteenth-century Philadelphia, focusing on the patterns of three distinct groups: Negroes, Irish, and Germans. The research was recently expanded to include native-white–Americans in order to study, in the most comprehensive comparative perspective, the relationship between social mobility and social stratification, industrialization, family structure, and neighborhood.

5. Edward Needles, *Ten Years' Progress: A Comparison of the State and Condition of the Colored People in the City and County of Philadelphia from 1837 to 1847* (Philadelphia, 1849), pp. 7–8.

6. Pennsylvania Abolition Society, *The Present State and Condition of the Free People of Color of the City of Philadelphia and Adjoining Districts* (Philadelphia, 1838), 40 pp.

7. Needles, *Ten Years' Progress*, pp. 7–8.

8. Society of Friends, *Statistical Inquiry into the Condition of the People of Colour of the City and Districts of Philadelphia* (Philadelphia, 1849), 44 pp.; Benjamin Bacon, *Statistics of the Colored People of Philadelphia* (Philadelphia, 1859), 2nd ed., rev., 24 pp.

9. Sam Bass Warner, Jr., *The Private City* (Philadelphia, 1968), see chap. 7, "Riots and the Restoration of Order," pp. 125–57.

10. Society of Friends, *Statistical Inquiry,* p. 7.

11. There was also a net population loss for blacks of .17 percent between 1860 and 1870; the white population in the same decade, however, increased some 20 percent.

12. This fact precludes the use of simple economic class analysis in determining social stratification in the black community. Social distinctions indispensable to the study of social stratification do exist among this 60 percent of the household population; however, they do not emerge along economic lines. Households averaging $30 of total wealth are not distinctively different from households worth $20 or $50. Important social distinctions can be determined by using specific non-economic measures such as church affiliation or a more general non-economic measure such as "life style," which, in turn, is described by a number of other variables: residence, family structure, education, occupation, etc.

13. The unequal distribution of wealth was not unique to the black population. Stuart Blumin, "Mobility and Change in Ante Bellum Philadelphia," in *Nineteenth-Century Cities,* Stephan Thernstrom and Richard Sennett, eds. (New Haven: Yale Univ. Press, 1969), found greater inequality among a sample of the entire Philadelphia population in the U.S. Census for 1860 than I did among all blacks in the Abolitionist and Quaker censuses in 1838 and 1847.

14. Ninety-nine percent of all male-headed households were two-parent households as well. Female-headed households in the Abolitionist and Quaker censuses were invariably one-parent households.

15. The data necessary to answer a series of important questions concerning the black men and women who lived and worked in white households as domestic servants will soon be available. Their age structure, marital status, mobility, social status, and the possibility of their families' living close-by will be examined. It will be valuable to know whether "live-in" service was a short-term or long-term experience and to determine its effects on family building, family structure, and child-rearing techniques. Perhaps the most important question, and one which relates this form of employment to the experience of other ethnic groups, is whether such employment was seen by blacks as severely limiting, demeaning, and poor-paying—engaged in only because there were no other occupational alternatives available to them—or if they embraced such work as their own domain, desirable, and were pleased by the standard of living it afforded them.

16. *The Daily Sun,* November 10, 1849. I am indebted to Bruce Laurie who originally came across this letter.

17. *Register of the Trades of the Colored People in the City of Philadelphia and Districts* (Philadelphia, 1833), pp. 1–8.

18. Appendix to the *Memorial from the People of Color to the Legislature of Pennsylvania,* reprinted in *Hazard's Register* 9 (1832): 361.

19. Benjamin C. Bacon, *Statistics of the Colored People of Philadelphia* (Philadelphia, 1859), 2nd ed., pp. 13–15.

20. Needles, *Ten Years' Progress,* p. 2.

21. The data describing the ex-slaves and the free-born, although compre-

hensive, are not complete; specific age, specific place of birth, and length of residence information are not included in the census. Such data will become available for a significant number of individuals only after linkage between censuses (especially between the Quaker census of 1847 and the U.S. Census of 1850) is accomplished because the latter began in 1850 to list age and place of birth data for every individual. While no explicit data exist in any of the censuses describing the length of residence, linkage will provide approximations of this information, especially for in-migrants (those not listed in 1838 but found in ensuing censuses).

22. The data describing church affiliation are derived from the Abolitionist and Quaker census categories "name of religious meeting you attend" and "number attend religious meeting." These terms and the very high percentage of positive respondents make it clear that we are not dealing here with formal, dues-paying church membership, but rather with a loose affiliation with a church.

23. Admittedly crude at this stage of research, the population density technique of analysis nevertheless yields interesting and important information; and with refinement promises to be an invaluable tool for the study of neighborhood, and its relation to social mobility, class ecology, and community structure.

24. The construction of meaningful occupational categories has thus far proven to be the most difficult part of the research. While constructing such categories for the Irish, Germans, and native white American work force (currently underway) is certainly complex, one at least has the benefit of considerable occupational differentiation which provides vertical distance, a prerequisite for the study of social mobility and social stratification. Some 13 vertical categories including white collar/skilled/unskilled, non-manual/manual, proprietary/non-proprietary, and combinations of these schema, and 102 horizontal categories including building-construction, food, clothing, and domestic service were constructed for the study of the black occupational structure.

25. See the discussion of the "hiring-out system" in Richard C. Wade, *Slavery in the Cities* (New York, 1964), pp. 38–54. It is highly likely that many of the ex-slave household heads who bought their freedom had, in fact, experienced the hiring-out system first-hand and migrated to Philadelphia.

26. There is some reason to believe that the total number of ex-slaves (1,141 or one out of every five persons who migrated to Pennsylvania) is understated. The year 1838 was not too early for free blacks to fear being sent South illegally or legally as runaway slaves. It is understandable, therefore, that despite the fact that Philadelphia blacks were asked by their clergymen to cooperate with the two census takers (a white Abolitionist, Benjamin Bacon, and the black minister of the First African Presbyterian Church, Charles Gardner), many blacks who had in fact been born slaves reported instead that they had been born free.

27. To determine the effect of slavery on the slaves as compared to blacks

who were born free or who won their freedom before the Civil War, we would have to look some place after 1865. No one has yet found any data for the post-Emancipation period which distinguishes the Freedmen from the free-born (or from those freed before the Civil War). We can make the assumption that because 94 percent of the blacks in the South were slaves in 1860, a significant percentage of the migrants from the South after the Civil War were exslaves. But even if we discount the fact that if the migrants came from Maryland, Delaware, or the District of Columbia they were more likely to have been free before the Civil War (55 percent of all blacks in these areas were free in 1860), we are still left with with the problem of representativeness. To put it another way, even if we had data which distinguished the Freedmen from the free-born we would still be left with only the typical migrant, not the typical ex-slave. There is every reason to believe that Carter Woodson was correct in his observation that the migrants who came to the cities of the North before the Great Migration were not typical at all but, rather, representatives of the "Talented Tenth." The migrants who came after 1910, and especially after 1915, although not "typical" of the millions of Southern blacks who did not migrate, were nevertheless far more representative of Southern blacks than those who migrated before them.

28. Herbert Gutman, "The Invisible Fact: Negro Family Structure Before and After the Civil War," paper read at the *Association for the Study of Negro Life and History* (Birmingham, October 1969) and in a revised form at the *Organization of American Historians* (Los Angeles, April 1970).

29. Richard Wade, *Slavery in the Cities,* pp. 243–82.

30. A major interest of my research is to develop and make explicit for the city the characteristics of an "urban component" which distinguishes the urban from the rural experience. There is certainly general agreement that urban conditions differ from rural ones in significant dimensions: family structure, sex ratios, mortality, fertility, housing conditions, diet, educational and occupational opportunities, plus the intangibles of values and expectations. In future work, however, I hope to demonstrate that it is seriously misleading to treat these urban/rural differences monolithically. The racial discrimination and structural inequality of the city affected each ethnic group differently. The advantages of the city were never equally available for all.

Dennis J. Clark

7

The Philadelphia Irish:
Persistent Presence

Despite the fact that the Irish were Philadelphia's largest foreign-born group for fifty years, and that they have had a vigorous and continuous prominence as a minority in the city extending from prior to the Revolutionary War to the present, this group has attracted very little study by historians.[1] The Irish engagement with the life of the city extends from the pre-industrial period through the decades of active industrialization in the nineteenth cenutry, and through a delayed cycle of minority achievement into the twentieth century. Their greatest demographic and institutional impact followed their heavy influx after the potato famine in Ireland in 1846–47.[2] As the first large-scale immigrant group to challenge the city's tolerance and its capacity for social adjustment, the Irish experience may reveal some signal features of Philadelphia's development. This paper will be limited to a presentation of information and some guarded conclusions about facets of this protracted Irish experience in the period from 1840 to the present. The presentation deals with the issues of how the Irish adjusted to urban life, and how they formed an ethnic business-political tradition promoting urban growth.[3]

The rural background of the Irish was distinctive.[4] As a nation they resisted urban concentration. In the nineteenth century the overwhelming bulk of the immigrants came from the farms and fields that retained an ancient rural character, for cities in Ireland were historically the seats of invaders, aliens, and the administration of the oppressing Ascendency class. The transition to America thrust the Irish into urban centers that were utterly novel. The rapidity and eccentric character of this transition from time-heavy ruralism to thriving urbanism invests the Irish with special interest. How did the immigrants respond to such a radical change of locale? Obviously, no general answer to such a broad question is

135

warranted at this stage of our knowledge, but a partial response based on Philadelphia for one time period is feasible.

The study of the famine generation, that huge group affected by the "hungry forties," has drawn the attention of various historians.[5] The arrival of the famine generation in Philadelphia coincided with a period of rapid physical expansion and industrialization in the city. This generation of Irish-born people in the city witnessed the political annexation and consolidation of the city in 1854, the growth of the Republican party that was to dominate the city for almost a century, and the events of the Civil War on the Philadelphia scene. The Irish arrival represented the first great influx of immigrants to the city in numbers that were to presage the heavy immigration of later decades. The years from 1840 to 1870 were not only the "take-off" period for Philadelphia economically and industrially, they were also years of great social diversification and change. The city was transformed in this period, and the adaptation of the Irish to its energetic growth demonstrates the resilience of ordinary people and the cultural resources of minority groups.

The evidence dealing with the adaptation of the Irish to urban life reveals that an important portion of the Irish population of Philadelphia had begun a positive process of social advancement prior to 1870. In terms of property acquisition, occupational diversification and institutional activity, a significant element of the Irish population had begun to take advantage of opportunities in the city and to create an ethnic subcultural complex that would persist for generations. Although the data does not permit generalizations about the proportion of the city's Irish population engaged in the process of active social development, it does clearly testify to the evolution and vitality of that process.

With respect to the residential adjustment of the immigrants, the Irish experienced all the misfortunes of slum conditions as an introduction to urban living. As undesirable newcomers, they were consigned by economics and custom to the least desirable areas at the edge of the city proper.[6] Their concentration in these districts, especially in Moyamensing, Southwark, and Grays Ferry, created the city's first pattern of ethnic ghetto living. In the worst streets of these districts, overcrowding, dilapidation, and disease exacted a grim toll.[7]

But even in the 1850s, property-holding by the Irish was substantial in these districts. In Moyamensing and Grays Ferry between one-third and one-half of the properties examined in a sampling were owned by persons with Irish names.[8] In addition, various contemporary observers confirmed that Philadelphia did make better housing available to a larger proportion of its working people than other major Eastern cities.[9] The relative economy of the city's pattern of row house construction permitted extensive residential building. The steady expansion of the city made residential improvement a practical possibility for workers' families. This is especially notable in view of the fact that the immigrants actively joined in organizing and patronizing building and loan associations that made financing a home feasible. These popular associations were widespread, many bearing Irish names such as the Shamrock Building and Loan Association or the Daniel O'Connell Building and Loan Society. Some were adjuncts to Catholic parishes. They provided a means for the residential upgrading and mobility of thousands of Irish families, for hundreds of such associations existed in the city by 1870.[10]

The dispersion of Irish people through the city's neighborhoods in the Civil War period is indicated by the tabulations of Sam Bass Warner showing that no ward in the city in 1860 had a population composed of more than 28 percent Irish-born, and that seventeen of the city's twenty-four wards had Irish-born populations of between 10 percent and 28 percent.[11] By 1864 the numerous street railways of the city enabled many of the Irish as well as other citizens to journey relatively long distances between home and job.[12] The building of thirteen Catholic churches between 1850 and 1870, nine of which were outside the heaviest areas of Irish population concentration existing in 1850, indicates the residential dispersion of the Irish urbanites.[13] It is also worthy of note that some affluent Irishmen had homes in the most fashionable residential district in the center of the city, and that others lived in adjacent middle-class areas or outlying upper-class neighborhoods.[14]

These residential opportunities provided the immigrants with a very important vehicle for social advancement and a device for maintaining an equilibrium in urban life. Although the ghetto districts in Moyamensing, Grays Ferry, and Port Richmond persisted, populated by those unable to become mobile and a steady stream of newly arriving immigrants, for many of the Irish home ownership in a decent neighborhood was a practical goal, a goal that encouraged thrift, propriety, and family cooperation. Better housing brought the benefits of improved health and family life. A decent home, whether rented or owned, gave the immigrant or his son an increased stake in the community and a degree of social stability hardly attainable in the turbulent slum districts. Philadelphia's housing opportunities presented the Irish immigrant with a ladder for advancement that led to a residential situation in which home, school, and church were linked in institutional support of relatively attractive neighborhood life.

Philadelphia, because of the scale and variety of its economic activity, had a great capacity to absorb and advance the immigrant worker. During the years 1840 to 1870, the city was in the midst of one of its most active periods of economic development.[15] As a transportation nexus for canals and railroads and as a major port, it attracted an immense traffic. As a center for the manufacture of metals, textiles, and all the goods that the new industrialized system produced, the city was dotted with mills, factories and warehouses. The subsidiary financial and commercial services related to the industrial establishment stimulated and abetted its activity. All of these enterprises required unskilled labor, and immigrant labor was readily available.

While approximately one-third of the Irish males in the city were laborers and unskilled workers in 1850, occupational samples drawn from the South Philadelphia Irish population show that there was increasing diversification of employment over the next twenty years.[16] The Irish began to obtain jobs in factories, fabricating plants, and some of the technical trades associated with metal production and textiles. The industrial geography of the city was such that the immigrant living areas were not isolated, but were near a large variety of plants and businesses. The rapid extension of street railway lines between 1858 and 1870 permitted at least some of the better-paid Irish workers to reach employment that was relatively distant from home. The economy of the city was characterized by a high rate of labor mobility at the time, and this occasioned a diversified choice of job opportunities. In a time of economic growth and industrial expansion, new kinds of jobs were being invented rapidly as technology and production systems became more specialized. Thus, even though the city used great numbers of unskilled workers, its economy created opportunities open to immigrants at a variety of levels.

The beginning of occupational diversification among Irish wage earners was matched by a notable degree of small business activity and some large, substantial businesses under Irish ownership. Grocers, dry goods dealers, real estate brokers, commission merchants, as well as manufacturers and members of the professions were not uncommon among the Irish in the 1850s and 1860s.[17] There were some wealthy Irishmen, but a fact of more significance is that large numbers of the Irish were attracted to business in an age when individual enterprise was a potent and prevalent ideal.

The occupational and economic diversity reflected in the city's Irish population was part of an upgrading cycle that was in progress. The unskilled and uneducated Irish in the slums, suffering from exploitation, unemployment, and privation, could look forward to entering semi-skilled or skilled work. By becoming part of the skilled labor force of the industrial age, they and their Irish fellow citizens in business could begin to share in the residential, educational, and social benefits of urban life. The breadth and pace of this development and the proportion of the Irish population involved in it is a subject that must await the clarification of further research. The conclusion stressed in this paper is that the process of occupational dispersion by which the immigrants achieved economic mobility was begun in a substantial way before the Civil War. From backgrounds almost exclusively rural, the immigrants were becoming part of industrialized society.

Part of the earnings gained by the Irish were contributed to the network of parish churches that they constructed throughout the city. The dispersion of large numbers of Irish Catholics beyond the original immigrant enclaves resulted in the construction of twenty-four churches between 1840 and 1870 in Philadelphia.[18] To this parish network was appended a school system completely supported by the Catholic population, and a number of hospitals, asylums, charitable organizations and social groups. The extent and organizational complexity of this Catholic structure is in itself surprising. The construction of a religious and cultural matrix with a strong residential base, with schools reaching from primary grades to the college level, and providing a considerable array of social and welfare services, was no mean achievement. The fact that the achievement was carried out by that segment of the city's white population that was the least affluent, the most beset by social problems, and with the least recourse to power and influence in the city makes the performance remarkable. In furthering this Catholic religious and educational work, the Irish were the primary agents and chief contributors.[19] Their religious and educational institutions perpetuated traditions of voluntarism, clerical leadership, and social service that had their roots in the history of the Catholic Church in Ireland.

That a group of immigrants from a rural society could build such an institutional system in an urban setting testifies to its adaptability and inventiveness. While the Catholic schools served to provide the literacy, training, and skills needed for further urban adjustment, the parishes and religious associations bound the immigrants together in a subculture that linked education, the home, the neighborhood, and a circuit of institutional facilities and associations that functioned on a city-wide basis.

This religious network was a comprehensive medium aiding the immigrants in the attainment of careers and social stability in the urban environment. If Catholic institutions existed as a separate, partially segregated system in the city, they were not notably different in this respect from the facilities of other denominations.[20] If Catholic morality and opinion tended to be conservative and rigidly dedicated to its version of religious certitude, this was not untypical of other Victorian religious denominations. Its strict attitudes toward sex, the total abstinence movement against alcohol, and a preoccupation with propriety gave to Irish Catholicism features that were compatible with the social emphasis of much of the city's Victorian Protestantism. These aspects of Irish Catholicism, encouraged by the strong and concerted leadership of the clergy, left an impress not only upon the new Catholic middle class, but also upon the working-class Catholics for which that middle class served as a model for imitation and aspiration.

In addition to the extension of Catholic institutional and educational structures, the immigrants also promoted a congeries of fire companies, beneficial associations, Irish ethnic groups, and nationalist societies. These organizations were another sphere for association and social advancement. They preserved the ethnic traditions and identity of the Irish and provided organizational ties for them at a variety of social levels for a variety of purposes. There were groups that were unacceptable to the general public and to most of the immigrants as well, such as the conspiratorial Fenians and the criminal gangs of the slum areas, who helped to sustain the stereotype of the Irishman as an antic and erratic figure. The coming of the Civil War, however, was the occasion for immigrant military service that impressed public opinion and gave the Irish a more favorable image.

The political participation of the Irish in the city involved the development of a grass roots system of electoral activity at the neighborhood and ward level based upon the saloon and the fire company. These two local community fixtures became the vehicles for an intense political aptitude that initially was chiefly of benefit to the Democratic party.[21] This effort was carried out under local bosses who were the prototypes of a long line of political machine leaders who became masters of urban party manipulation. The advent of the Irish immigrant political organization coincided with the reshaping of urban political life. Expansion of the city and its services and the necessity of initiating a diverse urban population into the processes of party campaigning and exercise of the franchise required the creation of a broad and flexible mechanism for political participation. In the fashioning of this mechanism, which was to accommodate the political aspirations of ethnic groups and the new masses of industrial workers in the city, the Irish played a leading role.

The fact that the Irish adhered initially to the Democraitc party was to have very significant results for the political history of Philadelphia. The Democrats were unable to consolidate the Irish immigrant faction with the older party elements that continued the tradition of the Jacksonian democracy in the city. The Civil War and the identification of the Democrats with Southern secession struck a grave blow at the party.[22] The rising appeal of the Republicans, identified with the victory of the Union and the ascending forces of the Industrial Revolution, captured the political allegiance of the majority of Philadelphians after the Civil War. The Irish Democrats remained a political minority and their influence dwindled as the Republican hegemony became more complete. By the late 1870s, Irish Catholics were rising to prominence in the local Republican machine. Thus, the Irish as an ethnic group were politically split. The Republicans drew more and more of them into their ranks, but, because the Irish did not represent a sufficiently large minority to dominate the city's politics, they did not readily rise to ultimate positions of power as Republicans. The broad base of Republican support in Pennsylvania extended beyond the city and the Irish never constituted a major numerical element in the spectrum of Republican strength. Hence, even if the Irish Catholics did become intermittent leaders of local Republican factions, the preponderant Republican power base among native Americans, Protestants, and middle- and upper-class groups prevented any Irish domination.

This permanent denial of commanding political power significantly affected the Irish and the city. It consigned the Irish Catholics either to political futility in the ranks of an ineffectual Democratic party, or to the status of permanent minority stepchildren within the ranks of a Republican organization dominated by Anglo-Saxon business interests or Scotch-Irish bosses of the state-wide Republican empire. In Philadelphia the Irish Catholics did not dominate the urban machine as they did in Boston and New York.[23] This permanent minority political status induced among the Irish an ambiguity of purpose. On the one hand, they could not hope to dominate or control the city's life; on the other, they did have access to some patronage and offices through the Republican party. The resulting ambivalence frustrated that combative morale and single-minded pursuit of power that Edward Levine finds a characteristic of Irish politicians.[24] The Irish in Philadelphia remained handmaidens of a machine that they did not control, a group with blunted political ambitions and fragmented political impact.

The picture that emerges from the evidence gathered about the Irish in Philadelphia in the mid-nineteenth century, then, is one of modest but promising progress in the residential and economic life of the city. Through a cultural and religious network, the immigrants had developed their own institutional dimension of urban life. Despite the continuing disability of a large unskilled minority among them, the Irish were creating a viable and accepted subculture within a major American industrial city. If they could not break through to achieve political control of the city, they could function satisfactorily within the existing political framework, while enjoying an acceptable degree of latitude for social and economic advancement.

The problems raised by comparative assessment of immigrant history in different cities are formidable. It is at least worth the struggle to set up the hypothesis that the Irish adjustment to Philadelphia was less aggrieved and more rapid economically and socially than was the adjustment of the Irish to Boston, for instance.

The full testing of this hypothesis requires some Herculean labors, but my conjecture, based upon the data I have been able to assemble thus far, is that it would be affirmed.[25]

In Boston there was less industrial capacity to absorb the unskilled immigrants, less occupational diversification, and less opportunity for immigrant penetration of business. Mobility in the housing market appears to have been greater for the Irish in Philadelphia, and the construction of Catholic churches, schools and institutions proceeded at a more rapid pace. Not only was the death rate lower, but living was apparently better for the Irish in Philadelphia than in Boston.

A further illustration of the revealing factors embedded in ethnic history can be provided by a reassessment of the "contractor-boss." One of the central figures in the history of the American city is the contractor-boss, the builder-developer with strong political ties and influence. There has been produced a considerable literature delineating the political boss, the machine chieftain whose influence is variously interpreted as nefarious or socially beneficial depending upon which historian or political scientist one reads.[26] The contractor as a builder, as an agent of urban expansion and development, however, has rarely been examined against the background of ethnic and political affiliations.

An examination of the occupational statistics concerning immigrants compiled by Edward P. Hutchinson shows a notable concentration of Irishmen as builders and contractors. According to the 1870 and 1880 U.S. Census figures summarized by Hutchinson, the Irish led all other immigrants in this occupational category. By 1890 the Irish had twice the proportion of builders and contractors that other immigrant groups had.[27]

For many men anxious to improve themselves, an opportune route out of the unskilled labor pool was to become a small-scale building contractor. It was not too far from the truth to say that any man with his own shovel and wheelbarrow styled himself as a "contractor." Such a pursuit required little capital, but aggressiveness and strong backs were important, and these the Irish had. They also had easy access to fellow countrymen who, after the initial adjustment to city life, had developed skills in stone-cutting, bricklaying, iron work, and most of the trades associated with building. Because of discrimination and their fidelity to Catholicism, the overwhelmingly Catholic Irish felt impelled to construct an entire parallel network of churches, schools, and welfare institutions in the major cities. This they did with alacrity, and the building work for these institutions provided a continuing source of construction operations for the Irish contractors. The political proclivities of the Irish quickly identified them with the municipal machines that would be fruitful sources of contracts for public works. An illustration of this process of the evolution of the Irish construction magnate can be found in the City of Philadelphia, a city whose rich Colonial past has obscured its interesting history during the period of industrialism and urban expansion.[28]

As early as 1852, Irish contractors were monopolizing most of the public construction work in the Port Richmond district.[29] In 1853 builder Thomas Dugan was selling three-story houses in the Kensington area for $1,200 each.[30] In 1856, James Tagert advertised in the Philadelphia *Evening Bulletin,* "There is not a man in the consolidated City of Philadelphia but can avail himself of a Home if he desires." Tagert, born in County Tyrone, was President of the Farmers and Mechanics Bank and a promoter of various building activities.[31]

Financing for homebuilding operations did not come easily. In the mid-nineteenth century most banks were wary of lending mortgage money to ordinary working people. This produced in Philadelphia an extraordinary proliferation of that local business invention, the building and loan association.

Homebuilding, however, had its limitations. Its market uncertainties were proverbial. Railroad and public works construction offered a large-scale area for more lucrative operation. Tipperary-born Thomas Costigan did much railroad work, as did William J. Nead and Francis McManus.[32] The large pool of Irish pick and shovel laborers in the city provided practically the only resource needed for a smart contractor to organize an excavation crew to perform the enormously arduous work of digging cuts, grades, and tunnels for the railroads.

The business of Patrick McManus indicates the kinds of jobs the contractor could become involved in. McManus was born in Pottsville, Pennsylvania, of Irish parents in 1847. His first major project was the building of stockyards in Philadelphia. He laid special tracks to serve the grounds of the Centennial Exposition in 1876 in Fairmount Park. Later, he and his partner, James B. Reilly, built stone bridges over the Schuylkill River, and built track lines and stations for the railroads, including the Reading Company's line to Atlantic City.[33]

In a period when business and politics were closely allied, the contractors were frequently engaged in public works. Edward J. Lafferty, from the Irish community in South Philadelphia, helped build the city's famous water works. Martin Maloney, who started as a simple mechanic, invented a gas burner for street lamps. He went into the business of laying gas utility lines and helped organize the United Gas Improvement Company in the city.[34] The continuing expansion, renovation and improvement of the urban landscape afforded such men repeated opportunities for public work. Corruption, fraud, and shady practices were not uncommon. Seymour Mandelbaum has maintained that the only way that the burgeoning cities could be controlled politically and ordered physically was by resorting to massive pay-off schemes.[35] Philadelphia's Republican politics became a national byword for corruption. Although the dollar costs of public gouging can be calculated in some cases, the social cost of not expanding and building the city can only be conjectured. Whatever the malpractice involved, many of the contractors did produce. They built, and the city is still full of their works, aging but utilitarian, a century after their erection.

By 1900, 63 percent of the building firms in the nation were located in 200 cities, and urban construction was 90 percent of the national total.[36] What had transpired since the 1840s was an unprecedented urban development, and the Irish contractors had ridden the wave of this growth. Asa Briggs, in his *Victorian Cities,* has pointed out the primary role that the provision of sanitation, utility and public works facilities played in such growth.[37] It was in these areas of construction that the Irish contractors made a heavy contribution. They were one of the new categories of "talent and connection" that the city expansion called forth.[38] Starting in the ditches as excavators, they had gained command of a flexible medium for meeting the fast-changing construction needs of the cities. Construction activity has historically been a speculative and economically eccentric field, more sensitive to cycles of boom and bust than most other areas of the economy. This has led to an old saying in the field that a construction man must be a gambler. A sudden contraction of credit, a hard-rock strata struck in excavation, a laborers' strike could jeopardize not only a single project, but a whole business. Competition in a field where heavy capitalization was not required for entry was always keen. The contractors could attempt to stabilize their work by obtaining jobs through political preference, but the high risk element remained.

The contracting business interacted with politics in a system of mutual reinforcement. The system suited the Irish admirably. In Philadelphia, the Irish political fortunes were divided, however. Their early strength in the Democratic party identified them with pro-Southern sentiment during the Civil War. The ensuing ascendency of an unbeatable city Republican machine in an impervious Republican State, cast the Irish under a cloud.[39] But gradually they did emerge, and as the new immigration from Southern and Eastern Europe commenced, they took up the role of political intermediaries as an ethnic group.[40] In contracting also, they were intermediaries as well as principals. In hiring labor, in presiding over subcontractors, in reconciling architects, engineers, union bosses, and clients, they demonstrated the same facility for maneuver and mobilization that they displayed in politics.

An example of the contractor-boss interaction can be seen in the career of James P. "Sunny Jim" McNichol, the first Irish Catholic to become a powerful figure in the Philadelphia Republican party. McNichol, born in 1864 in the tough Tenth Ward, formed a building firm with his brother, Daniel, as a young man. Between 1893 and 1895, his business forged ahead, doing six million dollars worth of work in those years.[41] From 1898 to 1902, McNichol served on the Select Council of the city, then in the State Senate. The factional disputes within the Republican Party, and the shifting alliances of the Democrats who were intermittent handmaidens of one Republican cohort after another, made McNichol's political life a stormy one. In 1908 when he was at the height of his power, "Sunny Jim" faced challenges and patronage fights involving the Commissioner of Wharves, Docks and Ferries, the police, the City Solicitor, and the anti-saloon forces in the city. He was able to show that one of his antagonists, D. Clarence Gibboney, Secretary of the Law and Order Society and a candidate of the "reform" City Party, was a stooge as well as a hypocrite in the pay of contractor rivals of McNichol.[42] Through it all "Sunny Jim" maintained the geniality suggested by his soubriquet. About one-fourth of the Republican City Committee, over which McNichol presided, was composed of Irish Catholics, and "Sunny Jim's" reputation as a dispenser of jobs through his government contacts and through his huge contracting business stood him in good stead.[43]

In 1907 McNichol was reported to have said after a controversy involving municipal contract work, "Never again under any circumstances will I go after municipal contracts." [44] But business sense overcame political irritation. In 1908 McNichol was completing the subway excavation from City Hall into South Philadelphia, building the million-dollar Torresdale water filtration plant, performing extensive sewer and utility pipe-laying work, handling asphalt and granite block paving contracts, and conducting a half-million dollar garbage disposal business through the Penn Reduction Company.[45] A total of more than two and one half million dollars in contracts was thus handled by McNichol. During his career McNichol also built the subway tunnel for the Market Street subway, the imposing Benjamin Franklin Parkway, which is still one of the most appealing features of the city, and the eight-mile long Roosevelt Boulevard, which opened up the broad fields of the Northeast section of the city to automobile traffic and residential development.[46] In terms of urban construction, few men in the last century changed Philadelphia's physical aspect and orientation more extensively than "Sunny Jim" McNichol.

After McNichol, a series of contractors emerged whose careers and construction contributed notably to the development of the city. Their activities transcended the city, and several gained national prominence in politics and business. Perhaps the most widely known and attractive was John B. Kelly, Olympic sportsman, Democratic candidate for mayor and leader of a talent-rich family.[47] A keen competitor of Kelly was Matthew H. McCloskey, National Democratic Finance Committee Chairman from 1955 to 1962, builder of the Penn Center transportation complex, and U. S. Ambassador to Ireland in the Kennedy administration.[48] The largest contractor of all, John McShain, assembled a huge financial and building operation, handling over one billion dollars of construction including the eighty-million-dollar Pentagon building and hundreds of other government structures.[49] These men, all sons of Irish immigrants, retained their identity as Irishmen.

The extent to which our cities have been structured physically and socially by the personal and social dynamics of the various ethnic traditions within them constitutes a broad area for exploration. The specific development roles of Jews, Italians, and Germans, as well as the economically emergent blacks and Puerto Ricans, can provide insights to many of the confusing aspects of our urban growth. The history of urban physical development has largely been considered in terms of technological innovations and architectural traditions.[50] Although a social dimension for the history of our cities has been growing through the study of sociological and political factors shaping urban patterns, the connection between urban expansion and the drives and tendencies of our ethnic groups has not been carefully examined.[51] Such study could take us behind the stereotype and reveal the reality and complexity of the influences acting upon powerful figures whose roles and decisions have had a lasting impact upon our urban system.

NOTES

1. From 1860 until 1910, Irish-born persons constituted between 10 and 15 percent of the city's population. Figures on the Irish population in Philadelphia are given by Irwin Sears, "The Growth of Population in Philadelphia: 1860–1910" (unpublished diss. Dept. of American Civilization, New York Univ., 1960), p. 66. The activities of Irishmen in the city are catalogued in a valuable volume devoted exclusively to this subject: John H. Campbell, *History of the Friendly Sons of St. Patrick and the Hibernian Society* (Philadelphia: The Hibernian Society, 1892). Histories of Roman Catholic churches in the city, such as Daniel J. Mahoney, *Historical Sketches of Catholic Churches and Institutions in Philadelphia* (Philadelphia: D. J. Mahoney, 1895), give much information on the group. The Irish are mentioned in general histories of the city largely with reference to two periods, the eighteenth century immigration of the "Scotch-Irish" whom James Logan, William Penn's administrator, found so distressing, and in connection with the anti-Catholic riots of the 1840s. See James G. Leyburn, *The Scotch-Irish: A Social History* (Chapel Hill, N.C.: Univ. of North Carolina Press, 1944), and Carl Bridenbaugh, *Cities in the Wilderness* (New York: Capricorn Books, 1964), p. 408. The venerable *History of Philadelphia: 1609–1884* by J. Thomas Scharf and Thompson Westcott, 3 vols. (Philadelphia: L. H. Everts Company, 1884), mentions the Catholic Irish largely in connection with the 1844 riots and Catholic church growth: 1:662–75, 2:1380, *passim*. Later books add little examination of original sources or further insight. See Nathaniel Burt, *The Perennial Philadelphians* (Boston: Little, Brown and Company, 1963), p. 75 and pp. 565–76; E. Digby Baltzell, *Philadelphia Gentlemen: The Making of a National Upper Class* (Glencoe, Ill.: The Free Press, 1958), p. 188.

2. The problems of the immigrants during industrialization are reflected in Elizabeth M. Geffen, "Violence in Philadelphia in the 1840's and 1850's," *Pennsylvania History* 36 (Oct. 1969): 381–410, and Sam Bass Warner, Jr., *The Private City: Philadelphia* (Philadelphia: Univ. of Pennsylvania Press, 1968), pp. 63–78 and 125–57.

3. My studies have largely dealt with the Irish Roman Catholics. I have not attempted to trace the history of those redoubtable Ulstermen, the Presbyterian "Scotch-Irish," in the city. This group has produced its own cadre of effective historians.

4. In 1841 only one-fifth of the Irish population lived in any kind of community that could be termed a town or village. See T. W. Freeman, *Pre-Famine Ireland: A Study in Historical Geography* (Manchester: Manchester Univ. Press, 1957), p. 25. The Irish antipathy to urbanism is examined by Sean O'Faolain in *The Irish* (New York: Devin-Adair Company, 1949), p. 26. O'Faolain says with exaggerated pungency, "The Irish never founded a town." In a poor country, the resources for urban growth were not readily attainable. See J. C. Beckett, *A Short History of Modern Ireland* (New York: Harper and Row, 1952), p. 133. But upon entry to the United States, the Irish became concentrated overwhelmingly in cities: "In no other group was urban concentration so complete as among the Irish." Maldwyn Allen Jones, *American Immigration* (Chicago: Univ. of Chicago Press, 1960), p. 21.

5. R. Dudley Edwards and T. D. Williams, eds., *The Great Famine* (New York: New York Univ. Press, 1957); William P. O'Brien, *The Great Famine in Ireland* (London: Downey and Company, 1896); Cecil Woodham-Smith, *The Great Hunger* (New York: Harper and Row, 1962); Radcliffe Salaman, *The History and Social Influence of the Potato* (Cambridge: Cambridge Univ. Press, 1949). For the emigration accompanying the famine, see Oliver Mac-Donough, *A Pattern of Government Growth: 1800–1860: The Passenger Acts and Their Enforcement* (London: MacGibbon and Kee, 1961).

6. The concentration of Irish-born in these areas is established in the *Seventh Census of the United States* (National Archives of the United States, microcopy no. 432, roll no. 809) for Philadelphia. For 1860 concentrations, see Warner, *The Private City*, table 12, p. 139.

7. Charles E. Rosenberg, *The Cholera Years* (Chicago: Univ. of Chicago Press, 1962), p. 121 and p. 136; *Report of the Sanitary Committee of the Board of Health of Philadelphia on the Subject of the Asiatic Cholera* (1848, microfilm, Archives of the City of Philadelphia, RG 37.195).

8. *Tax Assessors Ledger, Moyamensing, First Ward (1849–51)*, Archives of the City of Philadelphia, RG 214.5. A 10 percent sample of 450 properties showed these proportions of ownership for Cedar Street, Passyunk Road, Sixth and Eleventh Streets in Moyamensing. A similar sample for the Schuylkill (Grays Ferry) area was taken from

Tax Assessors Ledger, Moyamensing, Fifth Ward, Archives of the City of Philadelphia, R.G. 214.5, pp. 12, 13, 24, 25, 33, and 41.

9. *Philadelphia North American,* January 27, 1851; Ivan D. Steen, "Philadelphia in the 1850's as Described by British Travellers," *Pennsylvania History* 33 (Jan. 1966):37. As early as 1856 more than one-fifth of the employed persons in the city were members of Building and Loan Associations. Between 1849 and 1876 over fifty million dollars in housing investment flowed through Building and Loan Associations. By 1876 there were 450 such associations active in the city, and more than half the housing was owner-occupied: Lorin Blodgett, "Building Systems of the Great Cities," a paper read to the Philadelphia Social Science Association, April 5, 1877, now in the files of the Historical Society of Pennsylvania, pp. 10, 19, 21.

10. H. Morton Bodfish, ed., *History of Building and Loan in the United States* (Chicago: U.S. Building and Loan League, 1931), pp. 32–79. One Irishman was secretary of 35 such associations: Campbell, *History of the Friendly Sons of St. Patrick,* p. 507.

11. Warner, *The Private City,* table 12, p. 139.

12. Frederic W. Speirs, *The Street Railway System of Philadelphia* (Baltimore: Johns Hopkins Univ. Press, 1897), p. 16.

13. The growth of the city's parishes is reflected in *The Metropolitan Catholic Almanac* (Baltimore: L. Fielding, Jr., 1849), and the same almanac for 1860, pp. 167. Also, Scharf and Westcott, *History of Philadelphia,* 2:1374–1400.

14. A sample of fifty prominent Irishmen, chosen from Campbell, *History of the Friendly Sons of St. Patrick,* when spot mapped according to their residences on a map divided by residential class zones, showed that thirty-four lived in center-city upper- or middle-class areas or in such pleasant areas as Germantown or Darby. The residences of the fifty Irishmen were obtained from *McElroy's Philadelphia Directory: 1860* (Philadelphia: J. and E. C. Biddle Company, 1860). The map of class areas was taken from Norman Johnston, "The Caste and Class of the Urban Form of Historic Philadelphia," *Journal of the American Institute of Planners* 33 (Nov. 1966): 344–49. This finding accords with the relatively high rate of geographical mobility found by Stuart Blumin.

15. Geoffrey G. Williamson, "Ante-Bellum Urbanization in the American Northeast," *Journal of Economic History* 25 (Oct. 1965): 598. Descriptions of the city's developing industry are given in Edwin T. Freedley, *Philadelphia and Its Manufactures* (Philadelphia: Edward Young, 1859), pp. 15–43, and Sam Bass Warner, Jr., "Innovation and Industrialization in Philadelphia: 1800–1850," in *The Historian and the City,* Oscar Handlin, ed. (Cambridge: The M.I.T. Press, 1963), pp. 65–68.

16. This conclusion is based upon samples of the Irish-born males age fifteen to sixty-five for a section of the Second Ward in Moyamensing (South Philadelphia). The microfilm copies of the Census for 1850, 1860 and 1870 were scanned to compute the Irish-born males in a portion of the Second Ward (Seventh Census, microcopy no. 432, roll no. 809; Eighth Census, microcopy no. 653, roll no. 1153; Ninth

Census, microcopy no. 593, roll no. 1389). A 20 percent sample of
the Irish-born males, 15 to 65, was drawn and their occupations
listed and compared for the three Census periods. In 1850 the sample
showed thirty-two occupations among the Irish; in 1860, forty-nine
occupations; in 1870, sixty-two occupations. For details of this
computation, see Dennis J. Clark, "The Adjustment of Irish Immigrants to Urban Life: The Philadelphia Experience—1840–1870"
(unpublished diss., History Department, Temple University, Philadelphia, Pa., 1970), app. B. Sources such as the Septenniel Census
of the Commonwealth of Pennsylvania for the First, Seventh, Eighth
and Nineteenth Wards (South Philadelphia) indicate that the Irish
in the city had a smaller proportion of laborers than was true for
the Irish in Boston. Ibid., p. 109. Theodore Hershberg has shown
that three-fourths of the city's blacks were in unskilled occupations
during this same period.

17. Of 137 Irishmen visited by Jeremiah O'Donovan in Philadelphia in
1854, there were 17 grocers, 9 bootmakers, 8 tavern and hotel keepers, 4 tailors, 3 hatters, 2 lawyers, and 3 physicians. Jeremiah
O'Donovan, *A Brief Account of the Author's Interview with His
Countrymen* (New York: originally printed for the author in 1864,
reprinted by Arno Press, 1969), pp. 114–50. Of 44 Irishmen active
in the city from 1850 to 1870 listed in Campbell's *History of the
Friendly Sons of St. Patrick,* 24 occupations and businesses were
represented, including merchants, manufacturers, contractors, lawyers, teachers and others. *McElroy's Philadelphia City Directory*
for 1857 gives 22 percent of the grocers listed with recognizably Irish
names; 12 percent of the dry goods dealers and 8 percent of the real
estate brokers had such names. The percentage of grocers with such
names increased in the next decade. The occupational diversity,
business activity, and smaller proportion of laborers among the
Philadelphia Irish contrasts with the greater economic disability
found by Handlin among the Boston Irish in the same period.
Handlin, *Boston's Immigrants,* pp. 55–57, chap. 3, and table 13, pp.
350–51.

18. Scharf and Westcott, *History of Philadelphia,* 2:1374–1400.

19. In St. Patrick's parish, for instance, only six of the twenty-six priests
serving there between 1839 and 1870 were non-Irish: *Souvenir
Sketch of St. Patrick's Church: 1842–1892* (Philadelphia: Hardy
and Mahony, 1892), *passim.* As early as 1838 when St. Augustine's
Church was founded, more than half the congregation was Irish:
Rev. F. X. McGowan, O.S.A., *Historical Sketches of St. Augustine's
Church* (Philadelphia: The Augustinian Fathers, 1896), p. 84. By
the 1870s, five of the local parishes were German, while thirty-one
were largely Irish: Scharf and Westcott, *History of Philadelphia,*
2:1374–1400.

20. The religious and class demarcations in the city are shown by Norman
Johnston, "The Caste and Class of the Urban Form of Historic
Philadelphia," *Journal of the American Institute of Planners* 32
(Nov. 1966): 247–49.

21. For the significance of the saloon as a political vehicle, see Alexander B. Callow, *The Tweed Ring* (New York: Oxford University Press, 1966), p. 196. Irish saloons as political redoubts figured often in Philadelphia's politics. See Warner, *The Private City*, pp. 90–91. For a listing of fire companies, see Scharf and Westcott, *History of Philadelphia* 3:1911–12. The Irish Democrat faction is referred to in Nicholas B. Wainwright, "The Loyal Opposition in Civil War Philadelphia," *Pennsylvania Magazine of History and Biography* 88 (July 1964): 295, and Irwin Greenberg, "Charles Ingersoll: The Aristocrat as Copperhead," *Pennsylvania Magazine of History and Biography* 93 (April 1969): 194.

22. Wainwright, "The Loyal Opposition," p. 295; The *Evening Bulletin* (Philadelphia), August 8, 1866, provides an editorial illustrating the taint of disloyalty the Democrats bore.

23. The rise of the Irish to political control in Boston is traced by Geoffrey Blodgett in *The Gentle Reformers: Massachusetts Democrats in the Cleveland Era* (Cambridge: Harvard Univ. Press, 1966), pp. 53–55 and 61–63. The domination of New York machine politics by the Irish by 1890 is shown by Theodore Lowi, *At the Pleasure of the Mayor* (Glencoe, Ill.: The Free Press, 1964), pp. 34–40. See also Alfred Connable and Edward Silberfarb, *Tigers of Tammany* (New York: Holt, Rinehart and Winston, 1967), pp. 149–50, 173–96, for reference to Irish prominence in New York in the 1870s. Even in smaller, less cosmopolitan cities, the Irish became politically more potent than in Philadelphia. See Lyle Dorsett, *The Pendergast Machine* (New York: Oxford University Press, 1968), *passim*. It was not until 1964 with the accession of James H. J. Tate to the Mayor's office that the first Irish Catholic was to head the city government in Philadelphia.

24. Edward Levine, *The Irish and Irish Politicians* (Notre Dame, Ind.: Univ. of Notre Dame Press, 1966), pp. 188–89.

25. Oscar Handlin notes the relative absence of heavy industry in Boston in 1850: Handlin, *Boston's Immigrants,* p. 13 and table 1, p. 238. The industry in Philadelphia, by contrast, made possible a better economic adjustment. See Freedley, *Philadelphia and Its Manufactures*, pp. 15–43. For contrasts of unskilled labor, see Handlin, p. 57 and chap. 3 for Boston as compared with the employment data in this paper. Housing comparisons may be made between Handlin, pp. 99–114 and this paper. The death rate for the Irish-born in Boston was 37.7 per thousand in 1850, while in Philadelphia it was 12.2 per thousand: J. D. B. DeBow, *Mortality Statistics of the Seventh Census of the United States* (Washington, D.C.: A. O. P. Nicholson, 1855), p. 235. The number of Catholic parishes in Boston doubled between 1850 and 1870, while those in Philadelphia tripled; i.e., Boston: nine parishes to twenty; Philadelphia: twelve parishes to thirty-six. Clark, "The Adjustment of Irish Immigrants to Urban Life," p. 156.

26. The dour view of American city government held by Bryce is now seen to have been strongly biased. See Robert C. Brooke, ed., *Bryce's American Commonwealth* (New York: Macmillan Company, 1939), pp. 56 and 95. Zane Miller sees the machine and the boss performing

153   Dennis J. Clark

crucial functions: Zane L. Miller, *Boss Cox's Cincinnati* (New York: Oxford Univ. Press, 1968). For a discussion of the differing interpretations of boss rule, see Dorsett, *The Pendergast Machine*, introduction. Also, Levine, *The Irish and Irish Politicians*. Lloyd Warner elevates the boss to the status of the American archetypal figure of "Biggy Muldoon": Lloyd Warner, *The Living and the Dead: A Study of the Symbolic Life of Americans* (New Haven: Yale Univ. Press, 1959), p. 99.

27. Edward P. Hutchinson, *Immigrants and Their Children* (New York: John Wiley and Sons, 1956), tables 21, 25a, 29a, pp. 83, 103, 126.

28. For a critique of the preoccupation of historians of the city, see R. H. Shryock, "Historical Traditions in Philadelphia and in the Middle Atlantic Area," *Pennsylvania Magazine of History and Biography* 67 (April 1943): 115–42.

29. Board of Commissioners Minutes, Richmond District, 1852–54, R.G. 219.1, Archives of the City of Philadelphia, City Hall, Philadelphia, Pa. These minutes list contractors' invoices and payments.

30. Deed Book Th100 (1853), p. 549, Archives of the City of Philadelphia, City Hall, Philadelphia, Pa.

31. *Evening Bulletin* (Philadelphia) September 14, 1856, and Carl Wittke, *The Irish in America* (Baton Rouge, La.: Louisiana State Univ. Press, 1956), p. 231.

32. For reference to Thomas Costigan, see Wittke, *The Irish in America*, p. 228. For Francis McManus and William J. Nead, see Campbell, *History of the Friendly Sons of St. Patrick*, pp. 486 and 489.

33. J. St. George Joyce, ed., *The Story of Philadelphia* (Philadelphia: City of Philadelphia, 1919), pp. 436–7.

34. Campbell, *History of the Friendly Sons of St. Patrick*, p. 449. Wittke, *The Irish in America*, p. 231.

35. Seymour Mandelbaum, *Boss Tweed's New York* (New York: John Wiley and Sons, 1965), p. 58.

36. Edward C. Kirkland, *Industry Comes of Age* (Chicago: Quadrangle Books, 1961), p. 238.

37. Asa Briggs, *Victorian Cities* (New York: Harper & Row, 1970), pp. 16–17.

38. Eric Lampard, "Historical Contours of Contemporary Urban Society," *Journal of Contemporary History* 4, no. 3 (July 1969): 20.

39. The Irish Catholics in Philadelphia did not elect a mayor from their group until the 1960s, but in other cities the Irish were dominant in politics by the late nineteenth century. See Blodgett, *The Gentle Reformers*, pp. 53–55; Lowi, *At the Pleasure of the Mayor*, pp. 34–40.

40. Edward C. Banfield and James Q. Wilson, *City Politics* (Cambridge: Harvard Univ. Press, 1963), p. 39. See also Milton L. Barron, "Intermediacy: Conceptualization of Irish Status in America," *Social Forces* 27 (March 1949): 256–63.

41. St. George Joyce, ed., *The Story of Philadelphia*, p. 474. McNichol was one of a number of Republicans whose alliances within the party shifted in a continuous maneuvering for primacy.

42. The newspaper coverage of McNichol at the time was extensive.

Samples of political reportage on the events of 1908 can be seen in the *Philadelphia North American,* Jan. 2, 1908; *Public Ledger* (Philadelphia), Jan. 3, 1908; *Philadelphia Record,* Jan. 6, 1908; *Inquirer* (Philadelphia), April 12, 1908; *Philadelphia North American,* April 20, 1908. See also Edward Morgan, *City of Firsts* (Philadelphia: City of Philadelphia, 1919), p. 291.

43. *Evening Bulletin* (Philadelphia), April 15, 1908.
44. *Philadelphia North American,* Jan. 9, 1908.
45. *Philadelphia North American,* Jan. 9, 1908.
46. St. George Joyce, ed., *The Story of Philadelphia,* p. 474.
47. *Evening Bulletin* (Philadelphia), Oct. 29, 1934; Sept. 31, 1935. James Reichley, *The Art of Reform* (New York: The Fund for the Republic, 1959), p. 6. Reichley credits Kelly with inspiring the first true opposition party in the city since the Civil War.
48. *Evening Bulletin* (Philadelphia), March 10, 1936; June 10, 1962; Feb. 25, 1968.
49. *Evening Bulletin* (Philadelphia), May 29, 1963, and Thomas O'Malley, "John McShain: Builder," *Columbia* (February, 1955).
50. See, for instance, Sam Bass Warner, Jr., *Street Car Suburbs* (Cambridge: Harvard Univ. Press, 1962); Blake McKelvey, *The Urbanization of America* (New Brunswick, N.J.: Rutgers Univ. Press, 1963); and *The Emergence of Metropolitan America* (New Brunswick, N.J.: Rutgers Univ. Press, 1966). Christopher Tunnard, *The American Skyline* (Boston: Houghton Mifflin, 1955).
51. Some attention has been devoted to this subject by Edward J. Logue, "The Impact of Political and Social Forces on Design in America," in *Who Designs America,* L. R. Holland, ed. (New York: Doubleday Books, 1966), pp. 236–56.

8

"A Peaceful City":
Public Order in Philadelphia from Consolidation
Through the Civil War

Philadelphia in the middle of the nineteenth century was likely to impress the observer as an orderly city. Visitor and inhabitant alike tended to perceive in the neat regularity of the famous checkerboard street pattern and in the rows of rectangular houses reflections of the deeper nature of the Quaker City. Charles Dickens found everything so interminably neat and orderly that he "would have given the world for a crooked street." [1] William Russell of the *Times* of London saw the city as a "vast extent of the streets of small, low, yet snug-looking houses. . . . Philadelphia must contain in comfort the largest number of small householders of any city in the world." [2] The native literary luminary Charles Godfrey Leland saw

a very well-shaded, peaceful city, not "a great village," as it was called by New Yorkers, but like a pleasant English town of earlier times, in which a certain picturesque rural beauty still lingered. The grand old double houses with high flights of steps, built by the Colonial aristocracy—such as the Bird [Burd] mansion in Chestnut Street by Ninth Street—had a marked and pleasing character, as had many of the quaint black and red-brick houses, whose fronts reminded one of the chequer-board map of our city.

It seemed characteristic of the city that Leland had gone to a Quaker school in Arch Street, where the master stressed natural philosophy and chemistry but "objected to our reading history, 'because there were so many battles in it.' " [3]

Yet those who knew the city realized, as do those who know its history, that the deliberately cultivated outward aspect of orderliness in small things and large was deceptive. In 1854, when the old City of Philadelphia between the Delaware and Schuylkill Rivers, Vine and South Streets, was consolidated with Philadelphia

County by act of the Pennsylvania General Assembly, the appearance of orderliness had been belied for more than a decade by intermittent spasms of violence.

> Whoever shall write a history of Philadelphia from the Thirties to the end of the Fifties [said the same Charles Godfrey Leland] will record a popular period of turbulence and outrages so extensive as to now appear almost incredible. These were so great as to cause grave doubts in my mind whether the severest despotism, guided by justice, would not have been preferable to such republican license as then prevailed in the city of Penn.[4]

Leland referred to such events as the anti-black riots in Philadelphia and the neighboring borough of Moyamensing in August, 1834; the two anti-black riots of the depression months of 1837; the rioting and burning of the Pennsylvania Anti-Slavery Society headquarters in May, 1838; new anti-black riots precipitated by a Negro celebration of Jamaican Emancipation Day in August, 1842; rioting by Irish weavers in 1843 and the famous anti-Irish, anti-Catholic riots in Kensington in May and Southwark in July, 1844; chronic election rioting; and chronic anti-black outbreaks, reaching another culmination in 1849. In the intervals between outright rioting, street gangs fought each other and mugged passers-by, and the volunteer fire companies were often taken over by thugs who converted them into fighting gangs. Echoing the sentiments of Charles Godfrey Leland, the fastidious diarist Sidney George Fisher mused: "These things must happen under a democracy, which is inconsistent with order or wise arrangements in a city." [5]

To restore to Philadelphia the image and reality of a tranquil Quaker City after the violent 1830s and 1840s required a civic tour de force. To accomplish the restoration, despite Leland's and Fisher's elitist misgivings, through the democratic political process became possible in part because party, civic, and business leaders of all political complexions united during the fifties in a common revulsion against violence and a common campaign to restore public order. Political leaders of all parties behaved as though they thought that electoral success in the Philadelphia of the fifties depended on the diligence they displayed in the search for order. In the general revulsion against violence, this political judgment was probably correct.

Already there had appeared a tendency, in later years to become appallingly evident, for many of Philadelphia's business and social elite to divorce themselves from political activity; but some of the usually apolitical elite joined in the effort of political leaders of all parties (each party having convinced itself it could profit from the measure) which prevailed upon the General Assembly at Harrisburg to pass the Consolidation Act of February 2, 1854. The desire to restore public order was the primary motive behind this statute; even its conservative opponents had had to propose substitute schemes for controlling Philadelphia's violence in order to support their effort to forestall it. By amalgamating twenty-nine separate municipalities into the city and eliminating the tangle of their jurisdictional boundaries, the Consolidation Act immediately erased an impediment to law enforcement which had aggravated all the major riots. The consolidation charter gave the mayor of the consolidated city command of the police force and ample police powers, including authority to call upon any citizen of appropriate age and abilities to assist in quelling disturbances, to summon the commander of the Philadelphia militia district to mobilize his troops, and to disperse groups of twelve or more persons whom he found "riotously or unlawfully" assembled. More to the point than the latter emergency powers, the first mayors after consolidation, with the financial cooperation of the Select and Common Councils, used the new charter to create the beginnings of a modern professional police force.[6]

The first consolidation mayor, Robert T. Conrad (1854–56), a businessman and journalist, represented a Whig-American coalition and the idea that controlling the disorderly tendencies of the foreign-born would be an essential ingredient in a return to tranquility. He set out to recruit a police force of 900 men, and he introduced a police and fire telegraph alarm system connecting 163 outlying police stations with the new central police headquarters. He indulged his nativism by trying to restrict the police force to native Americans and by using the force vigorously in support of a complex of Sunday blue laws. The consequent police interference with Sunday recreation appears to have annoyed enough native Americans as well as immigrants to contribute to Conrad's failure to win renomination and to his coalition's defeat in the mayoralty election of 1856. Thereupon the new Democratic mayor, Richard Vaux (1856–58), like his father Roberts Vaux a man identified with a variety of reform causes, set out to show that Democrats could at least equal Whigs and Know-Nothings in the pursuit of law and order, albeit with Irish-born rather than exclusively native policemen. Vaux created a police reserve squad to make better use of the police telegraph, raised the force for a time to about a thousand, enhanced their pride by putting the police into blue uniform coats, and so identified himself with the consolidated and improved Philadelphia police force that to the populace they became "Dick Vaux's police." All the political parties could now claim to be law-and-order parties.[7]

Probably the steps toward a modern police force contributed much to ending the cycle of riots and violence. Whatever the reasons for the end of the cycle, Philadelphia in the 1850s did regain its image of tranquility in the reports of its visitors. Among the inhabitants, however, there persisted through the fifties an uneasy conviction that the city had regained and retained its cohesion by an extremely narrow margin, and that a descent into violence could all too easily recur. It was important to the political parties, therefore, that they cultivate an identification with law and order, because law and order could not be taken for granted, and a party's association with contrary forces might cause it severe damage at the polls. For Philadelphians, unlike visitors, the memories of rioting were still fresh, and the growing sectional crisis in national politics aggravated their city's tensions. When the Panic of 1857 struck, Sidney George Fisher feared it would cause "riots & popular tumult" which would throw the city "under the rule of vigilance committees or martial law." [8] When the Pennsylvania Anti-Slavery Society scheduled a public meeting at National Hall, 1229 Market Street, to mark the hour of John Brown's execution in 1859, the third consolidation mayor, Alexander Henry (1858–66), decided that the preservation of order demanded the presence of 120 policemen to keep away antiblack, antiabolitionist hecklers.[9]

The sectional crisis produced an accelerating series of renewed threats to order. When Mayor Henry learned that another meeting was called to pay honor to John Brown's body as the corpse passed through the city on its way from Virginia to New York, and that a Philadelphia undertaker was to prepare the body for burial, he assembled a large police detachment at the Broad and Prime Streets railroad station to meet the body, and he saw to it that the Philadelphia undertaker's work was called off, so that Brown's remains would be hurried through the city without pause. At that, he helped arrange for a decoy coffin to draw the crowds away before the real coffin moved quietly from the railroad station to the Camden ferry. When two weeks later George William Curtis spoke for abolitionism in a rally at National Hall, and a counter-rally of an estimated 5,000 people gathered outside the hall amid rumors that Curtis would be muzzled, the mayor stationed 400 police around the building and in the rear of the hall, scattered 50 more through the audience, arrayed another 50 in front of the speaker, and placed himself at the speaker's side. When the antislavery men proposed to bring Curtis back to the city the next year, Mayor Henry told them: "If I possessed the lawful power I would not permit his presence on that occasion"; and he managed to have the speech cancelled.[10]

With the exception of the riots of 1843 and 1844, the storm center around which all the major disturbances since the 1830s had swirled was the Philadelphia black community and its antislavery friends. The black community was proportionately the largest in any Northern city, 22,185 out of the 1860 population of 565,529, or about 4 percent of the total. While this proportion of blacks hardly seems large by the standards of twentieth-century American cities, it was notable that the black population was concentrated within the original boundaries of the city and just across their southern edge. Most of the blacks lived immediately adjacent to the business, commercial, and upper-class residential heart of the consolidated city, where they were most visible and closest to the principal institutions of the city's life. In the Fourth Ward of the consolidated city, the old district of Southwark from South Street to Fitzwater Street and from the Delaware River to Broad Street, nearly 10 percent of the inhabitants were black, 2,299 of 23,461. In both the Seventh and Eighth Wards, the westerly reaches of the old city from Chestnut Street to South Street and west from Seventh Street to the Schuylkill (these two wards being divided by Spruce Street), more than 11 percent of the inhabitants were black, 3,621 of 31,267 and 3,104 of 27,770, respectively. In the Fifth Ward, the nucleus of the city, between the Delaware River and Washington Square and from Chestnut to South Streets, 21 percent were black, 5,229 of 24,792.[11]

The blacks concentrated especially around Lombard Street, which ran east and west through the Fifth and Seventh Wards, and in the alleys nearby. But as their presence in the Eighth Ward indicates, they were numerous throughout the old city. The riots directed at them may help account for the minuscule rate of growth of the black population during the 1840s, a mere .36 percent. During the better policed 1850s, the growth rate of the black population rose to slightly over 12 percent. The white growth rate remained much higher—38 percent from 1850 to 1860—but there was an evident enough increase of blacks during the fifties to have caused disquiet among those whites on the lower rungs of the economic ladder who felt threatened by them, who had rioted against them intermittently for twenty years preceding consolidation, and who impressed cautious Philadelphians as likely to riot again. The Irish, themselves so spectacularly the targets of violence, were notorious for their dislike of the blacks.[12]

The black presence disquieted also the economic, social, and political leaders of the city in the 1850s. To those who valued the city's restored law and order, the blacks represented a danger because so frequently they had provided the spark which touched off disruptions of the city's tranquility. To the first families of the city, the blacks and their antislavery friends were a source of unease also because the first families of Philadelphia were tied closely to the South both socially and economically and shared Southern attitudes on the issues of race and slavery.

In the Philadelphia of the 1850s, the old first-family upper class of Biddles, Cadwaladers, Ingersolls, Peppers, Wistars, and Wisters remained the commercial and financial elite. The upheavals of the Civil War and its aftermath would soon provide opportunities for the financial rise of newcomers such as the Drexels (whose firm had been founded in 1837) and Jay Cooke, but in the fifties the old Philadelphia upper class still retained financial preeminence. The banking and commercial interests of the old Philadelphians had been directed heavily toward the South since long before the time when overextension of credit to the South did much to precipitate the final collapse of the Bank of the United States, rechartered in Pennsylvania; and that debacle had not prevented a continuation of the Southern ties. Social connections with the South accompanied economic ones. Except for the Ingersolls, the upper-class families of Philadelphia had strikingly few connections of origin or marriage with New England or even with New York. Many of the first families, however, established bonds of intermarriage linking them with the South.[13]

The tone of community thought in Philadelphia followed the

business and social leanings of the upper class. None of the major newspapers of the city in the late 1850s endorsed antislaveryism, save for the *Times* in its brief period as Republican party organ in the election campaign of 1856, an adventure which was followed promptly by the paper's collapse. The only clergyman in Philadelphia to speak out against slavery during the fifties was a transplanted New Englander, William Henry Furness of the First Unitarian Society. Preoccupation with the Hicksite schism had turned the consciences of the Society of Friends inward and thus muted their antislaveryism. In any event, Quaker antislaveryism had been combined consistently with belief in the inherent inferiority of the black race to the white, and Quaker philanthropy was conducted consistently upon the principle that the races should be segregated. Despite the Friends' traditional distaste for slavery, there was little in the customary beliefs of Philadelphia Quakerism to develop bonds of understanding between the white and black inhabitants of the city.[14]

In politics the leadership of the upper class was predictably less firmly rooted than in other areas of the city's life, but even in the political arena the strength of the old Philadelphians was still considerable in the 1850s; "the withdrawal of the gentlemen from the political arena into the counting house"[15] had begun but was far from complete. The first three mayors of the consolidated city, Robert T. Conrad, Richard Vaux, and Alexander Henry, were all gentlemen, especially the latter two. Vaux's first-family credentials were incontestable, and Henry was a scholar of Greek and Hebrew whose evident good breeding and cultivation were sufficient to impress Sidney George Fisher.[16] During the fifties and early sixties, a Cadwalader and a Biddle represented Philadelphia in Congress. Of twelve Philadelphia members of the Thirty-third through Thirty-sixth Congresses, at least half had the institutional connections and memberships of thoroughly respectable gentlemen.[17]

The political sentiments of Philadelphia in the 1850s were consistent with both a Southern-oriented upper-class leadership and a fear and dislike of the city's own black presence as a threat to public order. No one party established a consistent ascendancy; Democrats, Whigs and Know-Nothings moved in and out of office. There was a certain tendency for old Philadelphians of Whig affiliations to become Democrats as the Whig party expired, but nevertheless it was a law-and-order coalition of old Whigs, Know-

Nothings, and high-tariff Republicans calling itself the "People's party" that elected Alexander Henry mayor in 1858. As an anti-slavery party, the new Republican party made no progress in Philadelphia. In 1856, William B. Thomas received less than 1 percent of the vote as the first Republican candidate for mayor. In the October election of that year, the Democrats campaigned candidly as the white man's party and won four of the five Philadelphia Congressional districts. In November, Pennsylvania's favorite son Presidential candidate, James Buchanan, captured 53 percent of the Philadelphia vote, to 36 percent for the American party candidate, Millard Fillmore, and only 11 percent for the Republican, John C. Frémont. As late as the Presidential election of 1860, the Lincoln ticket in Pennsylvania felt obliged to call itself the People's party and to play down antislaveryism; a Republican ticket under the Republican name and led by William Thomas again went nowhere. The People's party mayor, Alexander Henry, was reëlected in the spring of 1860 but refused to identify himself with the Lincoln ticket in the fall. The Democrats still polled 51 percent of the Philadelphia vote in the October, 1860, gubernatorial election. As the People's party Presidential candidate, Lincoln did win 52 percent of the Philadelphia vote in November, but he did so against a Democratic opposition that was not only divided nationally but further confused and undermined in Philadelphia by the flirtation of one of its major local leaders, the newspaperman John W. Forney, with the Lincoln party.[18]

Through these political vicissitudes, most of the political leadership of Philadelphia, and especially the political leaders with upper-class credentials, remained consistent in their friendship for the South and their opposition to agitation of the slavery issue. Mayor Henry felt it was wise to prevent a return appearance by the anti-slavery orator George W. Curtis in December 1860; but when South Carolina led the secession movement that month, the City Councils, including half the People's party councilmen, called for a conciliatory rally in Independence Square, at which most of the speakers stressed the legitimacy of the South's grievances in view of Northern offenses against the South. At the beginning of the new year, a meeting of business leaders at the Board of Trade petitioned the General Assembly of Pennsylvania to repeal any legislation which might be deemed unfriendly to the South. On

January 16 a mass meeting of anticoercionists received encouragement from George M. Wharton, Charles Ingersoll, and William B. Reed, active upper-class politicians.[19]

Thus far there was no conflict between sympathy for the South and that determination to restore and retain public order which had characterized local politics during the fifties. On the contrary, sympathy for the South in national politics paralleled fear of Philadelphia's black population and of abolitionists as sources of disorder on the local scene. The diarist Sidney George Fisher, in fact, saw the Southern sympathies and the anti-antislaveryism of his fellow upper-class Philadelphians primarily as expressions of their intentness upon preserving law, order, and security.[20] But the secession crisis of 1861 presented an obvious danger to the continuation of a parallelism between pro-Southern politics nationally and the desire for public order at home. With the Southern states in rebellion against the Union and Philadelphia situated close to the border between the seceding and the loyal states, civil war obviously might become a greater and more immediate threat to Philadelphia's tranquility than the presence of the city's black population. Obvious though that possibility might seem, however, Philadelphia's upper-class political leaders mainly continued to be guided by their Southern sympathies, and to interpret antislaveryism and the black presence in the city and the country as remaining the principal threats to the future tranquility of both their city and the country.

When secessionist guns fired against Fort Sumter in April 1861, Philadelphia like all Northern cities reacted with an outpouring of popular patriotic emotion. At that moment it was pro-secession newspapers that the police had to protect against threats of mob violence, and displays of red, white, and blue at windows and on lapels became almost indispensable for ensuring the safety of person or property.[21] But once the intense enthusiasm of the Fort Sumter crisis began to fade, the Philadelphia electorate seems to have moved toward an ambivalence and apathy regarding the Civil War suggestive of a puzzlement about where their city's interests really lay. As the Union cause became the emancipation cause, did it not threaten Philadelphia's public order in the presence of the city's own black population? For those who might not have thought of it otherwise, this question was enunciated by the city's upper-class political leaders with their traditional Southern ties, both life-long Democrats and a former Whig such as William B. Reed.

Not surprisingly, Pierce Butler, who was as much a South Carolinian and Georgian as a Philadelphian, was the first of the Philadelphia aristocrats to become conspicuous for vocal opposition to the war. Partly because by August 1861 Butler seemed far from alone in his opinions, on the 19th of that month federal authorities in the city availed themselves of the President's suspension of habeas corpus to take Butler away to a cell in Fort Hamilton in New York harbor, without a hearing or a trial. During the following months they proceeded with arrests of additional anti-war Democrats, eventually including Charles Ingersoll, a son of former Congressman Charles Jared Ingersoll.[22]

During the summer of 1861 when the arrests began, Lincoln's appointment of E. Joy Morris as United States Minister to the Sublime Porte necessitated a by-election in the Second Congressional District. The Democrats elected an old Philadelphian, Charles John Biddle, over a Republican party wheelhorse, Charles O'Neill. Although Biddle was serving as colonel of the 42nd Pennsylvania Regiment in the Union army, after he took his seat in Congress he distinguished himself by opposition to any war measure which threatened to touch slavery. A major tenet of his opposition was his conviction and fear that emancipation in the South would stimulate race hatred and terminate racial tranquility both South and North. He believed the South would have returned to the Union if her people were offered "a spectacle of entire contentment and security upon this negro question." He declared that slavery had been planted in America by the Providence of God, and that only gradual action by the states could safely uproot it. He believed that the federal government was moving toward both constitutional and social revolution, and he opposed both: "I would leave to my children the Union that our fathers left to us." "Sir, the repugnance to negro equality is as strong in the middle states as it is in the South." Emancipation in the South, Biddle feared, would inundate his own state with black men.[23]

In July 1862 the Democratic state convention of Pennsylvania, with Philadelphia leadership conspicuous, resolved that "Abolitionism is the parent of secessionism," and "That this is a government of white men, and was established exclusively for the white race;

that the Negro race are not entitled to and ought not to be admitted to political or social equality with the white race." That year Frederick Douglass remarked that "There is not perhaps anywhere to be found a city in which prejudice against color is more rampant than in Philadelphia." Another observer offered much the same idea in verse:

> I found, most gladly, no secession;
> But hatred strong of abolition,
> A willingness to fight with vigor
> For loyal rights, but not the nigger.[24]

But what if "the repugnance to negro equality . . . as strong . . . as it is in the South" and the unwillingness to fight for "the nigger" should collide with the willingness to fight with vigor for loyal rights? Would the Philadelphia electorate then continue to follow pro-Southern upper-class leadership? When Sidney George Fisher, who did not share Southern sympathies, argued with his brother-in-law Charles Ingersoll that the Legal Tender Act was necessary to carry on the war, Ingersoll replied: "But we don't want the government to carry on this war." [25] Public statements of Democratic leaders were less candid, but among Philadelphia upper-class Democrats they pointed in the same direction. In October 1862 the Republicans won four of Philadelphia's five Congressional seats, and Charles J. Biddle was among the defeated Democrats.

Still, the Philadelphia Democratic leadership did not allow the Congressional election to discourage it or to alter its course. They found encouragement when the Pennsylvania legislature elected a Democrat, Charles R. Buckalew, to the United States Senate over Simon Cameron in January 1863. After the Senatorial election, Fisher found the recently liberated Charles Ingersoll "in a state of great exultation at what he considers the triumph of the Democratic Party & [Ingersoll] said that soon they will resort to mob law & physical force to carry out their views." [26] On January 8, a week after the final Emancipation Proclamation, a circle of upper-class Philadelphia Democrats of Southern proclivities organized the Central Democratic Club through which they hoped more effectively to assert their leadership of the city's Democratic party. In the ensuing months the club fulfilled their hopes by functioning as the most influential organization within the local Democratic party. Charles Ingersoll was its president, George W. Biddle, John C. Bullitt, and George M. Wharton vice-presidents. These men secured the election of Charles J. Biddle as chairman of the Democratic State Central Committee. In March they launched an ambitious attempt to create a major newspaper voice for their views, the Philadelphia *Age*.[27]

These activities continued to be conducted in part in the name of domestic tranquility and public order, to ward off the threat of an enlarged and more assertive black population implicit in emancipation. But threats of "mob law & physical force" were a strange means of demonstrating continued dedication to public order, and Fisher was not alone in finding such threats emanating from the Democratic leadership. On March 5 another diarist, the businessman George W. Fahnestock, recorded:

The opposition of the Democratic party to the Administration is daily becoming more apparent. Some, indeed, fear a revolution in the North. Dark hints are thrown out about arms being secretly collected in New York, to be used against the Government in case any attempt is made to incarcerate a Democrat in Fort Lafayette. In the Democratic Clubs in this city, I am told that the most treasonable sentiments are avowed.[28]

The Democratic party of Philadelphia seemed to be squandering the image it had earned through its contributions to the consolidation movement and as the party of Dick Vaux's police. When in June the city learned of the advance of General R. E. Lee's Confederate army toward Pennsylvania, anti-war Democrats rejoiced openly at the anticipated invasion and Confederate triumph.

Unhappily [wrote Fahnestock], so strong has grown the feeling of opposition to the present Administration, that many men are pleased with the prospect of invasion, carnage, blood, and smoking ruins! They walk our streets today, radiant with joy, led on by W. B. Reed, Charlie Ingersoll, Wharton and a horde of old worn out Peace Democrats. Nothing would rejoice them more than to see our whole government in ashes! [29]

In the face of Lee's invasion, Fahnestock found the mass of people of the city "as quiet and apathetic as if it was all a false report. Thousands of able bodied young fellows are ever parading in the streets, but no enlistments go on with spirit." [30] Sidney George Fisher found that:

The streets presented a strange aspect, most of them deserted, but Chestnut Street thronged with crowds of men, chiefly of the working classes, many of them vicious & ill-looking, wandering about apparently without a purpose. Recruiting parties were marching about with drum & flag, followed only by a few ragged boys—recruiting offices empty, taverns & grog shops full. The people looked careless & indifferent. There was no excitement. The same street presented a very different scene in April 1861 when the war broke out. Then it was fluttering with flags & filled by a crowd of agitated, earnest men. War was a novelty then; it is an old story now, and the demagogues have spread abroad the opinion that the administration is corrupt & imbecile, that it is impossible to conquer the South & that we ought to have peace now on any terms.[31]

The laments of state and federal officials charged with rallying the city for defense confirm the impressions of the diarists. Pennsylvania found itself unable to rally respectable bodies of militia from Philadelphia or elsewhere to defend Harrisburg and the line of the Susquehanna.[32] Yet despite the city's lethargy, the open rejoicing of the anti-war Democrats at the Union's adversity may have been a grave mistake. For the peace Democrats to align themselves with Lee's invading army hardly restored credibility to their image as friends of the city's public order. The lethargy of the city under the threat of invasion may have signified continued popular irresolution about the war and the conjoined cause of black emancipation; but following Lee's invasion, there took place a remarkable resolution and clarification of the wartime political convictions of the Philadelphia electorate. The clarification took shape to the distinct disadvantage of those Democrats who, while they claimed to be concerned for the city's tranquility against the Negro, nevertheless proved willing to embrace an invading enemy army.

A straw in the wind involved the enlistment of black soldiers in the face of Lee's invasion. On July 17, 1862, Congress had authorized recruiting of Negroes, and the Lincoln administration had been encouraging such recruiting since it issued the Emancipation Proclamation. Philadelphia hesitated to accept the idea of black men in arms. Some of the city's Negroes began drilling, but the establishment of companies of black soldiers in the city seemed an uninviting prospect in the context of the search for tranquility. Or rather, it did until Lee threatened Philadelphia with invasion and whites proved slow to come forward for the city's defense. Then for the first time "several hundred colored men in procession march[ed] up Sixth to Chestnut, and up Chestnut Street. They were not uniformed nor armed, but were a good looking body of men. They had a drum and fife, and [were] carrying inspiriting banners." They were on their way to a camp for colored troops at Chelten Hills, the later LaMott, just outside the city, where they would drill with arms as well as drum and fife.[33]

As late as July 6, 1863, the city was still uncertain of the outcome of the clash of arms it learned had occurred between Lee's army and the Union army at Gettysburg. On the 7th, Philadelphia received increasing confirmation that Gettysburg had been a Union victory and Lee had abandoned the invasion of Pennsylvania, and the same day word arrived of the Confederate surrender of Vicksburg. Banners again appeared in the streets. The banners were still flying and Philadelphia was still rejoicing in its deliverance from invasion when the draft riots began in New York on July 13. The New York riots raged as much against the black man as against the draft, and Philadelphia's previous record of turbulence and antiblack feeling made it appear a likely scene of similar disturbances. But the draft also began to be enforced in Philadelphia that July, and there was no rioting. About the same time, Republican Congressman William D. Kelley became the first major Philadelphia political figure to address a mass meeting of blacks in company with black leaders; he did not thereby damage the beginnings of a highly successful political career.[34]

In October following Lee's invasion, an upper-class peace Democrat from Philadelphia, Judge George W. Woodward, carried his party's standard into the Pennsylvania gubernatorial election. Philadelphia nevertheless gave a 7,000-vote margin to the Republican incumbent from upstate, Andrew Gregg Curtin, and Curtin won a second term. This victory proved to be the first of a long line of Republican electoral triumphs, both in the city and in the state. Reacting to the election and to the changing atmosphere of the city, the Philadelphia Democratic party shifted course and moved toward forthright support of the war. More plebian leaders than those who had lately directed the Democracy, notably the Irish politician Lewis Cassidy, decided that the peace Democrats were leading the party toward disaster. The Cassidy group revitalized a Democratic organization called the Keystone Club and used it to recapture the leadership of their party in Philadelphia from the upper-class Central Democratic Club. Significantly, they chose as president of the Keystone Club Colonel William McCandless, a twice-wounded veteran of the Union army.[35]

If Cassidy was moving in the direction necessary to save the Philadelphia Democracy, the move came too late to recapture the party's former ascendancy. In the October elections of 1864, Philadelphia returned to Congress its delegation of four Unionists and one Democrat, and as the "National Unionists" the Republicans for the first time won clear majorities in both the Select and Common Councils. In November, Lincoln carried the city again.

The next spring, unluckily, on the evening before the assassination of Abraham Lincoln, Charles Ingersoll's brother Edward reiterated the charge that the war against slavery and the South was unconstitutional, in a speech delivered in New York. The *Evening Bulletin* promptly wrote of Ingersoll's ideas as "the Ingersoll and Booth doctrine." On April 27, a Philadelphia crowd hooted and shouted as Edward Ingersoll got off a train at the Ninth and Green Streets station, and Ingersoll became involved in a caning fight with a Union army captain. The police took Ingersoll into custody, partly for his own safety. When Charles Ingersoll approached the police station to visit his brother, a mob attacked him and beat him badly. Charles was, of course, the man who according to his brother-in-law's testimony had once threatened to invoke mob action against Republicans.[36] However inoffensive he had become since the decline of the Central Democratic Club, he remained the same kind of threat to the public order that the blacks had been: his very presence in the city was likely to provoke mob violence, and did. He had become a political pariah like the blacks; for since 1850, the Philadelphia electorate gave its approval only to those parties and leaders who remained identified with the restoration of law and order.

NOTES

1. Charles Dickens, *American Notes and Pictures from Italy* (London: Oxford Univ. Press, 1957), p. 98.
2. William Howard Russell, *My Diary North and South,* Fletcher Pratt, ed. (New York: Harper, 1954), pp. 16–17.

3. Charles Godfrey Leland, *Memoirs* (New York: D. Appleton, 1893), pp. 9, 30.

4. Ibid., p. 216.

5. Sidney George Fisher, *A Philadelphia Perspective: The Diary of Sidney George Fisher Covering the Years 1834–1871*, Nicholas B. Wainwright, ed. (Philadelphia: Historical Society of Pennsylvania, 1967), p. 257 (May 4, 1856); W.E.B. DuBois, *The Philadelphia Negro: A Social Study* (New York: Schocken, 1967), pp. 26–31; Elizabeth M. Geffen, "Violence in Philadelphia in the 1840's and 1850's," *Pennsylvania History* 36 (Oct. 1969): 381–410; J. Thomas Scharf and Thompson Westcott, *History of Philadelphia, 1609–1884*, 3 vols. (Philadelphia: L. H. Everts, 1884), 1: 637–39, 641–42, 647, 650–52, 654–55, 660–61, 664–73, 691–93.

6. Eli K. Price, *The History of the Consolidation of the City of Philadelphia* (Philadelphia: Lippincott, 1873); *Laws of the General Assembly of the State of Pennsylvania, 1854* (Harrisburg: A. Boyd Hamilton, 1854), pp. 21–46, especially pp. 24–25, 26–28; *Journals of the Select Council, 1855*, 2, app., pp. 15–17. An Act of May, 1850, had sought to provide for the consolidation of the police forces of the city and the neighboring municipalities, but it did not accomplish this limited aim effectively.

7. *Journals of the Select Council, 1854*, app., pp. 85–87; *1855*, 2, app., pp. 8–9, 15–22, 107–8; *1855–1856*, app., pp. 316–19, 327; *1856*, app., pp. 298–99; *1856–1857*, app., pp. 187, 195–206; *1857–1858*, app., pp. 135–67; *1858*, app., pp. 263–64; Ellis Paxson Oberholtzer, *Philadelphia: A History of the City and its People*, 3 vols. (Philadelphia: S. J. Clarke, 1912), 2: 319–22; Scharf and Westcott, *History of Philadelphia*, 1: 719–21; Howard O. Sprogle, *The Philadelphia Police: Past and Present* (Philadelphia: n.p., 1887), pp. 100–13.

8. Fisher, *A Philadelphia Perspective*, p. 279 (Oct. 1, 1857); Austin E. Hutchinson, "Philadelphia and the Panic of 1857," *Pennsylvania History* 3 (July 1936): 182–94.

9. Ira V. Brown, "Miller McKim and Pennsylvania Abolitionism," *Pennsylvania History* 30 (Jan. 1963); 68–69; William Dusinberre, *Civil War Issues in Philadelphia, 1856–1865* (Philadelphia: Univ. of Pennsylvania Press, 1965), pp. 83–89; Scharf and Westcott, *History of Philadelphia*, 1: 732.

10. Alexander Henry to Wm. H. Allen *et al.*, Dec. 11, 186[0], Curtis Lectures File, box 1, Alexander Henry Papers, Historical Society of Pennsylvania; George William Curtis to Henry, Dec. 16, 1859, ibid.; Dusinberre, *Civil War Issues*, p. 90; Scharf and Westcott, *History of Philadelphia*, 1: 733.

11. *Population of the United States in 1860 . . . Eighth Census* (Washington, D.C.: Government Printing Office, 1864), pp. 431–32.

12. Ibid.; DuBois, *The Philadelphia Negro*, p. 50; Dennis J. Clark, "The Adjustment of Irish Immigrants to Urban Life: The Philadelphia Experience, 1840–1870" (diss., Temple University, 1970), pp. 199–200.

13. Herman Leroy Collins and Wilfred Jordan, *Philadelphia: A Story of Progress,* 4 vols. (New York: Lewis Historical Publishing Co., 1941), 1: 292; Bray Hammond, *Banks and Politics in America from the Revolution to the Civil War* (Princeton: Princeton Univ. Press, 1957), pp. 538–39. Nathaniel Burt, *The Perennial Philadelphians: The Anatomy of an American Aristocracy* (Boston: Little, Brown, 1963), pp. 20–21 and *passim*, notes frequently the Southern connections of the Philadelphia upper class. Fisher, *A Philadelphia Perspective,* offers numerous examples of such connections both in Fisher's own family—with his mother's roots in Maryland—and in others. The terms "upper class" and "elite" are used herein in the sense employed by E. Digby Baltzell, *An American Business Aristocracy* (New York: Collier Books, 1962), pp. 20–22 (first published as *Philadelphia Gentlemen: The Making of a National Upper Class,* Glencoe, Ill.: Free Press, 1958). "The *elite* concept refers to those *individuals* who are the most successful and stand at the top of the *functional* class hierarchy. . . . The *upper class* concept, then, refers to a group of *families,* whose members are descendants of successful individuals (elite members) of one, two, three or more generations ago."

14. *The Liberator,* Oct. 19, 1855, citing the New York *Tribune,* comments acidly but accurately on the Philadelphia press and Philadelphia pro-Southern proclivities. See also Dusinberre, *Civil War Issues,* pp. 40–45; Elizabeth M. Geffen, *Philadelphia Unitarianism, 1796–1861* (Philadelphia: Univ. of Pennsylvania Press, 1961), pp. 184–209. On the Friends' attitudes toward race, see Winthrop Jordan, *White over Black: American Attitudes Toward the Negro, 1550–1812* (Chapel Hill: Univ. of North Carolina Press, 1968), pp. 132–33, 419–22. The research of Harry Silcox, an Ed. D. student at Temple University, toward a dissertation on black schools and school desegregation in Philadelphia tends to confirm Jordan's conclusions about the segregationist views of the Society of Friends as far as the Philadelphia Quakers of the nineteenth century are concerned.

15. Peter Drucker, *The Future of Industrial Man* (New York: John Day, 1942), pp. 242–43, quoted in Baltzell, *An American Business Aristocracy,* p. 58.

16. Fisher, *A Philadelphia Perspective,* p. 344 (Jan. 6, 1860); microfilm biographical sketch of Henry in Historical Society of Pennsylvania.

17. The citizens of Philadelphia who served in the Thirty-third through Thirty-sixth Congresses were Thomas D. Florence (D. First District, 1853–59); Joseph R. Chandler (W. Second District, 1853–55); John Robbins Jr., (D. Third District, 1853–55); William H. Witte (D. Fourth District, 1853–55); Job R. Tyson (W., later D., Second District, 1855–57); William Millward (American, W. Third District, 1855–57; R. Fourth District, 1859–61); Jacob Broom (American, W. Fourth District, 1855–57); John Cadwalader (D. Fifth District, 1855–57); Edward Joy Morris (W., R. Second District, 1857–61); James Landy (D. Third District, 1857–59); Henry M. Phillips (D. Fourth District, 1857–59); and John P. Verree (R. Third District,

1859–61). Cadwalader, of course, was of the upper class. Broom was the son of James Madison Broom, a Princeton graduate and member of the Ninth and Tenth Congresses, who moved his family from Baltimore to Philadelphia in 1819. Robbins was a graduate of a private academy and became president and a director of the Kensington National Bank. Morris was a Harvard graduate whose legal career included a term as member of the board of directors of Girard College; he was to become United States Minister to Turkey, as will appear later in the text. Phillips was a lawyer who became a trustee of Jefferson Medical College, member and president of the Fairmount Park Commission, director and president of the Academy of Music, and a director of the Pennsylvania Railroad Company. Verree, born at "Verree Mills" on Pennypack Creek, was an iron and steel manufacturer who became president of the Union League. The members of the Select and Common Councils in the late 1850s already appear to have been mostly politicians of less distinguished nonpolitical associations and accomplishments.

18. Dusinberre, *Civil War Issues,* pp. 40–45, 67–69, 83–102; Roy F. Nichols, *The Disruption of American Democracy* (New York: Macmillan, 1948), pp. 43–47, 55–57, 61–63, 86–87, 203–5.

19. Dusinberre, *Civil War Issues,* pp. 105–10; Scharf and Westcott, *History of Philadelphia,* 1: 740–53.

20. Of his cousin Joshua Francis Fisher, for example, the diarist said: "For the sake of preserving the Union and peace and order, which in reality means his own property and enjoyments, he is willing to sacrifice the right and the truth, to yield to all the demands of the South and to maintain slavery without so much as asking whether it be not in itself a wrong and a crime:" *A Philadelphia Perspective,* p. 343 (Jan. 1, 1860).

21. Dusinberre, *Civil War Issues,* pp. 116–19; Scharf and Westcott, *History of Philadelphia,* 1: 753.

22. Fisher, *A Philadelphia Perspective,* pp. 400 (Aug. 20, 1861), 433–37 (Aug. 25–Sept. 1, 1862); Irwin F. Greenberg, "Charles Ingersoll: The Aristocrat as Copperhead," *Pennsylvania Magazine of History and Biography* 93 (April 1969): 197–99; Scharf and Westcott, *History of Philadelphia,* 1:777, 781.

23. *Congressional Globe,* 32, pt. 2 (37th Congress, 2nd Session), pp. 1169, 1644–45, 2503–5; Nicholas B. Wainwright, "The Loyal Opposition in Civil War Philadelphia," *Pennsylvania Magazine of History and Biography* 88 (July 1964): 296.

24. Dusinberre, *Civil War Issues,* pp. 137–40, for the Democratic State Convention; Frederick Douglass quoted in James M. McPherson, *The Negro's Civil War: How American Negroes Felt and Acted during the War for the Union* (New York: Pantheon, 1965), p. 255; (Anonymous), *Rifle Shots at Past and Passing Events by an Inhabitant of the Comet of 1861* (Philadelphia: n.p., 1862), p. 110.

25. Fisher, *A Philadelphia Perspective,* p. 431 (Aug. 1, 1862).

26. Ibid., p. 446 (Jan. 14, 1863).

27. Greenberg, "Charles Ingersoll," pp. 203–4; Wainwright, "The Loyal Opposition in Civil War Philadelphia," pp. 298–301.

28. George Wolff Fahnestock Diary, March 5, 1863, Historical Society of Pennsylvania.

29. Ibid., June 15, 1863.

30. Ibid., June 27, 1863; see also entries for June 25 and 26.

31. Fisher, *A Philadelphia Perspective*, p. 455 (June 29, 1863).

32. *The War of the Rebellion: A Compilation of the Official Records of the Union and Confederate Armies*, 4 series, 70 vols. in 128 vols. (Washington, D.C.: Government Printing Office, 1880–1901), 27, pt. 2, pp. 211–19; pt. 3, pp. 68–69, 76–80, 97, 111–13, 130–42, 162–67, 169, 187–88, 239–40, 243, 264, 329–30, 342–44, 347–48, 363–65, 391–92, 408, 436, 448, 480–81, 527; Frank H. Taylor, *Philadelphia in the Civil War* (Philadelphia: The City, 1913), pp. 40, 215–20, 242–51.

33. Fahnestock Diary, June 30, 1863 (See also ibid., March 26, 1863); Dusinberre, *Civil War Issues*, pp. 160–65, 169–70; Taylor, *Philadelphia in the Civil War*, pp. 186–88.

34. Fahnestock Diary, June 29–July 7, 1863; Fisher, *A Philadelphia Perspective*, p. 456 (July 6, 8, 1863); Dusinberre, *Civil War Issues*, pp. 169–70; Scharf and Westcott, *History of Philadelphia*, 1:800, 809.

35. Philadelphia *Age*, June 6, 8; July 12, 13; August 2, 31, 1864; Greenberg, "Charles Ingersoll," pp. 208–10.

36. Fisher, *A Philadelphia Perspective*, pp. 493–96 (April 21–28, 1865); Greenberg, "Charles Ingersoll," pp. 211–12.

John F. Sutherland

9

Housing the Poor in the City of Homes:
Philadelphia at the Turn of the Century

Throughout the nineteenth and early twentieth centuries, Philadelphia enjoyed a reputation as "The City of Homes." This reputation was symbolized by row after row of neat brick houses. The easy expansion provided by the city's geographic location facilitated the horizontal development of the city, in contrast to the crowded high-rise New York tenements. Yet behind the neat row houses there existed decaying slums. It was to these areas that the late-nineteenth century immigrants and blacks often came to live. That these slums were frequently owned by the immigrants themselves is testimony to the complexity of Philadelphia's housing situation.

Philadelphia's modern housing problems cannot be understood without reference to the city's early history. William Penn had sought to found a city of homes, although the title seems to have been a creation of the post-Civil War era. Penn's famous dream of houses surrounded by land "for gardens or orchards or fields, that it may be a green country town," was undoubtedly nurtured by memories of the Fire of London. However, his dream ignored the commercial facilities which so many of the settlers desired, and Philadelphia's original site was not as large as he had hoped. Few people wanted to live far from the center of business, communication, and transportation. Lots were therefore placed close together and were very deep. Secondary streets and alleys soon disrupted the neat gridiron pattern, and the famed Philadelphia row house made its first appearance in 1691. Overcrowding quickly became a problem in older areas.[1]

The problems of housing and overcrowding were intensified following the Revolution. The new state legislature auctioned off land in the Northern Liberties. Speculators then bought up plots of land and built long rows of identical, often shoddy (but profitable) houses. Furthermore, the city took possession of many of the small alleyways. It then subdivided and sold them, permitting commercial traffic unfit for such narrow thoroughfares. Throughout the nineteenth century Philadelphia extended her grid system, and the city was marked by large houses for the well-to-do, smaller ones for the skilled workers and middle classes, and, less obvious, back-alley shacks and shanties for the poor.[2]

The back-alley dwellings represented a particularly difficult problem. They took several forms. Owners of houses fronting on main streets might simply add on buildings in the rear to the end of the lot, creating a dark, unpaved, unsewered alley. A more famous Philadelphia rear-dwelling was the band-box, or "father, son, holy-ghost" house. These houses rarely fronted the streets, but instead were built in back yards and formed little courts, which were often invisible from the street. Of three, or less frequently two, stories, they contained only one room per floor, with an unenclosed stairway leading from one floor to another. They could be suitable for one small family, but they were unfit for the poor who often crowded into them. These rear courts multiplied as the city's original large lots were subdivided. They were probably built both for speculation and for servants' quarters. Of great significance is the fact that they were rear dwellings, often obscured from the view of passers-by.[3]

Despite her housing problems, the Quaker City enjoyed advantages which enabled her to project an image of the city of homes. The horizontal expansion of the city relieved the pressure of congestion which New York had to combat with high-rise multiple dwellings. As late as 1898, Philadelphia had 83,000 acres upon which to build, while New York had only 25,000. The small row house could be extended on adjacent, inexpensive land. What was true for houses also applied to industry. Machinery and textile mills were centered in Kensington, locomotive and metal shops in the northwest, and additional textile mills in Southwark and Moyamensing. These industrial clusters may have been significant in breaking down the old close-knit community structure of the original city. On the other hand, they aided in relieving congestion and served to encourage a horizontal, rather than a vertical expansion.[4]

Geographic advantages were not the only factors which led to Philadelphia's reputation as a city of homes. Building and loan associations were also of major importance. The first association

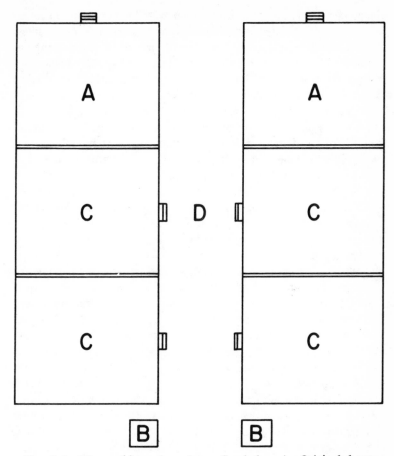

FIG. 9.1 The making of a slum. Symbols: A. Original house facing street. B. Original outhouse, intended for one building, now serving three. C. Rear houses added on in former yard, facing alley. D. Alley. Source: W. E. B. DuBois, *The Philadelphia Negro,* p. 294.

in the United States was founded in Philadelphia in 1831. Build-and loan associations later spread throughout the country, but they remained most significant in Philadelphia, where in 1874 there were 400 such organizations. Again, the contrast with New York is important; land in New York was costly and therefore too expensive for such ventures. In Philadelphia however, the individual of modest means could invest his savings in shares of the association and borrow up to the matured value of those shares at a moderate interest rate. In this way, thousands of middle-income workers could purchase small houses at prices ranging from $1,000 to $2,500. The local custom of ground rents also helped the small home buyer. Instead of purchasing the lot, he could rent it for a nominal sum over a long period of time.[5]

The impact of the building and loan associations upon the attitudes of Philadelphians cannot be over-emphasized. The associations fostered an optimistic view that people of humble means could benefit from the institutions of free enterprise and private property. Furthermore, civic groups and the news media used the publicity attending the associations in an effort at social control —an attempt to implant bourgeois attitudes upon the lower classes. It is ironic that a much-touted spirit of individualism was nourished by what were essentially cooperative ventures. One charitable organization applauded the associations, because they helped "to make men independent and self-helpful. There is nothing pauperizing about them." Because every man was his own landlord, the city's citizens were "steady, thrifty, forehanded, and domestic in their habits." The small homes of Philadelphia, in contrast to the tenements of New York, promoted a "bourgeois spirit, and inspired the people to rise." Organized labor would not succeed, assured the *Public Ledger,* because "the separate home feature of the city detracts very much from the attractiveness of union headquarters, and once there, with his working clothes off and his slippers on, the average workingman is just as likely to stay in as he is to go out." [6]

The flaws in this enthusiasm were obvious. Building and loan associations might do very well for low-paid clerks, teachers, and skilled workers, but they did not begin to fulfill the needs of the unskilled or the poor. Such people could hardly be expected to offer security for loans or pay 6 percent interest in order to provide themselves with a row house. One author, while claiming on the one hand that the "wage earner and man of humble means" could easily own his own house, admitted that he was describing the man who earned an average wage of $25.00 per week in 1891.[7] Obviously there existed in Philadelphia a class of people about whom many citizens were unaware. These people, often unskilled immigrants or blacks, lived in degrading conditions.

Few people ventured behind the façades of the rows of brick houses to confront the surface drainage and privys in the hidden, festering alleys; consequently, little publicity was given to the increasing slum problems in the pre-Civil War period. Visitors to the city joined the citizens in praising the symmetry and beauty of the city. One visitor did notice "some small low-class houses here and there," but they were "fewer in proportion than in any other town" of his acquaintance. In fact, some found Philadelphia's attractiveness boring. Gustave de Beaumont declared that the city's "sole defect is to be monotonous in its beauty," while Alexis de Tocqueville observed that "the regularity is tiresome, but very convenient," and Mrs. Trollope complained of the "extreme and almost wearisome regularity." Thus the remarks of travelers reinforced Philadelphia's view of itself as a city of homes.[8]

A few concerned citizens did take notice of the growing slums. The industrialist Mathew Carey made a study in 1837 of 64 tenements which contained 92 families and 473 inhabitants. Of these, "there are THIRTY TENEMENTS containing FIFTY-FIVE FAMILIES and TWO HUNDRED AND FIFTY-THREE INDIVIDUALS *that have not the accommodations of a privy for their use!!*" But most observers related such conditions to idleness and drunkenness. In 1853 a grand jury, in cooperation with the *Evening Bulletin,* investigated some slums in the Fifth Ward. The report described Dickensonian conditions of such incredible squalor that they "are not fit to be the abiding places of swine"—with which they were often shared. Small overcrowded hovels without windows, ventilation, furniture, or "even a straw to lie upon" were described. Yet the jury only recommended the establishment of a repressive House of Correction and the "total abolition of the groggeries. Rum is at the root of the trouble, strike *there* and the battle is half won." The report did not speculate on how to win the other half. Such attitudes supported the comfortable satisfaction of the city. New immigration and worse overcrowding would be required to shake its complacency.[9]

Philadelphia's housing problems were intensified following the Civil War by the influx of two groups—blacks and immigrants. The Negro population of the city climbed from 31,699 in 1870 to 84,459 or 5.5 percent of the total population in 1910. The blacks were primarily poor migrants from the upper South. They settled throughout the city, often as domestic servants. The particularly poor blacks, however, moved into the core city. By 1900 they were being pushed by Russian immigrants from the Fifth Ward into the Seventh and Thirtieth Wards. These wards contained the heaviest concentration of blacks. The upper Fifth and lower Seventh Wards were regions of abject poverty, inhabited by recent migrants from the rural South who had no preparation for urban life.[10]

Immigration from Southern and Eastern Europe also added to the crowded poverty areas of the city. Philadelphia did not share in this immigration as heavily as did New York or Chicago. One scholar has estimated that close to 70 percent of the city's population in any given year from 1860 to 1910 was made up of native white migrants or native-born Philadelphians. However, after 1880, the growth from Great Britain and Northern Europe either declined or proceeded at a much slower rate than that from Russia and Italy, the two major contributors of the new immigration. The absolute increase is also instructive. For example, the city's Russian-born population vaulted from 94 in 1870 to 90,696 in 1910. Most of these were poor Russian Jews. The change in Philadelphia's foreign-born population has been summarized by a recent scholar.

The change in source of foreign-born ingredients by the turn of the twentieth century is revealed in the fact that, in 1860, natives of southern and eastern Europe numbered only 831 and represented only 0.14 percent of Philadelphia's aggregate population, while by 1910, a similar group of nations had supplied some 176,288 persons to the city, or 11.4 percent of its aggregate population. By contrast, immigrants from northern and western Europe numbered 167,797 and represented 29.7 percent of Philadelphia's aggregate population in 1860, while in 1910, this group numbered 202,604 and represented only 13.1 percent of the city's aggregate population.[11]

The new immigrants settled in south Philadelphia in areas already marked by poor housing. The heaviest concentration of Italians was in the Second Ward, with the market at Ninth and Christian streets serving as the center of their settlement. Large numbers of Italians were also found in the Third and Twenty-sixth Wards. The Russians settled heavily in the First Ward with smaller important settlements in the Third, Fourth and Fifth Wards. As mentioned, the Russian immigration had a marked effect upon the black community. Social workers in the Fifth Ward noted that the St. Mary Street Library and the James Forten School, both of which had catered largely to blacks, were by 1890 serving more and more Russian Jews. In 1891, the James Forten School had been 50 percent black and 50 percent Jewish. By 1899, the number of blacks had declined to 13 percent.[12]

In spite of the increased immigration, Philadelphia's housing picture still seemed better than that in other large cities. In 1895, reformers pushed a bill through the state legislature which practically ensured the exclusion of high-rise tenements with narrow air shafts, poor lighting, and insufficient ventilation.[13] Moreover, most studies presented a bright picture of the city's housing. One study revealed that of 102,259 new buildings erected between 1887 and 1901, 93,898, or 91.8 percent were two- and three-story buildings. The same study examined four residential wards

TABLE 9.1   Areas of Black, Russian, and Italian Settlement in South Philadelphia, 1910

| | WARD | | | | |
	One	Two	Three	Four	Five
Black	208	689	1,501	2,542	763
Russian	16,398	8,427	5,093	5,269	5,149
Italian	2,346	11,527	6,538	3,732	197
	Six	Seven	Eight	Nine	Ten
Black	75	11,553	1,839	844	593
Russian	1,533	1,036	177	35	639
Italian	55	158	88	51	162
	Eleven	Twelve	Thirteen	Fourteen	Fifteen
Black	99	249	670	3,085	2,698
Russian	2,863	3,658	4,173	1,288	1,262
Italian	45	35	120	85	356
	Twenty-six	Thirty-six	Thirty-nine		
Black	5,191	5,840	906		
Russian	680	1,076	7,522		
Italian	7,274	524	375		

SOURCE: U.S. Bureau of the Census, *Thirteenth Census, 1910, Population,* pp. 111, 605–8

and discovered that the vast majority of landholders owned properties assessed at less than $5,000. Philadelphia's reputation for horizontal development was enhanced in 1900 when the Director of Public Safety reported that half of the home construction in the city for the previous year occurred in the four wards west of the Schuykill. The U.S. census indicated that more people owned their own homes in Philadelphia than in New York, Boston, and Chicago, although the figure never exceeded 25 percent. More significant is the average number of occupants per dwelling; after 1870, this figure never exceeded six. It dwindled from 6.01 in 1870 to 5.2 in 1910, and it always bore a reasonable resemblance to the average number of members per family. In addition, Philadelphia's congested wards (Two through Twenty, except Fifteen) actually lost population between 1870 and 1890. Finally, the thirteenth census revealed that south Philadelphia never reached two families per house in any ward.[14] Thus most citizens paid little heed to the warnings of reformers.

This confidence was nourished by the contrasting state of affairs in other cities. Housing authorities were universal in their declarations that New York had the worst housing conditions of any major U.S. city. The "dumbbell" tenement was the notorious symbol of New York's slums. Originally designed as a plan for a model tenement, the dumbbell was actually a front and rear tenement connected by a narrow passageway. It was characterized by dark, ill-ventilated halls and rooms, insufficient narrow air shafts, and a lack of space for play and recreation. This attempt to crowd as many people as possible into a 25x100-foot lot was no reform at all, and one architect remarked: "If the dumbbell is the best, then 'how much is the best worth'?" A very few of these buildings existed in Philadelphia, but the act of 1895 made them illegal. Thus the Quaker City was spared the necessity of correcting a major error which plagued New York for decades.[15]

"After New York, Boston has the worst tenement house conditions of any American city," remarked one report in 1901. Although New York's six- and seven-story tenement was rarely seen, the Hub City's problem's were severe. Half of the homes in the South End were tenements which had formerly been fine one-family dwellings. Some of the smaller streets and alleys were simply passageways for rows of tall tenement buildings. The damp cellar dwelling was a particular problem, because most of the

South End, or the old "Neck," had originally been reclaimed from the sea. The most severe problem in the North, South and West Ends was the one-family house which had been improperly converted into a tenement. Often toilet and water facilities adequate for one family were shared by four to eight families. There were rear dwellings, but they differed from those in Philadelphia. Boston's rear houses were erected in yards, and the original homes were often replaced by four- to six-story tenements. When a house was set in the middle of a plot, its front and back yards would simply become surrounded by dwellings, thus filling the lot and creating problems of light and ventilation. Overcrowding was a problem in Boston, a fact attested to by its average occupancy of 8.4 persons per dwelling.[16]

Chicago also had serious slum problems. The expansion of manufacturing and commercial enterprises around the "Loop" created a need for more land. As a result, homes were crowded onto less space, especially in the river wards. In 1900 a writer for the Chicago *Tribune* proclaimed Chicago's slums more horrifying than any in Europe. Overcrowding was serious and frightening. Like Philadelphia, New York, and Boston, Chicago had rear tenements, but they took a different form. Often the original frame house was moved to the rear of the lot while a larger brick tenement was erected in front. This blocked light and ventilation from the rear house, which was usually situated among privies, garbage, and manure piles. Unpaved, uncleansed, and unsewered alleys resulted. One-family houses were partitioned for two or even three families, and in some cases children actually suffocated for want of sufficient cubic air space. An ominous aspect was

TABLE 9.2 Home Occupancy in Philadelphia, New York, Boston, and Chicago

CITY	OCCUPANTS PER DWELLING				PERSONS PER FAMILY			
	1880	1890	1900	1910	1880	1890	1900	1910
Philadelphia	5.79	5.60	5.4	5.2	5.13	5.10	4.9	4.7
New York	16.37	18.52	13.7	15.6	4.96	4.99	4.7	4.7
Boston	8.26	8.52	8.4	9.1	4.99	5.00	4.8	4.8
Chicago	8.24	8.60	8.8	8.9	5.19	4.99	4.7	4.6

SOURCES: U.S. Bureau of the Census, *Eleventh Census, 1890, Abstract*, p. 88; *Twelfth Census, 1900, Abstract*, p. 90; *Thirteenth Census, 1910, Abstract*, p. 261

the introduction of the dumbbell (or double decker, as it was called in Chicago) into the city. One study of a small area on the West Side discovered eighty-seven of these buildings. In that same section, houses covered more than 90 percent of the space of 144 lots. It is little wonder that Jane Addams spoke enviously of the "happy condition of Philadelphia" in 1902.[17]

Philadelphia's outward appearance did compare favorably with other large cities. The reason for this, however, was the absence of large tenements and the invisibility of the rear alley slums. Yet almost every other problem was present—small alleys and courts with their rear dwellings; a total absence of paving and sewers in some cases; unspeakable toilet facilities; overcrowding—all could be observed in a careful walk through the southeastern wards of the city. The report which had noted the prevalence of two- and three-story homes in Philadelphia also warned that "the devotion to dwellings of this type . . . has not prevented congestion in the older parts of the city, where the three-story houses have been adapted to tenement house methods of life." [18]

A typical turn-of-the-century rear alley court might begin with a three- or four-story house facing the street; in the past it might have been a fashionable home. Now it was subdivided for several families. Its former spacious yard was probably filled in with back-to-back rear brick dwellings. The same might be true of the house beside it. The result would be a row of brick houses deriving their light and air from a narrow alley. Or the back yard might be filled with a court of two- or three-story band-box houses. While band-boxes usually contained only one family, some could be found with two or more families gaining access to their rooms by the staircase of the room below. The small yards of the courts might be clean, or they might be garbage and ash heaps supplemented by the ubiquitous privy vault. Worse yet was the back yard which had been haphazardly filled in with tumble-down wooden shacks and lean-tos. Damp cellar dwellings existed, and the cellars or first floors of some houses might contain bakeries, butcher shops, goats, pigs, chickens, and geese. Push cart operators often stored their produce in their dark rooms. In 1895 there were 171 such small alleys and courts in the Fifth Ward and 88 in the Fourth. The single block bounded by South, Lombard, Fifth, and Sixth Streets contained fifteen crowded courts and alleys.

If the low-income family was fortunate enough to live in a reasonably clean apartment, it might still be overwhelmed by the insanitary conditions surrounding it. The city was slowly paving and sewering its streets, but thousands of courts and alleys were privately owned and remained as cobbled passageways. Landlords frequently refused to install the necessary plumbing even when sewers were available. Filth and waste were trapped in the cobbled alleys. Pools of waste material and garbage would stagnate in the summer, freeze in the winter, and thaw in the spring. These hostels for disease were made more horrifying by antiquated toilet facilities. The thousands of privy vaults in south Philadelphia were excellent examples of the reluctance of a city to face up to the facts of urbanism. One vault could serve several families or indeed an entire tenement. Their close proximity to kitchen and bedroom windows often made those rooms unbearable. When water closets did exist, they were frequently outdoors and inoperable in the winter because of freezing. The poor water supply was also a major factor in the lack of cleanliness so often deplored by more fortunate citizens. Indoor facilities were frequently totally absent, and one outdoor hydrant might serve ten families. Indoor faucets were at times inoperable because of broken pipes, and they sometimes contained no traps. The seriousness of that situation becomes obvious when one realizes that the discharge pipes of kitchen sinks were often connected to sewers, or worse yet, privy vaults. Although they might be inefficient vehicles for water, the pipes became excellent conductors of foul odors and sewer gas. Of course many water fixtures contained no outlets at all and merely discharged their waste into the courts to mix with the other surface drainage.[19]

In 1904, a well-publicized study focused on some of Philadelphia's slums. The Octavia Hill Association, named after the famous English reformer, commissioned Miss Emily W. Dinwiddie, a New York social worker, to study three sections of the city. They were the blocks bounded by Carpenter, Christian, Eighth and Ninth Streets in the Second Ward; North American and New Market between Vine and Callowhill in the Eleventh Ward; and from Sixteenth to Eighteenth and Lombard to Rodman Streets in the Seventh Ward. The first district was in the center of the major Italian settlement. The second was inhabited by a mixture of Russian and Austro-Hungarian Jews, as well as Germans, Poles,

Irish and natives. The third was a black neighborhood. Five hundred and sixty-five houses were inspected. The study provides a look at Philadelphia's slums as well as a contrast between different ethnic neighborhoods.[20]

At first glance, the Dinwiddie conclusions appear comforting. Of 565 dwellings, 453 or 80 percent housed only one family. Only 25 were over three stories high. Most of the rooms were clean. But these figures do not tell the entire story. Forty-one out of 167, or almost 25 percent of the houses in the Italian district were tenements. (The word "tenement" in this study follows that of the 1895 housing law, i.e., "every building which, or a partition of which, is occupied or is to be occupied as a residence of three or more families, living independently of each other and doing their cooking on the premises.") Only four of these had fire escapes. Furthermore, 28.42 percent of the Italian families lived, slept and cooked in one-room apartments. Over half of the toilets in the entire study were outdoor privies, 87 percent of which were described as offensive. Of the 342 privies, only 48 leaked and 55 were full or overflowing. Nevertheless, most of them were close enough to the houses to contaminate the air of the living quarters. Most water fixtures were outdoors and inoperable much of the time. The halls and stairways were often dark and dirty. In the Italian district, forty-eight instances of six families sharing one toilet were discovered. Over 65 percent of the toilets in that area were shared with one to five other families. Thirty-nine percent of the living quarters in the study housed two or more persons per room. Similar studies in Chicago and Jersey City reported only 24.3 percent and 23.6 percent, respectively. Clearly the city of homes had its share of undesirable dwellings.[21]

The Dinwiddie study revealed differences among the three districts. The Italian district had the greater number of tenements, while 62 percent of the houses in the mixed district were rear-alley dwellings. The black neighborhood had witnessed an increase in its black population since W. E. B. DuBois' monumental study of the Seventh Ward in 1899. Although the lower section of the district had been a criminal haven, much of the area had included fine residences. Fewer tenements and rear houses were located here, but all but one of the furnished rooming houses were in this district. Overcrowding was worst in the Italian district; in that area, 104 one-room apartments were found in one block. One common urban evil, however, was not much in evidence; only one actual sweatshop, a tailor shop in the Italian district, was discovered. In sixty-three other cases, or 7 percent of all apartments, some home work was discovered, but it was carried on only by members of the family.[22]

Miss Dinwiddie was careful to point out that these families were not shiftless. Only seven heads of families were reported as having no occupation. Thirty-nine percent were unskilled laborers, 39 percent skilled, 16 percent engaged in commerce and 6 percent miscellaneous. Only one person, an aged woman, was receiving charity. Yet it was clear that proper housing was not available for many of these families. Furthermore, the Dinwiddie study noted that most of the rooms were clean, despite difficult conditions. This was particularly true in the black neighborhood, a fact which Miss Dinwiddie attributed to the employment of many black women in domestic service and to the lack of tenements. Yet how was a housewife supposed to keep her rooms habitable when the privy leaked, the hydrant was broken, and underground drainage was not available? One reformer chided the more fortunate citizens of Philadelphia by asking: "Is it not we who are "dirty" when we give [immigrants] no better chance . . .? We ask the foreigners to come here—If they spread disease and vice, it is not *they* who are responsible, but we." [23]

An evaluation of Philadelphia's housing results in some ambivalence. It is true that few Philadelphians were crowded into high-rise tenements. Even the slum wards did not reveal the overcrowding that existed in comparable wards in other cities. But other indices were not as comforting. A comparison of Boston, New York, Philadelphia, and Chicago indicates that Philadelphia's mortality rate, while declining in the first decade of the century, was higher from 1906 to 1910 than any of the other cities except Boston. One reason for this was the extremely high typhoid rate which resulted more from the poor water supply than from actual slums. But the Quaker City also led in tuberculosis deaths. This is important, because tuberculosis was usually associated with dark crowded rooms such as those found in the tenements of New York. However, small houses could be just as dark and unhealthy, and Miss Dinwiddie warned that flies could assist in the spreading of typhoid by carrying

TABLE 9.3   Mortality Rates

CITY	1901–05	1906–10	1907	1908	1909	1910
ANNUAL AVERAGE TOTAL DEATH RATE PER 1,000 (EXCLUSIVE OF STILLBIRTHS)						
Philadelphia	18.1	17.7	18.6	17.3	16.4	17.4
Boston	18.8	17.9	18.6	18.3	16.8	17.2
New York	19.0	16.9	18.3	16.3	16.0	16.0
(Manhattan)	19.5	17.4	18.7	16.8	16.6	16.5
Chicago	14.5	14.9	15.7	14.5	14.6	15.1
ANNUAL AVERAGE DEATHS FROM TYPHOID PER 100,000						
Philadelphia	52.0	41.4	60.3	35.2	22.3	17.5
Boston	22.1	16.2	10.2	24.7	13.8	11.3
New York	18.1	13.5	17.1	11.9	12.1	11.6
(Manhattan)	16.0	13.1	16.8	11.1	11.3	11.4
Chicago	28.8	15.7	18.2	15.8	12.6	13.7
ANNUAL AVERAGE DEATHS FROM TUBERCULOSIS PER 100,000						
Philadelphia	239.6	234.5	251.7	232.2	215.6	216.9
Boston	250.5	210.1	214.4	209.9	190.2	204.7
New York	248.0	226.1	236.4	226.7	214.3	211.0
(Manhattan)	234.5	225.3	238.5	229.8	215.8	216.9
Chicago	179.9	186.7	197.2	186.6	181.0	178.0

SOURCE: Department of Commerce: Bureau of the Census, *Mortality Statistics, 1910*, pp. 15, 24, 47.

the germ from the privies. These mortality figures cast some doubt upon the quality of living conditions in the City of Homes. It appeared clear that both municipality and landlord had to assume greater responsibility. Yet landlords generally opposed housing reform. The following study may provide some suggestions as to why.[24]

The picture of the greedy landlord is one which has persisted throughout the twentieth century. Indeed, the slumlord has served a scape-goat function for reformers. Philadelphia's reformers contributed to this image. Bernard Newman, executive secretary of the Philadelphia Housing Commission, continually cited statistics showing a low rate of home ownership in Philadelphia's slum wards. This, he declared, proved that "the men who are opposed to [housing reform] are big property owners." A city councilman argued that "good profits" from slum properties were the cause of opposition to reform. The *Evening Ledger* harped upon the "selfishness and greed" of landlords and warned of impending disaster "whenever gold is set above men."[25]

Actually, many reformers were far less certain of the omnipresence of the "big property owner." Jane Addams wrote of her difficulties in persuading Italian immigrants that they should improve their tenements. Edith Abbott found that many Chicago landlords lived in the worst rooms in their tenements. Some poor tenement owners told her that owning a house made them feel like "real Americans" and "better citizens." Jacob Riis wrote, often in bigoted tones, of the Irish, and especially the Jewish slumlords of New York. He described the tenement problem as primarily one of educating the landlords. Lawrence Veiller, the great New York reformer, seconded this, describing the small property owner as "limited in his intelligence, his own standard of living, and his knowledge of sanitary science." Roger Baldwin's efforts to abolish privy wells in St. Louis were opposed by Jewish immigrants, while most of the new tenements going up in New Haven in 1911 were built by Italians, Russians, and Slavs, "who by pinching economy have saved enough to make these investments pay." Thus the tenement owner was often described as being of the same background as his tenant.[26]

The following study deals with 84 Philadelphia tenement owners who had been charged with housing violations in 1914.[27] The number of properties owned by these landlords ranged from one to 41; the number of buildings from one to 71; and the taxable value from $1,600 to $149,150. However, the median figure does not reflect a "big property owner." The median landlord owned two properties, three buildings, and his total real estate value for tax purposes was $8,500. The clearest results can be seen in table 9.4. Fully 52 (or 61 percent) of the owners owned only one or two properties. Fifty (or 60 percent) owned four or fewer buildings. Forty-eight (or 58 percent) owned properties valued at less than $10,000. Thus the average landlord in this study, while he was more prosperous than the housewife who took in boarders to make ends meet, clearly was not an exceptionally wealthy man.

The location of the properties under complaint is predictable. Of the 105 properties whose wards could be determined, 75 (71 percent) were in the Second, Third, Fourth, and Fifth Wards, which were centers of Italian and Russian immigration.[28] The

TABLE 9.4   Philadelphia Tenement Owners, 1914 (Selected)

Properties	Owners	Buildings	Owners	Total Value	Owners
1	34 (40%)	1	8 (10%)	Under $5,000	24 (29%)
2	18 (21%)	2	24 (29%)	$5,000–$9,999	24 (29%)
3	8 (10%)	3	12 (14%)	$10,000–$19,999	17 (20%)
4	3 (4%)	4	6 (7%)	$20,000–$49,999	11 (13%)
5	5 (6%)	5	4 (5%)	$50,000–$99,999	7 (8%)
6–10	7 (8%)	6	4 (5%)	$100,000 and over	1 (1%)
11–20	5 (6%)	7	3 (4%)	Total	84
21–41	4 (5%)	8	2 (2%)		
Total	84	9	2 (2%)		
		10	1 (1%)		
		11–20	10 (12%)		
		21–43	7 (8%)		
		71	1 (1%)		
		Total	84		

Seventh Ward is interesting; only five complaints appeared in that ward, the eastern part of which was heavily populated by poor blacks. However, it will be recalled from the Dinwiddie study that few legally defined tenements existed in that ward. A study of housing violations among non-tenement properties might yield different results. The owners also tended to hold most of their properties in the same geographic area. Of the 39 owners who could be located in the city or telephone directories, 11 (28 percent) lived in the houses under complaint. The absolute figure itself would be so low as to be meaningless, were it not for the fact that it compares favorably with a study made in 1914 by the chief of the Philadelphia Division of Tenement House Inspection. He examined four-fifths of the city's licensed tenements and found that 27 percent were inhabited by their owners.[29] Of the 84 owners whose total holdings could be determined, 34 (40 percent) owned only one property. Twenty-four multiple property owners (29 percent) had holdings in only one ward, 26 (31 percent) in more than one ward. Yet those 26 who owned properties in more than one ward generally owned them in nearby wards. Overwhelmingly, they were located in south Philadelphia. Thus those tenement owners who could be located lived in or near the wards in which their holdings were located.

The names of the owners were examined to determine ethnic origin. Of 99 names, 50 were Jewish-sounding names and 20

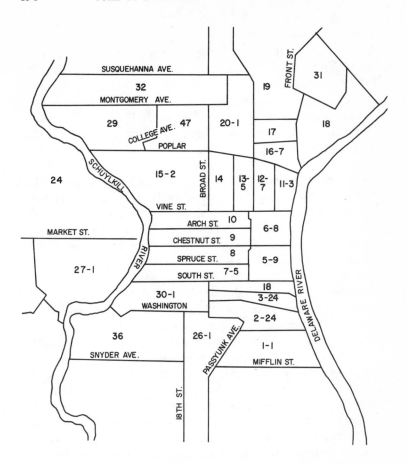

FIG. 9.2. Tenement violations, by ward, 1914. The first number indicates the ward, the second indicates the number of violations.

were Italian. Thirteen were labeled WASP or black, 13 unknown, and three Irish.[30] Of course there were wide variations in each group. If, for example, Newman wanted a "big property owner," he might have selected Charles C. A. Baldi. Baldi had immigrated from Italy in 1876 and had started out as a lemon hawker. By 1914 he had become a successful banker, undertaker, politician, and husband of a native Philadelphian named Luisa Sorbenheimer. The colorful and flamboyant Baldi also possessed extensive real estate holdings. He owned 24 properties and 45 buildings which were valued at $149,150. Although the holdings were fewer in number than some others on the complaint list, they had the highest value of any. This is because of their diversified nature. In addition to several houses (two of which were on the complaint list), Baldi owned a hotel, a factory, five stores, an office building, a warehouse, and other profit-producing buildings. If the holdings of other members of his family were included, the list would be even more extensive. Wielding vast economic and political power, Baldi did indeed fit the description of a "big property owner." [31]

But Baldi was atypical. So was A. Edward Newton, the only WASP of any note on the list. President of one company and treasurer of another, Newton enjoyed his passion as a bibliophile on his "Oak Knoll" estate in Doylesford. He was also an absentee landlord who owned 20 properties containing 25 houses, many of them in courts, on Callowhill Street in the fifteenth ward. There were also three Jews, two of them realtors and one a dentist, who owned properties valued at over $50,000. But much more common (and in some respects more fascinating), are forgotten figures with names like Giacomo Frantanduono and Rosa Jacobawitch who exist only in the dusty tomes of the assessor. [32]

A study of the holdings and their value for owners with Jewish- and Italian-sounding names does not reveal stark contrasts. As shown in table 9.5, both groups were heavily concentrated at one or two properties, but Jews covered a wider range on the property scale than did Italians. Only one Italian, Baldi, owned more than five properties, compared to seven Jews. The same is generally true for buildings. One reason for the wider range of holdings by Jews may be reflected in the occupational status which was discovered for 39 owners. Of the five property owners engaged in real estate, two were Jews with heavy holdings and only one, Baldi, was an Italian. Aside from Baldi, the Italians generally held lesser jobs, whereas the Jews ran the full scale, from shoemaker to physician.

The table of taxable property values, however, does not reflect large differences. It is true that of the lesser holders, 43 percent of those with Jewish-sounding names owned properties valued at between five and ten thousand dollars compared to only 20 percent for the Italians, and thus the small Italian property holder seems to have been less prosperous than his Jewish counter-

TABLE 9.5 Tenement Owners by Sound of Names

	Jews	Italians
Properties Owned		
1	17 (40%)	7 (35%)
2	10 (24%)	5 (25%)
3–5	8 (19%)	7 (35%)
6–10	3 (7%)	0
11–20	2 (5%)	0
21–41	2 (5%)	1 (5%)
Total	42	20
Buildings Owned		
1	3 (7%)	2 (10%)
2	12 (29%)	5 (25%)
3	6 (14%)	4 (20%)
4	4 (10%)	2 (10%)
5	4 (10%)	0
6	1 (2%)	2 (10%)
7	1 (2%)	1 (5%)
8	2 (5%)	0
9	0	2 (10%)
10	0	0
11–20	6 (14%)	1 (5%)
21–53	2 (5%)	1 (5%)
71	1 (2%)	0
Total	42	20

TABLE 9.6 Occupations of Tenement Owners

junk and		meat	2J	dentist	2J
rags	1I	livery	2J	physician and	
fruit	1I	confectionary	1J	pharmacist	1J
baker	1I	newsdealer	1J	trust company	
shoemaker	1J	grocer	3J, 1W-B	official	1U
tailor	1J, 1I, 1U	hotel	1J	company presi-	
presser	1J	apartments	1J	dent	1W
letter carrier	1J	manager	1J	unknown busi-	
dining	1U	woolens	2J	ness	2J
liquor	1J	furniture	1J		
		real estate	2J, 1I, 2U		

SOURCE: City Directory and Telephone Directory, 1914.
SYMBOLS: J=Jew, I=Italian, W-B=Wasp or Black, W=Wasp, U=Unknown.

part, but for holdings under $20,000 both groups are almost even at 80 and 85 percent. While the Jews lead in holdings over $20,000, 45 percent of the Italians held properties valued at more than $10,000, compared to 38 percent for the Jews. And the Italians would lead in that bracket even without Baldi (see table 9.7). Of course the figures for the Italians are so small, they might be dismissed as meaningless, but a look at the types of properties owned might provide a clue to the Italians' ability to hold their own.

In all, 39 landlords owned 86 stores, 65 of which were part of dwellings. Others owned stables and shops. A total of 62 landlords owned 114 buildings which served some function other than dwellings. Sixteen Jews, or 38 percent of them, belonged in this category. But a full 50 percent of the Italians also owned buildings other than dwellings. This helped to increase the value of their holdings.[33]

In one respect the Jews stood in marked contrast to the Italians. The holdings of the Jews were more diffuse than those of the Italians. Both were heavily concentrated in south Philadelphia. The Jewish properties under complaint were primarily scattered throughout the Third, Fourth, and Fifth Wards. However, 20 (83 percent) of the Italian properties were in the heavily Italian Second Ward. The same holds true when multiple property holders are considered. Twenty-five (57 percent) of the Jews were multiple property holders compared to 13 (68 percent) of the Italians. Yet 51 percent of the multiple property holders with Jewish-sounding names owned properties outside of the original ward of complaint, compared to only 31 percent of the Italians. Thus, although the Italian tenement-law violators seemed to

TABLE 9.7   **Property Values of Tenement Holdings**

Value	Jews	Italians
Under $5,000	8 (20%)	7 (35%)
$5,000–$9,999	18 (45%)	4 (20%)
$10,000–$19,999	7 (17%)	6 (30%)
$20,000–$49,999	6 (14%)	2 (10%)
$50,000–$99,999	3 (7%)	0
$100,000 and over	0	1 (5%)
Total	42	20

venture into multiple holdings more readily than their Jewish counterparts, they also chose to remain more heavily concentrated in one ethnic center (see tables 9.8–9.9).[34]

Thus, it would appear that the word "big property owner" is too nebulous and sweeping a generalization to be applied to the Philadelphia tenement owner. There were wealthy landlords, and they may have been formidable opponents of reform. It is also true that all of the smaller owners banded together might have offered effective opposition to reform. Indeed, there was an "International Tenement House Owners' Association" in Philadelphia; it is unfortunate that no membership rolls are extant. Yet the very name of the body is significant. Bernard Newman admitted that the title "was intended to designate the variety of nationalities grouped in the Association." This study suggests that the tenement owner was often a member of an ethnic minority. His holdings were not extensive. When he was an

TABLE 9.8   Ownership of Property Under Complaint by Ward

Ward	Jews	Italians
One	1	
Two	2	20
Three	13	3
Four	11	
Five	7	
Six	5	
Seven	1	
Eleven	1	
Twelve	1	
Thirteen	5	
Sixteen	1	
Twenty-six		1
Twenty-seven	1	
	49	24

TABLE 9.9   Ownership of Property in Wards Other than Original Wards of Complaint

Ownership in Other Wards:	Yes	No
Jewish multiple-property holders	13 (51%)	12 (49%)
Italian multiple-property holders	4 (31%)	9 (69%)

absentee landlord, he probably lived nearby, especially if he was an Italian. It may well be that he believed, rightly or wrongly, that increased repairs necessitated by reform legislation would adversely affect his economic status. This does not excuse slums; it only aids in understanding the opposition to reform. In the words of one scholar, "it is clear that the business of low-income residential property is not highly concentrated. There is no equivalent of General Motors or the A & P among slumlords." [35]

The portrait of the greedy slumlord and the exploited immigrant oversimplifies a complex subject. The run-down tenement was a problem for some immigrants, and one over which they had little control. Other newcomers, however, found an opportunity in slum housing. Real estate and landlordship offered a path of upward mobility, especially for Jews and Italians in Philadelphia. One Philadelphia immigrant (who was not a slumlord) became prosperous first in real estate and later as a land developer. He explained his passion for owning property.

> The ownership of real estate meant the gratification of an old ambition. In Russia a Jew could not legally hold title to property, but here, in this free land, one could purchase real estate and record a deed in his own name in the public archives. I knew a Jew in Russia who owned and operated large timber lands; but, because he could not legally hold title to them, he had vested the title in a loyal peasant laborer. However, the peasant died suddenly without a will. What peasant ever does have a will? His family claimed the timber land and the entire estate of the wealthy Jew, and he had no redress, for he could not legally contest their claim. He became a laborer on his own lands. For this reason open ownership held a great attraction for us Russian Jews. [36]

Thus America represented economic, as well as political freedom. And many immigrants, seeking economic freedom, probably owned slums in which their countrymen lived. Such were the opportunities and problems to be found in America's promised cities.

NOTES

1. Anthony N. B. Garavan, "Proprietary Philadelphia as Artifact," in *The Historian and the City,* Oscar Handlin and John Burchard, eds. (Cambridge: The M.I.T. Press, 1963), pp. 189–97; Nicholas Wain-

wright, "Plan of Philadelphia," *Pennsylvania Magazine of History and Biography* 80 (April 1956): 164; Sam Bass Warner, Jr., *The Private City: Philadelphia in Three Periods of Its Growth* (Philadelphia: Univ. of Pennsylvania Press, 1968), pp. 8–9, 15–18; Carl Bridenbaugh, *Cities in the Wilderness: The First Century of Urban Life in America, 1625–1742,* 2nd ed. (New York: Alfred A. Knopf, 1955), pp. 10, 148–49, 306; and *Cities in Revolt: Urban Life in America, 1743–1776,* 2nd ed. (New York: Alfred A. Knopf, 1955), pp. 13–16, 224–25; James A. Ford, *Slums and Housing* (Cambridge: Harvard Univ. Press, 1936), 1:255–57; J. Thomas Scharf and Thompson Westcott, *History of Philadelphia, 1609–1884* (Philadelphia: L. H. Evarts and Co., 1884), 1:88.

2. Garavan, "Proprietary Philadelphia," 197–98; Warner, *The Private City,* pp. 50–53.

3. William John Murtagh, "The Philadelphia Row House," *Journal of the Society of Architectural Historians* 16 (December 1957): 9; see fig. 9.1.

4. Adna F. Weber, *The Growth of Cities in the Nineteenth Century: A Study in Statistics,* 2nd ed. (Ithaca: Cornell Univ. Press, 1965), p. 139; Warner, *The Private City,* pp. 49–61; Warner, "Innovation and the Industrialization of Philadelphia, 1800–1850," in *The Historian and the City,* Handlin and Burchard, eds., p. 16.

5. Edith Elmer Wood, *The Housing of the Unskilled Worker: America's Next Problem* (New York: Macmillan, 1919), pp. 232–34; Philadelphia *Public Ledger,* April 24, 1893; Marcus T. Reynolds, "The Housing of the Poor in American Cities," *Publications* of the American Economic Association 7 (1893): 111–13; Harry P. Mawson, "Homes for the People," *Harper Weekly* 35 (November 7, 1891): 869–70; C. Bernard, "A Hundred Thousand Homes: How They Were Paid For," *Scribners Monthly* 11 (February 1876): 477–87; H. C. Cargill, "Small Houses for Working Men," in *The Tenement House Problem,* Robert W. DeForest and Lawrence Veiller, eds. (New York: Macmillan, 1903), 1:346.

6. Bernard, "A Hundred Thousand Homes," p. 478; *Public Ledger,* April 24, 25, 1893; *Charities* 2 (March 18, 1899):12; *The Monthly Register of The Philadelphia Society for Organizing Charity* 2 (November 5, 1880): 5.

7. Wood, *Housing and the Unskilled Worker,* pp. 233–34; Mawson, "Homes for the People," pp. 870–71.

8. Ivan D. Steen, "Philadelphia in the 1850's as Described by British Travelers," *Pennsylvania History* 33 (January 1966): 32–33, 37–38, 45–46; George W. Pierson, *Tocqueville and Beaumont in America* (New York: Oxford Univ. Press, 1938), pp. 457–58; Frances Trollope, *Domestic Manners of the Americans,* Michael Sadler, ed. (New York: Dodd, Mead and Co., 1927), p. 221.

9. Mathew Carey, *A Plea for the Poor* (Philadelphia: L. R. Bailey, 1837), *passim;* Grand Jury of Philadelphia, *The Mysteries and Miseries of Philadelphia* (Philadelphia: n.p., 1853), *passim.*

10. Irwin Sears, "Growth of Population in Philadelphia: 1860–1910," (unpublished diss., Department of History, New York Univ., 1960), pp. 48–49; W. E. B. DuBois, *The Philadelphia Negro: A Social Study* (New York: Schocken Books, 1967), pp. 58–62, 73–82, 305–6.

11. Sears, "Growth of Population," pp. 46, 64–65, 79–80, 87, 111.

12. Katherine B. Davis, "Some Facts About the Fifth Ward," *College Settlement News* 3 (July 1897): 1–3; Joan Younger Dickenson, "Aspects of Italian Immigration to Philadelphia," *Pennsylvania Magazine of History and Biography* 90 (October 1966): 454; St. Mary Street Library, *Annual Report, 1889, 1891;* Frederick W. Speirs, *The James Forten School: An Experiment in Social Regeneration Through Elementary Manual Training* (Philadelphia: n.p., 1901), pp. 7–9. See table 9.1.

13. Laws, Pa., 1895, No. 110, p. 178. After the act was passed, all tenement houses of more than four stories had to be made fire-proof throughout, adding significantly to the cost. Regulations were also included for light and ventilation. It is not the purpose of this paper to discuss housing reform or the reformers. A full examination of this topic may be found in my dissertation, "A City of Homes: Philadelphia Slums and Reformers, 1880–1920" (Temple University, 1973).

14. Anna F. Davies, "Land Values and Ownership in Philadelphia," Department of Commerce and Labor, *Bulletin* of the Bureau of Labor no. 50, 9 (January 1904): 115–30; Philadelphia Director of Public Safety, *Annual Report*, 1900; Weber, *The Growth of Cities*, p. 459; *Monthly Register* 11 (April 1888): 42.

15. Roy Lubove, *The Progressives and the Slums; Tenement House Reform in New York City, 1890–1917* (Pittsburgh: Univ. of Pittsburgh Press, 1962), pp. 28–32; Lawrence M. Friedman, *Government and Slum Housing: A Century of Frustration* (Chicago: Rand McNally, 1968), pp. 75–76.

16. Lawrence Veiller, "Housing Conditions and Tenement Laws in Leading American Cities," in *The Tenement House Problem*, DeForest and Veiller, eds., 1: 136–40; Robert A. Woods, ed., *The City Wilderness: A Settlement Study, South End, Boston* (Boston: Houghton Mifflin, 1898), pp. 2, 33–36, 59–67; and *Americans in Progress: A Settlement Study, North and West Ends, Boston* (Boston: Houghton Mifflin, 1902), pp. 72–103, 139.

17. Robert Hunter, *Tenement Conditions in Chicago: Report by the Investigating Committee of the City Homes Association* (Chicago: The Lakeside Press, 1901), pp. 11–12, 21–50, 73–75; Rudolph J. Vecoli, "Chicago's Italians Prior to World War One: A Study of Their Social and Economic Adjustment" (unpublished diss., Department of History, Univ. of Wisconsin, 1963), pp. 125–83; Jane Addams, "The Housing Problem in Chicago," *Annals of the American Academy of Political and Social Science* 20 (July-November 1902): 99–103; Veiller, "Housing Conditions," 1:131.

18. Davies, "Land Values and Ownership," p. 115; One immigrant recorded

his first quarters: "My lodging and my bed [was] a small couch in a corner of a room which served as kitchen, living room, store room, and bedroom. The couch was very much alive, and tired though I was, the activities within it usually kept me awake at nights." See Nathan Kushin, *Memoirs of a New American* (New York: Block Publishing Co., 1949), p. 49.

19. Emily W. Dinwiddie, *Housing Conditions in Philadelphia* (Philadelphia: n.p., 1904), *passim;* Gustavus A. Weber, "The Improvement of Housing Conditions in Philadelphia," *The American City* 1 (November 1909): 123–28; Philadelphia *Press,* March 12, 1895; Helen Parrish, Address to Church Conference of Women in Parish House of Holy Trinity Church, March 6, 1903, Handwritten ms. in Octavia Hill Association Papers, Philadelphia; Hannah Fox, Address Before the Industrial Exhibit at Horticultural Hall, December 10, 1906, Handwritten ms. in Octavia Hill Association Papers.

20. Dinwiddie, *Housing Conditions,* pp. 2–3.

21. Ibid., *passim.* The report is abstracted in Dinwiddie, "Housing Conditions in Philadelphia," *Charities* 14 (April 1, 1905): 630–38; see also Dickinson, "Aspects of Italian Immigration," pp. 460–62, and *News of the College Settlement of Philadelphia* 1 (March 1903): 2–3.

22. Ibid.; DuBois, *The Philadelphia Negro,* pp. 61–62.

23. Dinwiddie, *Housing Conditions,* pp. 22–23, 32–33; Fox, Address Before the Industrial Exhibit, in Octavia Hill Association Papers.

24. Dinwiddie, *Housing Conditions,* pp. 11–12; for mortality rates, see table 9.3.

25. Philadelphia *Evening Ledger,* December 4, 7, 11, 15, 1914; Bernard Newman to George W. Norris, April 29, 1914, in Housing Association of Delaware Valley Papers, Temple Univ. Urban Archives.

26. Friedman, *Government and Slum Housing,* p. 39; Jane Addams, *Twenty Years At Hull House,* Signet Classics ed. (New York : Signet Books, 1960), pp. 82, 209; Edith Abbott, *The Tenements of Chicago: 1908–1935* (Chicago: University of Chicago Press, 1936), pp. 363, 378, 380–82; Jacob Riis, *How the Other Half Lives: Studies Among the Tenements of New York,* American Centuries ed. (New York: Hill and Wang, 1957), pp. 16–17, 101, 205; Vecoli, "Chicago Italians," pp. 146, 156–157; Veiller, "Housing and Health," *Annals of the American Academy of Political and Social Science* 27 (January-June 1911): 260–61; Roger N. Baldwin, "New Tenants in Old Shacks," *Survey* 25 (February 18, 1911): 326; Emma W. Rogers, "The Foreign Invasion of a New England Town—New Haven," *Survey* 26 (June 3, 1911): 378.

27. The year 1914 was chosen because that is the first year for which a complete record of Assessors' Books is available. A list of 109 tenement complaints was taken from the files of the Philadelphia Housing Commission (now the Housing Association of Delaware Valley), a private, watch-dog reform agency. The owners were discovered by checking the addresses against the Assessors' Books in the

Philadelphia Records Storage Center. Four could not be located, and four institutions were ignored because their holdings in houses were not great. The one exception was a manufacturing company, and most of its holdings were large buildings. This left 101 names. Each name was checked against the Assessors' Books for all 48 wards to determine total property holdings. Nine names were so common that they could not be used in the final tabulation. Thus there remained 84 owners of 92 properties. The owners were then listed in three columns. One showed the number of taxable properties owned by each; another the number of buildings, and another the total taxable value of all properties owned. The number of buildings was differentiated from the number of properties, because one property might have both a house fronting on the street and a back building. One could conceivably own one property and two or more buildings. However, only one taxable value would be placed upon each property. The owners were then checked in the city directory and the telephone directory for residence and occupation. This was disappointing. Only 39 names were located in this manner.

28. Compare this with a study made by the Chief of the Philadelphia Division of Tenement House Inspection in 1914. The actual number of tenement houses in the city was more widely scattered than those under complaint. Furthermore, density does not mean that the tenement is prominent in a particular ward. "In the 13th ward, where the tenements are most thickly centered, they make up only 14 percent of the total number of dwellings in the ward, while in the next most congested tenement neighborhood, the 2nd ward, the tenements amount to but 6 percent of all the dwellings." See Philadelphia Bureau of Health, Division of Tenement House Inspection, *Annual Report, 1914.*

29. Ibid.

30. The author is well aware of the pitfalls involved in this type of impressionistic evidence. A Jewish-sounding name is only just that—a Jewish-sounding name. For example, a German Jew might be a member of an old established American family, while a Russian Jew is apt to be of more recent arrival. The unknown list may contain some Jews, but the author, relying upon his judgment and that of some colleagues, decided to use only those about whom he was fairly certain. The WASP category presents a particular problem. Four people with names like Harris, Needham, Scott, and Allen own property in the Seventh Ward. They may well have been black, but this cannot be determined. One final note—when more than one person owned a property, that property was counted only once. However for purposes of ethnic determination, all names, except for members of the same family, were considered separately. Hence the 99 names.

31. For Baldi's holdings, see Philadelphia Assessor's Book, 1915, ward 2, div. 1, pp. 9, 28, 55, 238, 365, 380, 413; div. 2, pp. 17, 84; ward 3, div. 1, pp. 202, 364, 369; ward 8, div. 2, p. 236; ward 42, div. 2, p. 48. I am grateful to Richard Varbero for supplying me with information

on Baldi's career from his forthcoming dissertation, "Urbanization and Assimilation: Philadelphia and Its Ethnic Minorities, 1918–1941."

32. For Newton, see Philadelphia *Inquirer,* September 29, 1940, and Assessor's Book, 1915, ward 15, div. 2, pp. 133–34, 150–53.

33. In a future study, I shall examine all of the names for a later year, in an attempt to determine whether the property holdings of the individuals increase, decrease, or remain the same. This would serve as another index to economic mobility.

34. Miss Dinwiddie commented upon the "cohesiveness of the [Italians]," in *Housing Conditions,* p. 31. She did not find a single Italian in the other two districts. In 1913, the Chief of the Division of Tenement House Inspection studied tenement house dwellers and found that 97 percent of the Italians preferred to live solely among each other, Philadelphia Bureau of Health, Division of Tenement House Inspection, *Annual Report, 1913;* for evidence that this cohesiveness continued into the second generation, see Herbert J. Gans, *The Urban Villagers: Group and Class in the Life of Italian-Americans* (New York: The Free Press, 1962), *passim,* especially chap. 10; and Nathan Glazer and Daniel P. Moynihan, *Beyond the Melting Pot: The Negroes, Puerto Ricans, Jews, Italians, and Irish of New York City* (Cambridge: The M.I.T. Press, 1963), pp. 186–216.

35. Bernard Newman to Lawrence Veiller, November 4, 1915, in Housing Association of Delaware Valley Papers, Temple Univ. Urban Archives; Friedman, *Government and Slum Housing,* p. 41.

36. Nathan Kushin, *Memoirs of A New American* (New York: Bloch Publishing Co., 1949), p. 79. Other research has indicated that immigrants may have sought status and advancement through real estate investments. Stephan Thernstrom discovered a suprising amount of investment in property among Newburyport's lower class citizens. See Stephan Thernstrom, *Poverty and Progress: Social Mobility in a Nineteenth-Century City* (New York: Atheneum, 1969), pp. 115–37, 194–201. Dennis Clark's examination of the tax assessors' ledgers for pre-Civil War Philadelphia revealed considerable property holdings for the Irish. See chapter 7 above.

Caroline Golab

10

The Immigrant and the City: Poles, Italians, and Jews in Philadelphia, 1870–1920

New York is excused for many of its ills because it is the metropolis, Chicago because of its forced development; Philadelphia is our "third" largest city and its growth has been gradual and natural. Immigration has been blamed for our municipal conditions; Philadelphia with 47% of the population native born of native parents, is the most American of our greater cities.—Lincoln Steffens, "Philadelphia: Corrupt and Contented," *McClures* (July 1903)

It is misleading, as well as unwise, to speak of Polish (or Jewish or Italian) immigration to Philadelphia without first exploring the broader and deeper forces which brought the immigrants to the cities of America. Millions of Southern and Eastern Europeans sailed for America between 1870 and 1920. The Poles were only one of many groups which came; Philadelphia was only one of many possible destinations. To appreciate the Polish experience in Philadelphia, therefore, it is necessary to remember two things: first, despite her size and industrial importance, Philadelphia was not a major center of the new immigration; secondly, her population possessed distinct ethnic and racial traits which were to characterize the city's development well into the eighth decade of the twentieth century.

Compared to other cities of the nation, Philadelphia housed a small immigrant population. Her percentage of foreign-born residents was the lowest of all large northern cities, averaging one-quarter of the total population from 1870 to 1920. Boston's foreign-born population averaged close to one-third for this same period; and, in some years, more than 40 percent of New York City's population was foreign-born. In the newer cities of America —Buffalo, Cleveland, Detroit, Milwaukee, Minneapolis, and Chicago—the percentages were even higher. For example, one-half of the persons living in Chicago in 1870 were foreign-born; if we include the native-born children of these foreigners, 75 to 80 percent of this city's population was of foreign stock (see table 10.1).

Philadelphia was not receiving her proportionate share of immigrants. Nevertheless, the composition of her immigrant population was distinctive, if not revealing. The foreign-born population never exceeded 27 percent, a peak which was reached as early as 1870. In that year the Irish, chief representatives of the old immigration, constituted more than one-half of all foreigners. In 1900 they were still more than one-third; in 1910, more than one-fifth. If one-quarter of all Philadelphians were foreign-born from 1870 to 1910, it was due to the foothold secured by the Irish at an earlier date. With Irish contributions diminishing after 1890, Philadelphia's foreign community could grow only if other groups replaced them. Many new immigrants, especially Russians and Italians, did move into the city. Given Philadelphia's total population, however, they did not do so to the extent that might have been expected. Abatement of the Irish influx, therefore, coupled with inadequate replacements on the part of other groups, contributed to the depressed level of the city's foreign-born population (see table 10.2).

According to the 1920 Census, Philadelphia's foreign-born population totaled 400,744. The leading groups were Russians (95,744), Irish (64,500), Italians (63,223), Germans (39,766),

TABLE 10.1 Percentage Foreign-born in Major Cities

City	1870	1880	1890	1900	1910	1920
Boston	35	32	38	35	36	32
Buffalo	36.5	33	35	30	28	24
Chicago	48	41	41	35	36	30
Cleveland	42	37	37	33	35	30
Detroit	44.5	39	40	34	34	29
Milwaukee	47	40	40	31	30	24
New York	44.5*	40**	42**	37	41	36
Newark	34.5	29.5	30.5	29	32	28
Philadelphia	27	24	26	23	25	22
Pittsburgh	32	28.5	31	26	26	20.5

SOURCE: U.S. Census, 1870–1920.
* Manhattan only.
** Does not include Brooklyn for 1880 and 1890.

TABLE 10.2   Philadelphia: Composition of Foreign-Born Population, 1870–1910

	1870	%	1890	%	1910	%
Total Population	674,022		1,046,964		1,549,008	
Foreign-born population	183,624	100.00	269,480	100.00	384,707	100.00
Austria [a]	519	.28	2,003	.74	19,860	5.60
Bohemia	101	*	189	*		
Belgium	117	*	365	.13	478	.12
British America	1,488	.81	2,684	.95		
Canada: French					301	*
Canada: British					3,735	.97
Denmark	192	.10	704	.26	1,119	.29
France	2,479	1.35	2,550	.94	2,659	.69
Germany [b]	50,746	27.60	74,971	27.80	61,480	15.98
Greece			31	*	589	.15
Great Britain and Ireland	123,408	67.20				
England	(22,034) [c]		38,926	14.40	36,564	9.50
Scotland			8,772	3.25	9,177	2.38
Wales			935	.34	1,033	.26
Ireland	(96,698) [c]		110,935	41.16	83,196	21.62
Holland	390	.20	260	*	349	*
Hungary	52	*	1,354	.50	12,495	3.25
Italy	516	.28	6,799	2.50	45,308	11.77
Norway	53	*	1,500	.55	1,144	.29
Poland [d]	146	*	2,189	.81		
Roumania					4,413	1.14
Russia [e]	94	*	7,879	2.90	90,697	23.57
Spain	107	*	136	*	200	*
Sweden	225	.12	1,626	.61	2,429	.63
Switzerland	1,791	.97	1,710	.63	2,013	.52

SOURCE: United States Census, 1870, 1890, and 1910.
* Less than .1 percent.
[a] In 1870, 1890 and 1910, "Austria" includes Galician Poles; in 1910 it includes Bohemia.
[b] In 1870, 1890 and 1910 "Germany" includes some German Poles.
[c] Figures in parentheses are those of Rev. Stephen Byrne, O.S.D., taken from his *Irish Emigration to the United States: What It Has Been and What It Is* (New York: The Catholic Publication Society, 1873), p. 162.
[d] In 1870 and 1890 "Poland" includes only those persons from Congress Poland or the Kingdom of Poland as set up at Vienna in 1815. Austrian Poles, German Poles and those Russian Poles living outside of the boundaries of the Congress Kingdom are not included, but are listed under "Austria," "Germany," and "Russia." In 1910 all Poles are included in the figures for "Austria," "Germany," and "Russia."
[e] In 1870, 1890 and 1910 "Russia" includes Poles from Russian administered territories.

Poles (31,112), English (30,886), Austrians (13,387), Hungarians (11,513), Rumanians (5,645), and Lithuanians (4,392). The vast majority of Russians were Jews who had fled the Pale and cities and towns of western Russia and the Ukraine. The Austrians, Hungarians, Rumanians, Lithuanians, and especially the Poles also included very large numbers of Jews. The number of East European Jews in the city, therefore, was more than 120,000; the number of Christian Poles was much less than the recorded 31,112. At most, the number of foreign-born Christian Poles in Philadelphia was 5,000 in 1910 and 15,000 to 18,000 by 1920.[1]

Jews, Italians, and Poles were the major representatives of the new immigration to settle in Philadelphia. The Jews, however, outnumbered the Italians by two to one, and the Italians outnumbered the Poles by more than four to one. The Polish community, therefore, was very small when compared to the city's Italian or Jewish groups. It was also small when compared to the Polish populations of other cities.

In 1903 Father Wracláw X. Kruszka, an early chronicler of the Poles in America, estimated that there were 250,000 Poles and Polish-Americans in Chicago; 70,000 in Buffalo; 65,000 in Milwaukee; 50,000 in Detroit and Pittsburgh, and 30,000 in Cleveland. He did not even mention Philadelphia. In 1908 the Polish *Press* estimated that the Chicago group numbered 350,000, and the New York City group 250,000. There were now almost 80,000 Poles in Buffalo, Detroit, and Milwaukee. Again, Philadelphia was not mentioned. By 1920 Chicago's Polonia was approaching 500,000, the Pittsburgh and New York groups were approximately 250,000, and Detroit, Buffalo, and Milwaukee each housed 100,000 Polish immigrants and their children. Philadelphia's Polish community, finally mentioned, was listed at 50,000, reflecting Polish immigration to the city between 1915 and 1920, a period of renewed industrial activity due to war orders pouring into city factories.[2]

For some reason, the Polish immigrant was avoiding Philadelphia. He was avoiding a city which was the second largest industrial matrix of the nation and a city which was a major port of entry, second only to New York in the number of immigrants who disembarked there. A study of ship records, port-of-entry statistics and city directories reveals that Poles were landing in

Philadelphia but were not remaining in the city. The Jews, in contrast, disembarked in Philadelphia and stayed. Virtually no Italians came through the Port of Philadelphia before 1909, and yet tens of thousands had made Philadelphia their home by that date. Why were the Poles avoiding Philadelphia when it was such an easy place for them to reach? Why did the Jews land there and decide to go no farther? And why were the Italians streaming to the city even though they failed to sail there initially? [3]

The Poles' negative response to the Philadelphia invitation is best understood in terms of the city's positive attraction for the Jews and Italians. A basic premise, however, underlies this approach: the immigrant did not exist in a vacuum. He brought much with him when he came to America, even if he carried all of it inside of him: a rich cultural heritage, previous work experiences in an industrializing Europe, and definite intentions as to why he came. He found much when he arrived here, including other people and a set social and economic structure. He had to react and to adapt to what he found on the basis of what he brought with him. His coming to America, his distribution across the continent, his settlement in a particular city or state—these experiences were not necessarily the result of random events and circumstances. There was an underlying method to what most Americans considered to be the madness of immigration fever.

Demographic, economic, and cultural forces were at work propelling certain groups in predictable directions and into predictable occupations. Indeed, the immigrant and the work he was to perform were directly related, if not often synonymous. The nature of this work had definite geographic locations. The availability of work often depended upon the immigrant's success in competing with other groups. Thus, to understand both the distribution of immigrants across the American continent and the reasons why the Poles avoided Philadelphia while the Jews and Italians decided to remain, we must know something about the relations of one group to the other, about the economic base of the area which attracted the immigrants, and about the cultural factors which caused the group to seek out or avoid certain occupations and forms of work.

A demographic analysis of fifteen major cities in the years

1870 to 1920 reveals two relationships which influenced immigrant settlement and distribution.⁴ First, there was an inverse relationship between the foreign-born and Negro populations of America's cities. Baltimore, Cincinnati, and St. Louis (and all large Southern cities, for that matter) differed from their northern colleagues in that they supported substantial Negro populations. Baltimore's Negro population averaged 15 percent from 1870 to 1920. Cincinnati's Negro population was more than 5 percent in 1910; St. Louis' was more than 6 percent (see table 10.3). Baltimore, with the largest portion of Negroes, had the smallest percentage of immigrants. St. Louis and Cincinnati also had high Negro percentages, but small immigrant populations. If Philadelphia's foreign-born representation was small when compared to that of other cities, her Negro population was large—almost 6 percent in 1910. Unlike her northern sisters, therefore, Philadelphia housed a large Negro community; in 1900 only Baltimore, Washington, D.C., and New Orleans had larger *absolute* Negro populations. Philadelphia had much in common with her Southern sisters.

A city's Negro population was a potential source of cheap, unskilled labor. Its size and the extent to which it was utilized determined the need for more unskilled labor—immigrant labor. Cities with large pools of Negro labor at hand were inclined to use these persons to fill vacancies in the unskilled labor force. This reduced the call for more unskilled immigrant labor and thus reduced the overall flow of immigrants to the city.

Throughout this period Philadelphia's Negroes were significantly employed in unskilled occupations.⁵ In the building trades (as of 1915) they were nearly one-fifth of all brick, cement, stone, paving, and road construction workers; 13 percent of those employed in general building construction and 10 percent in general railway construction. They were one-third or more of those employed in the manufacture of tallow and paving materials; one-fifth of those manufacturing bricks and oils; 13 percent of those making flour, grist mill products, and ice cream; and 12 percent of those employed in fertilizer manufacture. Negroes were 16 percent of those manufacturing iron and steel forgings and 20 percent of those working with cut stone. Substantial numbers were also employed by the steam railroads. Outside of industry they were street and sewer cleaners, trash collectors, livery men,

TABLE 10.3   Negro Population of Fifteen Selected Cities, 1890–1920

City	1890	%	1900	%	1910	%	1920	%
Baltimore	67,104	15.44	79,258	15.57	84,749	15.52	108,322	14.80
Boston	8,125	1.81	11,591	2.06	13,564	2.00	16,350	2.20
Buffalo	1,118	.43	1,698	.48	1,773	.40	4,511	.90
Chicago	14,271	1.29	30,150	1.77	44,103		109,458	4.10
Cincinnati	11,655	3.92	14,482	4.44	19,639	5.40	30,079	7.50
Cleveland	2,989	1.14	5,988	1.56	8,448	1.50	34,451	4.30
Detroit	3,431	1.66	4,111	1.43	5,741	1.20	40,838	4.10
Milwaukee	449	.21	862	.30	980	.30	2,229	.50
Minneapolis	1,320	.80	1,548	.76	2,592	.90	3,927	1.00
New York	23,601	1.55	60,666	1.76	91,709	1.90	152,469	2.70
Newark	4,141	2.27	6,694	2.72	9,475	2.70	16,977	4.10
Philadelphia	39,371	3.76	62,613	4.83	84,459	5.50	134,229	7.40
Pittsburgh	7,850	3.28	17,040	5.30	25,623	4.80	37,725	6.40
Providence	3,963	2.99	4,817	2.74	5,316	2.40	5,655	2.40
St. Louis	26,865	5.94	35,516	6.17	43,960	6.40	69,854	9.00

SOURCE: United States Census, 1890, 1900, 1910, 1920.

hostlers, and bootblacks. Women were mainly servants, cooks, and laundresses. Practically all of these industries and occupations employed significant numbers of immigrant laborers. In short, the Negro and the immigrant often competed for the same jobs in Philadelphia. The city's large indigenous Negro population, traditionally employed in certain lines of work, reduced the need for unskilled immigrant labor.[6]

Racial composition was not the only demographic factor influencing immigrant settlement. The immigrants themselves shared relationships which increased or decreased their propensity to settle in a certain area. There were relationships between old immigrant groups and new ones, and between groups of the same immigration period.

A large pool of labor "left over," so to speak, from the old immigration often deterred unskilled laborers of the new immigration from settling in a particular city. If jobs opened up which required unskilled muscle, older immigrants tended to be the first to fill them. Only if their supply fell short or if their wage demands were too high, were other unskilled laborers attracted to, or brought into, the city. Thus, in Philadelphia the presence of large numbers of Irish workers, a valued source of labor in railway and building construction, lessened employment opportunities for other unskilled immigrants (the Poles for one). The unskilled newcomer arriving in Philadelphia after 1890 had to compete not only with Negro labor, but also with Irish and Irish-American labor.

Relationships between groups of the same immigration period were also important. Italians and Poles, for example, often competed for the same jobs. If one group secured a foothold in the unskilled labor market due to political maneuvering and/or employer preferences, the other group could find entry difficult. This is basically what happened in Philadelphia. Because of their system of recruitment, via *padrone* and employment agencies centered in New York, the Italians were able to make deals with local politicians and thus obtained a monopoly on street construction, paving, and trash collection. The Poles lacked the effective mechanism of a *padrone* system. Moreover, once the Italians had secured their monopoly in certain industries, it was even more difficult for the Poles to find ample openings.

The Polish immigrant who wished to settle in Philadelphia had to compete with the Irish and the Negroes who were there before him and with the Italians and Jews who arrived with him. How well he competed, however, depended on two conditions: the type and number of jobs available in the city, and his qualifications with respect to these jobs—his skills or lack of them, his previous work experiences in Europe, and his personal preferences and dislikes.

Compared to her sister cities of the nation, Philadelphia was not receiving large numbers of immigrants, especially Polish immigrants. In contrast, Pennsylvania was receiving more Poles, Slovaks, Croatians, Slovenes, and Ukrainians than any other state of the Union—twice as many as New York and Illinois. Pennsylvania's Italian and Jewish populations were also very large; only New York housed greater numbers. Seventy-one percent of Pennsylvania's Polish and Italian immigrants lived in the smaller towns and villages of the state, outside of the two great cities of Philadelphia and Pittsburgh. Seventy percent of the Jews, however, lived in Philadelphia alone; the remainder resided in Pittsburgh and smaller cities of the state.

Pennsylvania was home to such vast numbers of immigrants precisely because it was a "Titan of Industry." The influx of Slavic and Italian workers coincided with the industrialization of the state. The consolidation of and technological advances in coal mining which enabled that industry to use large numbers of unskilled workers; the beginnings of iron and steel production and its innumerable manufactures; the incessant demand for railroads—and more railroads—to facilitate the inflow and outflow of coal and iron; the perpetual need to repair and to maintain these railways and to load and unload the freight cars; the manufacture of glass, cement, and chemicals: all of these activities demanded huge armies of laborers whose primary qualifications were strength and availability rather than knowledge and skill. Moreover, the size of these enterprises—a Carnegie Steel Company, a Pittsburgh Plate Glass Company, a Pennsylvania Railroad, an H. C. Frick Coke Company, a Westinghouse Air Brake Company, or a Pressed Steel Car Company—was enormous. Each employed tens of thousands of workers at a single point in space and time.[7]

Polish and Italian workers had the ideal qualifications for these industries. They were unskilled, plentiful, available, and geographically mobile. If 71 percent lived outside of Philadelphia and Pittsburgh, it was because Pennsylvania's industry and the nature of immigration were directly related.

In Philadelphia, industry and the nature of immigration were also closely linked. Whereas Pennsylvania's economy stressed bigness, required large numbers of unskilled workers, and was devoted to the more primary forms of industrial activity, Philadelphia's economy relied on old, well-established industries which stressed skill, diversity, precision, and quality. Philadelphia manufactured everything from "battleships to bon-bons," but the size of the city's enterprises was generally small. Of 8,341 firms in the city in 1915, only a dozen at the most employed more than 500 persons. Thus, there were very few firms capable of employing large numbers of unskilled workers. Finally, Philadelphia's economy was mature. Land, labor, and capital markets were saturated. Compared to newer cities, it was difficult for a large firm or industry, especially a heavy, primary one, to gain a foothold in the economy. Accordingly, no new industries were moving into Philadelphia. Any new firms which did spring up were variations or adaptations of existing industries. The lace curtain industry, for example, settled in Philadelphia only because of the skilled force of textile workers, mostly women, already there.[8]

Textile and clothing manufacture, machine shop and hardware manufacture, printing and publishing, and leather production were Philadelphia's four major industries. All required large pools of skilled and semi-skilled labor. Only the leather industry and certain branches of the metal industry employed substantial numbers of unskilled workers.

Textile and clothing manufacture employed more men and women than any city industry—one-third of all wage earners, or 103,000 persons in 1915. It accounted for more than 30 percent of the total value of all Philadelphia products. The most important branches were wool and woolen goods, men's and women's clothing, hosiery and knit goods, carpets and rugs, and cotton goods. Philadelphia, not New England, was the textile capital of America. By definition, however, the textile and garment industries required skilled or semi-skilled workers.

The principal iron and steel products manufactured in Philadelphia were (in order of value): foundry and machine shop products (including machinery); locomotives; rolling mill products; electrical machinery and supplies; steel ships; saws; stoves; cutlery; hardware and tools; files, safes and vaults; agricultural implements; bolts; rivets and washers; tin and terne plate; hatchets, axes, springs, and locks. More than 54,000 men and women were employed in the manufacture of these products in 1915. Only two, possibly three, of Philadelphia's metal firms could be considered primary producers—Midvale Steel Company, PennCoyd Iron Works, and Disston Saw Company. Only these were able to employ significant numbers of unskilled workers. Thus, the city's metal industry, like textile and clothing manufacture, also required skilled, not unskilled, labor.

By its very nature the printing and publishing industry required large numbers of skilled persons—printers, pressmen, proofreaders, and editors. These individuals had to speak, read, and write English fluently. Thus, this industry was the preserve of native-Americans, or English-, Irish-, Scotch-, and German-Americans. Of the 11,935 workers employed in printing and publishing in 1915, only 397 were foreign-born.

Seventy-five percent of the leather used by the United States government was processed in Philadelphia tanneries. The 1915 value of leather and its products manufactured in the city exceeded $45 million. This included tanned and finished leather, boots, shoes, trunks, bags, belts, and purses. The industry employed more than 15,000 persons. Unskilled workers predominated in the initial stages of leather manufacture, but skilled workers were needed to produce the final product.

The largest areas of employment open to the unskilled laborer in Philadelphia were not to be found directly in manufacturing. Philadelphia was a major railroad center, the home of three great continental trunk lines—the Philadelphia and Reading, the Pennsylvania, and the Baltimore and Ohio. She was the second major port of the nation and the home of one of the world's largest shipping terminals. And, as the nation's third largest city, she had to provide her citizens with countless public services—streets, sewers, transportation, and trash collection. Philadelphia's offering of unskilled jobs, therefore, included the construction and repair of streets, roads, bridges, buildings, railroads, and subways; the loading and unloading of ships and railroad cars; the cleaning of streets and sewers; the collection of trash and garbage.

A detailed examination of Philadelphia's labor force reveals that each immigrant group had its industrial and occupational preferences as well as dislikes. The Jews avoided unskilled activity such as construction, resorting to it only when absolutely necessary, and then only temporarily. The Jews were usually peddlers, hucksters, merchants, and shopkeepers. In industry the men were operatives in tobacco and cigar factories. The women, too, were often hucksters and peddlers and occasionally workers in cigar factories. The greatest number, however, found employment in the garment industry or "needle trades"; this included "the clothing trade and the manufacture of cloaks, waists, wrappers, skirts, shirts, overalls and underwear." In the 1880s and '90s, 40 percent of the city's Jews found work in some area of the garment industry. When the Metropolitan Life Insurance Company conducted a survey in 1915, it found that the men's and women's clothing industry alone employed 15,000 persons, most of whom were "Hebrews" and most of whom were women.[9]

Philadelphia's Italians were employed primarily as general laborers in unskilled occupations: construction work, especially street grading; sewer and subway construction; building and housing construction; street cleaning; street railway maintenance; snow shoveling; and scavenging (garbage and trash collection). Italian labor built City Hall, the Reading Terminal, and the Broad Street and Market Street subways. The Pennsylvania Railroad and the Philadelphia and Reading had miles of tracks and acres of railyards in the city. These also employed large numbers of Italians. Many of those brought in by the Pennsylvania Railroad (which, incidentally, was the single instrument most responsible for initiating the Italian influx to Philadelphia) did not stay with the Railroad for very long, but soon found better paying jobs in construction trades. In prosperous years such defections necessitated calls for more laborers and thus more Italians would find their way to Philadelphia.

The Italians were found most often in railroad and construction work because employers preferred them and expressed a desire for them.[10] On the other hand, because they were "less robust than the Slav, less hardy than the Irish," they were not considered exceptionally good performers in the mines and heavier activities of the steel industry. They were "rare in the rolling mills, whether because of their physical lightness, or as has sometimes been said, of a lack of nervous strength." [11]

Although not very powerful or well-developed in Philadelphia, the *padrone* system was also influential in channeling Italians to jobs; politicians were just as effective. Local political bosses would organize Italian newcomers into political clubs, garnering their support in exchange for job contracts with city-affiliated activities. As early as 1897 the Italians, through one of these arrangements, acquired "an exclusive claim on the work of keeping the streets of Philadelphia clean." [12] Another agreement secured them a monopoly on street grading and the construction and maintenance of the city's railway lines.

In addition to serving as general laborers, the Italians were most often hucksters, peddlers, venders, ragpickers, or shopkeepers; barbers, shoemakers, confectioners, waiters, and musicians; masons, stonecutters, and plasterers. In 1900 18 percent of the city's barbers and 8 percent of its masons were Italian.

Italian women, like their Jewish counterparts, were often hucksters and peddlers; they were also operatives in the silk, cigar, artificial flower, and candy factories. Their greatest concentration, however, was as seamstresses, tailoresses, and finishers in the various needle trades. Indeed, the garment industry played a major role in keeping the Italians in Philadelphia: while husbands were paving streets, building sewers or unloading ships, wives could supplement family income by taking needle work into the home. According to the Bureau of Labor, Italians were one-half of all women employed in the men's clothing industry of Philadelphia in 1910. Moreover, Italian men were by no means adverse to tailoring or needle work; they were second only to the Jews in the number of men so employed.[13]

Boyd's 1915 *City Directory* listed the names, addresses and occupations of 4,232 Polish persons (4,169 men and 63 women).[14] Less than 2 percent were engaged in professional, executive, or managerial occupations. Ten percent were self-employed, operating a small store or manufacturing business, or performing some service for the immediate community—insurance agent, notary, restaurant, or tavern keeper. Eight percent were employed in general and public service occupations and transportation. By far the largest number, 80 percent, or 3,389 men and women, were engaged in some industrial activity, either manufacturing, general labor, or construction (see table 10.4).

More than 1,300 persons, or 31 percent of all Polish workers, were employed in skilled and semi-skilled activities. Metal trades, textiles and leather manufacture were the chief employers. Almost two-thirds (217) of those in the metal trades were highly skilled machinists. Those in textile manufacture were most often dyers, weavers, spinners, and polishers. Those employed in the lumber

TABLE 10.4   Occupations of Polish Workers, 1915

CATEGORY	NUMBER	PERCENTAGE
Professional	57	1.30
Executive/Managerial	16	.37
Self-employed	405	9.59
Service occupations	354	8.37
Skilled and semi-skilled	1,314	31.06
Unskilled	2,075	49.03
Other	11	.26
Total	4,232	100.00

PROFESSIONAL (total 57)

actor	1	music teacher	2		publisher	1	
artist	2	musician	8		secretary	1	
chemist	3	nurse	1 (f)		stockbroker	1	
clergy	12	optometrist	1		teacher	3 (1f)	
editor	3	orderly	1		conductor Phila.		
lawyer	1	photographer	10		orchestra	1	
librarian	1	physician	3				

EXECUTIVE/MANAGERIAL (total 16)

executive	3	superintendent	1	purchasing agent	1
manager	10	bookkeeper	1		

SELF-EMPLOYED (total 405)

Mercantile/Manufacturing (total 338)

baker	48	furnishings	1	musical instru-	
baskets	1	furniture	4	ments	1
birds	1	grocer	59 (3f)	news	1
bottles	2	hardware	1	novelties	2 (1f)
brooms	1	harnesses	2	paints	1
candy	10 (4f)	home furnishings	6	poultry	1
church goods	1	horseshoes	1	pretzels	1
cigars	28 (3f)	huckster	7	produce	5 (1f)
coal	1	jewelry	3	shoes	16
druggist	5	marble	1	stationer	1
dry goods	20 (5f)	meat	47	trimmings	1
florist	1	men's furnishings	4	varieties	40 (6f)
flour	1	milk	5 (1f)	wagons	5
fruit	1	music	1		

NOTE: The 4,232 persons reporting occupations in Boyd's 1915 *City Directory* were engaged in 256 different tasks. The schema used in classifying these occupations was constructed with the following aims in mind: (1) the schema must reflect the economic development and economic structure of the Polish people within the larger Philadelphia economy. Such a classification, therefore, must give some indication of the skilled or unskilled nature of the occupations; it must also locate these occupations within their proper industries. (2) The schema must reflect the internal structure of the Polish community itself. It must indicate the level of development of the Polish community, its permanence or non-permanence, and the extent to which the community was self-servicing and self-sustaining.
    f = female

TABLE 10.4   Occupations of Polish Workers, 1915—Continued

Community services (total 67)

Professional and semi-professional:

insurance agent	6	printer	4	steamship agent	2
notary	1	real estate	5	undertaker	6 (1f)

Other:

dining	3 (1f)	livery	2	teams	1
liquors	28	pool	9		

SERVICE OCCUPATIONS (total 354)

General (total 194)

barber	39	elevator operator	1	porter	2
bellman	1	housekeeper	1 (f)	sexton	2
bartender	28	janitor	2	waiter	19
bootblack	4	meter reader	1	watchman	14
clerk	35	midwife	19 (f)		
cook	10	salesman	16		

Transportation (total 145)

chauffeur	4	mariner	1	fireman	29
conveyancer	1	motorman	19	stoker	3
driver	64	conductor	8		
hostler	1	engineer	15		

Public service (total 15)

collector	3	telephone		post office	
police	2	operator	1	clerk	1
post office		US Army	1		
carrier	3	US Navy	4		

SKILLED AND SEMI-SKILLED (total 1,314)

Building and contracting (total 78)

Brick, cement, and stone work:

bricklayer *	10	marbleworker	1	stonecutter *	3
cementworker	2	mason *	1		
Electrician *	4				

Painting and decorating:

painter *	13	decorator *	2	paperhanger *	7
Roofer *	9				

Plumbing and heating:

gas fitter *	1	pipefitter *	10	steamfitter *	1
heater *	1	plumber *	9		
Contractor *	4				

Chemicals and allied products (total 6)

gluemaker **	2	soapmaker	1	temperer **	1
paintmaker	2				

  * skilled
** semi-skilled

TABLE 10.4 Occupations of Polish Workers, 1915—Continued

Clay, glass, and stone products (total 42)

brickmaker **	4	glass blower *	2	glass worker	4
glass bottlemaker	1	glass cutter	1	glazier *	29
gasmaker **	1				

Food and kindred products (total 61)

bakers **	1	butcher *	16	icemaker	1
brewers **	1	meatcutter *	10	sausagemaker	1
bottler	12	confectioner	8 (1f)	sugarboiler	1

Leather and rubber goods (total 181)

hosemaker	1	rubbermaker	8	shoe operator	1
leatherworker	99	shoemaker *	62	tanner **	4
moroccoworker	6				

Lumber and its remanufacture (total 123)

cabinetmaker *	18	handlemaker	1	wagon builder *	3
carpenter *	76	joiner *	1	wagon maker	3
chipper	7	millwright *	1	woodworker *	9
cooper *	4				

Paper and printing industries (total 44)

boxmaker **	2	binder	3	pressman *	3
papermaker	16	engraver *	1	printer *	15
tag maker	2	lithographer *	1	stereotyper *	1

Textiles (total 232)

buffer	1	millworker	20	ropemaker	17
cordmaker	1	patternmaker *	3	spinner **	13
dyer *	25	piecer	1	stitcher	1
finisher **	1	polisher **	13	stripper **	1
ironer	1	presser **	2	textileworker	1
knitter *	4	roller *	1	weaver *	121
loomfixer *	5				

Clothing manufacture (total 75)

dressmaker *	10 (f)	hosiery operator **	3	tailer *	50
hatter	7	milliner *	3 (f)	stockingmaker	1
hosiery-worker **	1				

Metals and metal manufacture (total 347)

blacksmith *	46	filecutter	1	rivetmaker	1
hammerman *	2	grinder	1	sawmaker	9
boilermaker *	17	harnessmaker *	1	shovelmaker	1
brassworker **	3	instrumentmaker	3	smelter *	1
carbuilder **	2	locksmith *	4	springmaker **	6
coppersmith *	6	machinist **	217	tinsmith *	5
coremaker **	1	metalworker	3	watchmaker **	1
cornicemaker *	2	riveter **	8	wireworker **	3
filemaker	3				

TABLE 10.4   Occupations of Polish Workers, 1915—Continued

Tobacco and its products
cigarmaker   3

Miscellaneous and undefinable (total 122)

bambooworker	1	crane operator	6	oilclothmaker	4
reedworker	3	machine operator	4	oiler	1
basketmaker	3	driller *	4	packer **	2
boxman	1	estimator *	1	repairman	1
broommaker	2	foreman *	26	rigger *	7
buttonmaker	20	inspector **	6	umbrella-	
calker	3	gasworker	1	maker **	1
designer *	1	helper	1	upholsterer *	6
craneman	1	molder **	15	organmaker **	1

UNSKILLED (total 2,075)

foundryman	1	laborer	1,935	steelworker	28
ironworker	110	longshoreman	1		

OTHER (total 11)

farmer	4	miner	2	student	2
gardner	3				

industry were skilled craftsmen: carpenters, cabinet makers, wood-workers, and joiners. Those in the leather industry tended to perform the less skilled tasks. Only 75 of the 1,314 Poles reporting skilled occupations were employed in the clothing industry. Evidently, the Polish people were not a source of labor for the city's garment industry, an industry crucial to the city's economic welfare, employing thousands of its workers, and an industry which was the livelihood of the city's Jews and Italians.

One-half (2,075) of all Polish workers were unskilled. The vast majority of these 2,075 individuals were general laborers (1,935). The remainder were employed in the metal industry as iron workers and steel workers. Many of the 1,935 laborers were building and railroad construction workers, but greater numbers found work in chemical factories, petroleum refineries, and sugar refineries. They formed the bulk of those employed in Philadelphia's largest and finest primary producers: Midvale Steel Company and Blabon Oil Cloth Works in Nicetown; PennCoyd Iron Works in Manayunk; Baldwin Locomotive Works at Broad and Spring Garden Streets; the J.B. Brill Company in Southwest Philadelphia; Charles Lennig Chemical Company in Bridesburg; Cramps Shipyard in Kensington;

the Atlantic and Sun Oil Refineries and the Franklin Sugar House in South Philadelphia. Outside of industry the Poles, along with other Slavs, constituted the majority of the city's stevedores and longshoremen; they were also the largest group loading and unloading the cars in the large railroad terminal in Port Richmond.

Thus, if *unskilled,* as was 49 percent of the total, the Poles were employed as general laborers in the metal, leather, and chemical industries, or as stevedores and longshoremen. Unlike the Italians, they did not predominate in building and street construction or in railroad maintenance. *None* of the unskilled found work in the textile or garment industries. If skilled, however, the Poles were likely to be employed by the textile (but not the garment) industry, or as machinists and related workers in the metal industry.

Jewish, Italian, or Polish predominance in certain jobs and industries and their lack of representation in others was not fortuitous. More than chance—and more than purely demographic and economic factors—was influencing the ultimate occupational (and hence geographic) distribution of the immigrants. If this were not so, we would expect to find the immigrants distributed evenly throughout all industries and all parts of the country. Cultural factors were also at work. Each group possessed unique characteristics. These unique qualities were reflected in the nature of the group's emigration and in the work experiences of the group prior to emigration.

The Jews, for example, were literally forced from their homelands by poverty and pogroms. They arrived penniless, usually with wives and children in hand. Coming to America with the intention of staying permanently, they were true immigrants, not migrants. Moreover, long before they settled in the cities of America they had been moving from the Pale to the cities and larger towns of Poland and western Russia—to Łódź, Warszawa, Białystock, Grodno, Wilno, Kreslawki and Częstochowa. Here they found employment in cigar factories, toy factories, and textile mills. Those who disliked factory work took up peddling and huckstering or became small merchants and merchant capitalists. Rapid urbanization demanded skilled artisans: carpenters, joiners, roofers, masons, coppersmiths, blacksmiths, shoemakers, bakers, butchers, and tailors. The Jews filled these occupations in the cities of Europe just as they had traditionally done throughout the Pale, for the Russian and Polish peasant "aspired neither to commerce nor the handicrafts." [15]

The unique character of their immigration—their fugitive status, their poverty, their intention to leave Europe indefinitely, their urban orientation, and their possession of skills and crafts—explains why the Jews were concentrated in the larger port cities of the East, why they were not geographically mobile, and why, once landed in Philadelphia, they tended to go no farther. Moreover, given their experiences before emigration, it is not surprising to find the Jews engaged in the same occupations in America as in Europe. Migration from the towns and villages of the Pale to the cities of Eastern Europe was part of the same process which propelled them to the cities of America.

Indeed, with each passing decade of the nineteenth century, migration was ingraining itself deeper and deeper into the fabric of European life. No group was immune to it. This migration took the form of movements from farms to villages, villages to towns, and towns to cities; seasonal migration to other parts of Europe; and, finally, emigration to places beyond the continent of Europe. Migration had become such an integral part of life that it was rare to find a Pole who had not migrated to some other place in Europe —Germany, Russia, Denmark, Hungary, or France—before going abroad to the United States, Canada, Brazil, or Australia. America was merely another alternative in the list of available options. [16]

In contrast to the Jew, the Pole who came to America was, by tradition, a peasant-farmer, a tiller of the soil. From his point of view migration was an outgrowth of his complex relationships with the soil. Land was the focal point of his existence. Owning land meant economic security and independence, the freedom from want and hunger. Land was the source of social security: it determined status and delineated social position within the community. Because land was the primary organizing principle of economy and society, the Pole could not envision a life which was set apart from it. As Władisław Reymont said so well, "A man without land is like a man without legs: he crawls about and cannot get anywhere." [17]

In the middle decades of the nineteenth century, however, the land began to fail the Polish peasant. There was too little of it. It did not produce enough to support a wife and children. Moreover, the population was growing too rapidly—or so it seemed.

Births were not necessarily increasing, but people were living longer and children were surviving to maturity. Too many sons were now claiming the property. Smaller and smaller divisions resulted in decreasing productivity and efficiency. Crops and plots had to be mortgaged; debts continued to mount. The Polish farmer was up against a wall: in order to save his land and the life which was wedded to it, he had to seek work elsewhere. Migration presented itself as the only solution.

Viewed from the local level, therefore, migration was the Pole's response to his immediate predicament. In a larger sense, however, migration was a response to the industrialization which was overpowering Central and Eastern Europe at this time. It was a changing and transitional Europe which created a "peasant proletariat roaming the countryside, indeed the world, for employment in agriculture and industry." [18]

The Poles of Germany [19] headed for the coal mines, iron mills, and leather tanneries of Upper Silesia. Lack of land and lack of industry forced the Poles of Austria to move as settlers to eastern Galicia and the Bukowina; some furtively crossed the Dneiper River into Russia. When these areas became saturated in the 1870s, Austrian Poles headed for the mines and industrial regions of Bohemia, Moravia, Silesia, and Lower Austria; a few started for South America and the United States. Thousands of others, the *Sachsengänger,* migrated yearly to the large estates of Prussian Poland and Denmark. The Poles of Russia migrated to the provinces of Piotrokow, Warszawa, Lublin, and Radom. Piotroków, the most industrialized area of Poland, was the seat of the rich Dąbrowa coal basin and the textile capitals of Łódź and Częstochowa. Poland's largest and most productive steel mills and metal firms were also located in this province, near the Dąbrowa fields, or in Sosnowiec, Zgierz, Tomaszow, and Pabianice. Warszawa was another important industrial center with many refineries, tanneries, slaughterhouses and railroads. Ostrowiec in Radom province was literally one massive foundry.[20]

The men and women who crowded these cities and manned these factories were recruited from the countryside and from every province of Russian Poland. Heavy metal industries, oil refineries, sugar refineries and leather factories employed peasant labor, while the textile industries relied heavily on Jewish labor. Until 1900 it appeared as if internal migration and Polish industrialization would be able to absorb most of the surplus agricultural population. In that year, however, the Polish and Russian economies entered a severe depression. "Increasing numbers reason, 'If we must leave home, why not go further, wherever wages may be the highest, and stay until we have earned what we need.' So the father goes himself to America, or sends his son to get money to redeem or to enlarge the farm." [21]

Long before his trek to America, the Pole had been affected by urbanization and industrialization. There were many ramifications to these experiences. First, they changed the Pole from a peasant-farmer into a migrant-laborer. The Pole who came to America, therefore, was not an immigrant. He was a migrant, a temporary worker. Always, his intention, if not his dream, was to return to Poland with his American (or Silesian or Brazilian) savings and to buy land or rescue his property from debt. If this were not so, the Pole would have made greater efforts to seek out land and farms in America. Why should he settle in the city, the very antithesis of Polish life? Many returned to Poland and others were intending to do the same had not World War I and economic opportunity intervened.

Secondly, because of his status as a migrant laborer, the Pole was very mobile. He was unencumbered with wife and children, preferring to travel alone; more likely, he was not yet married. Nor was he poverty-stricken. He became a migrant precisely because he had known better times, or at least still believed in them. If he sought work abroad, he usually paid for his own passage. Thus, he was both willing and able to go wherever there was work. If this meant that he must go to America, to Chicago, or to the small towns of Pennsylvania, then this is where he would go.

Finally, because he was accustomed to migrating in an urbanizing and industrializing Europe, the Polish farmer had been exposed to towns, cities, factories, and machines. He was not totally unprepared for the type of work he would find in America. The industries which employed him in Europe were identical to those which would employ him in America. As in Poland, he headed for the cities and regions which supported heavy industrial activity. Instead of the Dąbrowa coal fields, however, he now mined the anthracite of central Pennsylvania. Instead of the factories and mills of Upper Silesia, Łódź, Warszawa, Częstochowa, Sosnowiec and Pabianice, he worked in the steel mills, iron foundries, sugar and oil refineries, leather tanneries, and slaughterhouses of Chicago, Detroit, Buffalo, Milwaukee, Cleveland, Pittsburgh, and even Philadelphia, U.S.A.

Summary

The Pole's chances for employment were crucial in determining whether or not he came to Philadelphia and stayed. His chances for employment, however, depended on how well he competed with other groups and how well he could fit himself into an economic structure which favored the skilled worker.

Irishmen and Negroes were available sources of unskilled labor. The Irish were employed in railway and building construction, the Negroes as street cleaners, garbage collectors, and laborers working with grease, tallow, and metals. Italians and Poles were also found in these industries. The Italians, however, far outnumbered the Poles in railway and building construction and street cleaning —major arteries of unskilled activity in the city. Given the manner in which they were hired—by employment agencies and railroad agents who showed definite preferences for them, and the *padrone* system with its political connections in South Philadelphia—it is not surprising to find that the Italians had preempted these lines of work. The Poles were at a disadvantage and were therefore excluded to a large extent.

Philadelphia's major industries were textiles, printing and publishing, and metal manufacture of the hardware and machine shop variety. None of these employed large numbers of unskilled laborers. Moreover, few new industries which could utilize such labor were entering the city. The Jews and Italians made their way in the needle trades. Comparatively, there were very few Polish tailors. Because the Poles, unlike the Italians, Jews, or Irish, were not inclined to work in textile mills or in the needle trades, they would tend to avoid Philadelphia. Those stayed, however, who could fit themselves into the cotton or woolen fabric of the city— Poles from Germany, for example, who had had previous textile experience in Europe. In short, textile and clothing manufacture had a negative, but selective, influence on Polish immigration to Philadelphia.

Polish women were more likely to make use of their needle, but if their men could not be employed in Philadelphia, they could not become a major source of labor for the garment industry. Polish women often worked in textile, paper box, and cigar factories before marriage or until the birth of the first child. Unlike Italian women, they were not as likely to staff the textile mills and needle trades after marriage. Once married or widowed, the Polish working woman was either a housekeeper, cleaning woman, laundress, etc.; or she was self-employed—she operated a grocery, candy, drygoods, or variety store.

Italian women, by contrast, deliberately avoided the cleaning trades and preferred clothing and textile manufacture. According to the MacDonalds, Italian women in the United States "avoided work as domestic servants since it was regarded as a threat to their chastity, a very serious consideration in the Southern Italian view." [22] They preferred to work in textile, garment or other factories where women would be the only workers, and where sisters, mothers, daughters, and other female relatives could work with them, serving as chaperones. If she did not work in the textile mills, the Italian women took piecework into the home.

As a major manufacturing center, Philadelphia had to compete with the rest of the state for unskilled labor. She had to compete with the steel mills, coal mines, cement and glass factories of central and western Pennsylvania. These industries were able to employ large numbers of unskilled workers. It is not surprising, therefore, to find that Pennsylvania had more Polish immigrants than any other state, or that 70 percent of them lived outside of Philadelphia and Pittsburgh. This distribution not only reflects differences in opportunities and nature of work, but also indicates the particular character of Polish immigration. Polish immigrants were predominantly unskilled, initially temporary, and came in search of quick economic gain. Moreover, they were influenced by previous work experiences in an industrializing Poland, and they were affected by cultural traits which shaped their occupational preferences.

The Jews avoided heavier manual occupations and thus offered no competition to the Poles. The Italians were considered physically unfit for certain types of work, especially in the mines and primary stages of steel manufacture. The Poles, larger in build and considered more stolid in temperament, supposedly performed better in these tasks. In addition, the Poles favored factory work, whereas the Italians disdained factory and foundry work, preferring outdoor activity which was close to the earth with which they so readily identified. Work with rock and stone, even rail, street, and building construction, fit this criterion, or had been familiar to them in Italy. The crafts, especially tailoring and masonry, were also common in Italy; in Poland these roles were performed by the Jews.

Those Poles who did settle in Philadelphia were able to fit themselves into the skilled occupations of the textile and metal industries, as weavers and machinists, for example. In this sense Polish immigration to Philadelphia was selective: it favored the skilled immigrant rather than the unskilled migrant. Most of these skilled workers were German Poles from Poznań and Silesia who were urbanized, skilled people who had worked in the textile mills of Germany prior to emigrating. Or they were Russian and Austrian Poles who had spent some time in the Pennsylvania hinterland, serving an apprenticeship as it were, before coming to Philadelphia in search of more stable, better-paying jobs.

Unskilled Poles who settled in Philadelphia were able to find work as steelworkers, ironworkers, leatherworkers, general construction hands, stevedores, foundrymen, and factory hands. Virtually all of these came from the Austrian and Russian sectors of Poland, especially from the three Russian provinces of Łomza, Płock, and Suwałki, the most unindustrialized sections of Poland. These Poles were peasant farmers who possessed few urban crafts. Nevertheless, they had been caught up in that pervasive institution of migration which characterized Europe before World War I. They had migrated to other parts of Poland or to Germany, Russia, France, and Denmark; they had been exposed to industrial activities in Europe, especially to primary ones such as mining, steel making, leather tanning, and meat packing.

In the final analysis, the Polish migrant avoided Philadelphia because there was little room for him. Competition from Irish, Italian and Negro labor was keen. Philadelphia's industries were biased in favor of the skilled worker. As a group, the Poles possessed few skills. Just as the skilled nature of the city's economy worked against large-scale Polish immigration, so did the unskilled quality and growing need of the state's industries work in favor of it. The Polish migrant, therefore, was more likely to seek out the central and western parts of the state rather than the city of Philadelphia.

NOTES

1. These figures are based on the records of Philadelphia's Polish Roman Catholic parishes and the listings of Boyd's *City Directory* for 1915. Note that they represent the foreign-born segment of the Philadelphia Polish community, not the *total* Polish community, i.e, foreign-born persons plus American-born children.
2. W. Kruszka, *Historja Polska w Ameryce* (Milwaukee: Kuryer Publishing Company, 1937), 2:174; Emily G. Balch, *Our Slavic Fellow Citizens* (New York: Charities Publications Committee, 1910), p. 264; anonymous estimate of the Chicago Polish *Press*, December 15, 1908; Paul Fox, *The Poles in America* (New York: George H. Doran, 1922), p. 63.
3. Information on immigrants disembarking in Philadelphia from: United States Treasury Department, *Annual Report and Statements of the Chief of the Bureau of Statistics on the Foreign Commerce and Navigation, Immigration and Tonnage of the United States for the Year Ending June 30. . . .* (1880–1892; 1894) Washington, D.C., Government Printing Office, 1880–1892; 1894).
4. This analysis includes five older cities of the Eastern seaboard—Boston, New York, Newark, Philadelphia, and Providence; seven newer cities, most of which were in the Midwest—Buffalo, Chicago, Cleveland, Detroit, Milwaukee, Minneapolis, and Pittsburgh; and three semi-Southern cities which were leading urban centers in the early days of the nation: Baltimore, Cincinnati, and St. Louis.
5. *Third Annual Report of the Commissioner of Labor and Industry of the Commonwealth of Pennslylvania, 1915,* part I: "Statistics of Production—Wages, Employees for the Year 1915" (Harrisburg, 1918).
6. What happened when World War One put an end to large-scale immigration further illustrates the relationship which existed between these two groups. Many Philadelphia industries—steel, railroads, and tanneries—found themselves hard-pressed for unskilled labor. New York employment agencies could not supply them with enough immigrant laborers. Consequently, railroad agents and employment agency representatives actively recruited Negro labor in the South and shipped these persons to Pennsylvania, New Jersey, and New York. The same institutions perfected to channel immigrant labor were now used to recruit Southern labor. Industries and occupations usually the preserve of the unskilled immigrant were now employing the Negro in increasing numbers. See S. T. Mossell, "The Standard of Living Among One Hundred Migrant Families in Philadelphia," *Annals* 98:173–75. From the spring of 1916 to the spring of 1918, 40,000 Negroes came to Philadelphia. Negro migration to the city stopped with the declaration of the Armistice, November 1918. See E. J. Scott, *Negro Migration During the War* (New York: Oxford Univ. Press, 1920).

7. For discussion of Pennsylvania's industrial activity and the labor which supported this activity, see S. K. Stevens, *Pennsylvania, Titan of Industry* (New York: Lewis Historical Publishing Co., 1948), vol. I; G. C. Whidden and W. H. Schoff, *Pennsylvania and its Manifold Activities* (Philadelphia: Twelfth International Congress of Navigation, 1912); V. R. Greene, *The Slavic Community on Strike: Immigrant Labor in Pennsylvania Anthracite* (Notre Dame, Ind.: Univ. of Notre Dame Press, 1968), chap. I; F. J. Sheridan, *Italian, Slavic and Hungarian Unskilled Immigrant Laborers in the United States*. U.S. Bureau of Labor *Bulletin*, no. 72 (September 1907); Pennsylvania Department of Labor and Industry, "Report of Division of Immigration and Unemployment" in *First Annual Report 1913* (Harrisburg, 1914).

8. For discussion of Philadelphia's economy and industry, see Whidden and Schoff, *Pennsylvania;* Stevens, *Pennsylvania;* H. L. Collins and W. Jordan, *Philadelphia: A Story of Progress* (New York: Lewis Historical Publishing Co., 1941), vol. 3; J. T. Scharf and T. Westcott, *History of Philadelphia 1609–1884* (Philadelphia: L. H. Everts, 1884), vol. 2; and, in particular, Philadelphia Chamber of Commerce, *Philadelphia Yearbook, 1917*.

9. J. H. Willits, *Steadying Employment,* with a section devoted to some facts of unemployment in Philadelphia (Philadelphia: The American Academy of Political and Social Science, 1916); for general background on occupations of Philadelphia's Jews, see Charles S. Bernheimer, *The Russian Jew in the United States* (Philadelphia: John C. Winston, 1905.)

10. For example, in 1906, a time of increased labor demand, the major railroads filed applications with New York employment agencies for thousands of Italian laborers. One agency received applications for 8,668 Italian laborers from 165 employers in New York, New Jersey, Connecticut, and Pennsylvania. Another agency received requests for 37,058 Italians. The demand for Italians was so high, however, that the agencies were unable to fill even one-third of the requests. See Sheridan, *Italian, Slavic and Hungarian Unskilled Immigrant Laborers in the United States,* pp. 416, 424.

11. U.S. Industrial Commission, *Reports,* 15 (Washington, D.C.: Government Printing Office, 1900–1902): 419; see also Robert Foerester, *The Italian Emigration of Our Time* (Cambridge, Mass.: Harvard Univ. Press, 1919), pp. 40, 343.

12. John Koren, "The Padrone System and Padrone Banks," *Bulletin* of the United States Department of Labor, 9 (1897): 123; Foerester, p. 355.

13. Information on Italian occupations in Philadelphia: *City Directories, 1880–1917;* for general background: Foerester, *The Italian Emigration of Our Time;* E. Lord, J. D. Trenor, and S. J. Barrows, *The Italian in America* (New York: B. F. Buck, 1905); Sister M. Agnes Gertrude, "Italian Immigration into Philadelphia," *Records of the American Catholic Historical Society* 58 (1947); for detailed infor-

mation on *padrone,* see John Koren, "The Padrone System and Padrone Banks," pp. 113–29.

14. For details as to the compilation and construction of this list, see C. Golab, *The Polish Communities of Philadelphia 1870–1920: Immigrant Distribution and Adaptation in Urban America.* (diss., Univ. of Pennsylvania, 1971), app. 1.

15. Moses Rischin. *The Promised City: New York's Jews 1870–1914* (Cambridge: Harvard Univ. Press, 1962), p. 25; chap. 1.

16. Perhaps more than any other scholar, Frank Thistlethwaite has worked to reconstruct traditional thinking about immigants and immigration history: ". . . trans-oceanic migration was only one aspect of a bewilderingly complex pattern of tidal currents which carried not merely Norwegian settlers to Minnesota homesteads and Irish immigrants to New York tenements, but Polish peasants to *and from* East German estates, Appalachian coal mines and Silesian steelworks, Italian labourers to and from Chicago, Illinois, and Homécourt, France, Italian hotel workers to and from Lausanne, Nice and Rio de Janeiro, Scotsmen to and from London and Buenos Aires, and Spaniards to and from Marseilles and Santos. We are a long way from a simple case of 'America fever.' " "Migration from Europe Overseas in the Nineteenth and Twentieth Centuries," *New Perspectives of the American Past,* vol. 2, S. Katz and S. I. Kutler, eds. (Boston: Little, Brown and Company, 1969). Interviews with hundreds of Philadelphia's Polish immigrants have yet to reveal one person who had not migrated to various places in Europe before sailing for America.

17. Wladislaw Reymont, *Chłopi (The Peasants)* (London: Alfred A. Knopf, 1924). Two early works continue to remain the best studies of conditions in Poland prior to emigration: William I. Thomas and Florian Znaniecki, *The Polish Peasant in Europe and America,* 5 vols. (Boston: Richard C. Badser, 1918–20); and Balch, *Our Slavic Fellow Citizens.*

18. Victor Greene, *The Slavic Community on Strike,* p. 26.

19. Theoretically, the Pole who emigrated before World War One was leaving a country which did not exist. Poland was wiped from the map of Europe in 1795 and was parcelled out among three powers, Austria, Prussia, and Russia. She was not fully reconstituted until Versailles, 1919. Because of these unique circumstances, each sector of Poland developed differently. These differences influenced which Poles emigrated, when they emigrated, and what became of them after their arrival in America. In general, Polish emigration progressed from west to east, from German Poland (Poznan, Silesia, West Prussia, and East Prussia) to Galicia (Austrian Poland) and the Russian provinces.

20. For discussion of land, peasant culture, and conditions in Eastern Europe prior to emigration, see Thomas and Znaniecki, *The Polish Peasant in Europe and America,* vol. 1; Balch, *Our Slavic Fellow Citizens;* U.S. Immigration Commission, 1907–1910, *Abstracts of*

Reports with Conclusions and Recommendations of the Minority (Washington, D.C., 1911); Polish National Committee of America (Wydzial Narodowy Polski w Ameryce), *Polish Encyclopedia* (Geneva: Atar, Ltd., 1906); Francis Bujak, *Poland's Economic Development* (Cracow: George Allen and Unwin, Ltd., 1926); *The Cambridge History of Poland,* W. F. Reddaway, J. H. Penson, O. Halecki and R. Dyboski, eds. (Cambridge: Cambridge University Press, 1941); Roger Portal, "The Industrialization of Russia", *The Cambridge Economic History of Europe,* J. J. Habakhuk and M. Postan, eds. (Cambridge: Cambridge University Press, 1965), vol. 6, chap. 9.

21. Balch, *Our Slavic Fellow Citizens,* p. 139.
22. John and Leatrice MacDonald, "Urbanization, Ethnic Groups and Social Segmentation," *Social Research* 29 (1962):466–48.

11

Philadelphia's Jewish Neighborhoods

The immigrant domicile that spread along Philadelphia's water-front continued long after William Penn's "greene country towne" became the largest city on the North American continent. Within a mile from the shores of the Delaware River, generation upon generation of immigrants inherited the housing of their predecessors. The descendants of earlier immigrants were constantly expanding the city and, in leaving their former homes, made way for the newcomers. Many older sites were gradually leveled and commercial sites arose where once stood pioneer homes. With each stage of European immigration, vast changes took place until the "greene country towne" vanished along with the primeval forest, the ancient navigable creeks and wooded Indian trails.[1]

Despite the changes that led to the disappearance of notable creeks such as the Cohocksink in the Northern Liberties and the old Dock Creek, once the city's produce center, Penn's checkerboard plan of streets remained inflexible.[2] Only former Indian paths transect the original geometrical plan and the creeks can still be traced by the crooked streets that follow their course to the Delaware River.

The colonial city, once a mixture of homes and private shops, was transformed into a mercantile axis designed to serve a community reaching into the hinterland of Pennsylvania and supply the ocean-going vessels that sailed and steamed up the Delaware. Lingering long after the consolidation of the city in 1854 were many homes of the colonials, their churches and business establishments that escaped destruction.[3] Architectural examples of the Federal period, instances of Egyptian and Greek revival, Gothic style and rows of Georgian houses mingled with houses built of wood. Amid these diverse structures were drab and monotonously-alike warehouses, stables, and a variety of unkempt buildings whose memory does not warrant recalling.

At the peak of West European immigration, following the consolidation of Philadelphia, the city counted 60,000 homes.[4] When
the South seceded from the Union, building in general was disrupted and both new housing and immigration sharply declined.
In 1864, building in Philadelphia was revived. The neat row of
uniform four-storey houses on Chestnut Street was scheduled for
remodeling into commercial sites,[5] the two-year-old Union League
of Philadelphia was erecting its handsome Broad Street house,[6]
and congregation Keneseth Israel, the only known synagogue built
during the war, completed its edifice at the end of the year.[7] But
it was not until peace was fully restored that the city entered into
a new phase of expansion.

In the decade that followed Appomattox, the city spread west-
ward and made a major thrust to the north. Plans for a new City
Hall were proposed, Rittenhouse Square was attracting the middle
class from the east of Broad Street, and the new bridges across the
Schuylkill River and improved transportation to West Philadelphia
made possible the establishment of the hospital of the University of
Pennsylvania in that part of the city in 1871.[8] Five years later the
Centennial of American Independence was celebrated in Fairmount
Park, exposing hundreds of thousands of visitors to a section of the
city known only to a few.

Following this great national event, the development of acres
of new residences added lustre to the Centennial City, but the
presence of urban retardation passed by unnoticed. Immigrants
from southern and eastern Europe, Jews in particular, poured into
an area that was a few minutes walking distance from the Delaware
River. "Jerusalem" in Port Richmond was an exception. Most of
the Jewish immigrants clustered in the deteriorating sections that
had resisted the many changes that took place during the first century of American independence.

"Jerusalem" in Port Richmond

To most Philadelphians, Port Richmond was an unattractive out-
post of the city, but to the industrial worker and the immigrant it
was a desirable place to live. Cramp's famous shipyard with a
number of others had sprung up in the vicinity where the Delaware
River turns east; freight yards were fed by the river traffic and in
turn hauled away tons of coal and other supplies. A variety of

industries took advantage of these facilities and crowded into Richmond. Many of the city's iron works, carpet factories, and distilleries were within walking distance of the new brick and stone dwellings which rose like magic following the Civil War. They were among the 2,706 two-storey homes and the 1,776 three-storey homes built in 1870 throughout the city, revealing the increased demand for new housing and the general postwar prosperity. To the new homes came the English, Scotch, and Irish workmen who were employed in the cotton, woolen and textile mills.[9]

The light and heavy industries attracted many residents from adjacent Kensington, and a new surge of immigrants turned to this industrial area for employment. Vast fields and farms along the Delaware River separated Richmond from Bristol and for country and river-front peddling the area was unsurpassed. For traders in scrap metals, for dealers in junk and vendors of small goods, the economy of the area was unexploited.

Following the Civil War, the new economic opportunity of Port Richmond attracted a small number of Lithuanian and Polish Jews. The first of their number, Yehzekiel Bernstein, had reached Philadelphia circuitously. From Poland's Suvalki province, he went to Canada, made his way across the Lakes to Detroit, following a route taken earlier by Bohemian Jews who went midwest. After peddling there for a number of years, he became a dealer in scrap metals. Bernstein was dissatisfied with the state of religious observance in Detroit and, with a number of friends, found his way to Philadelphia. He and his countrymen chose an area whose hub was at Tulip and Auburn streets, easily reached by going north on Frankford Avenue and east over Lehigh Avenue, two heavily-used highways that led into the lower Northeast. New housing had not yet reached this area of unpaved streets and walkways where horses and goats grazed undisturbed, and sewage was inadequate. Frequent flooding turned William street, the first exclusively Jewish street in Philadelphia, into a muddy canal through which rafts could be seen skimming after a severe shower of rain.[10]

The new immigrants were so successful at their occupations that very soon their friends and relatives from Suvalki and adjoining Kovno came at their urging. Within ten years, almost fifty Jewish families were living in the immediate vicinity of William Street. Other residents of Port Richmond dubbed the new settlement

"Jerusalem" and "Jew-Town," but the acrimonious description gradually lost its meaning even though it is still recalled by these names a century later. But to the immigrant Jews, the "Jerusalem" of Philadelphia was a special portion of America discovered by Bernstein who was their Columbus.

How the newcomers learned of this section of the city, far from the established center of Jewish life, is not certain. One of the factors that may have induced the new immigrants to settle here was the interethnic differences among Jews. German-speaking Jews and their descendants kept aloof from the few Yiddish-speaking Russians and Poles who trickled into Philadelphia before the Civil War. These folk clustered into the downtown section not far from Fifth and Catherine Streets near the Dutch Jewish synagogue.[11] They mustered sufficient strength for a mutual aid society to help their fellows in distress. Gradually they were absorbed into the existing Jewish structure and shared a common uneasiness in the presence of the newcomers. Perhaps it was as a result of this encounter that Bernstein chose the expanding industrial area of Richmond. It was a voluntary choice and not typical of the Jewish immigrants of other port cities who persisted in clustering close to the center of the city.

Country peddling and rag picking, the first occupations of the Jerusalemites, did not add sweetness to their lives, but their hardiness and determination overcame the difficulties of their trade. Their manner of peddling was not unusual and differed little from that of the Jewish peddlers who came from Germany a decade or two before. Only the terrain varied in that it was more localized and that the distance could be covered within a few days. From Monday to Friday the roads along the Delaware River between Richmond and Bristol were clogged by Jewish peddlers who covered the area in time to return to observe the Sabbath. Sundays were reserved for the reckoning of weekly accounts and the replenishing of stock. It was not unusual for the peddlers to make their rounds at Cramp's shipyard where the ironclad steamers of the American line, the *Illinois,* the *Indiana,* the *Pennsylvania* and the *Ohio* were being built. In a few years they would be transporting tens of thousands of Jewish immigrants on the run from Liverpool to Philadelphia.[12]

As the population of "Jerusalem" increased, the variety of occupations became more diverse. The old village cobbler became the neighborhood shoemaker, the town blacksmith became the local horseshoer and the water-carrier became the neighborhood teamster. There were coopers, tailors, leather-workers and cigar makers whose shops served Richmond. Umbrella repair men and glaziers vended their wares and services with the special cries they learned to recite in English. The "horse-radish" man with a heavy trestled grinder strapped to his back was rewarded when women folk responded to the clanging of his iron bell. It was not long before the hawkers of these services, the craftsmen, the artisan, and the peddler became the recognized shopkeepers and tradesmen. The need for hardware merchants, dealers in glass, dry grocers, and drygoods men was quickly supplied by the newcomers.

Other occupations transplanted from the old-world *shtetl,* the Jewish small town of the Russian Pale, were those provided by the religious functionary. A ritual slaughterer of poultry and cattle had come with Bernstein when "Jerusalem" was settled. A *hazzan,* one who chanted the prayers on Sabbath and holidays, was also among the original group. Later, when religious life flowered, two rabbis joined the community. A kosher butcher and a bakery were opened midway on William Street.

The compact Yiddish-speaking microcosm was completely new to Philadelphians. If bewigged women, or women wearing the Jewish equivalent of a mother Hubbard cap, were a strange sight to the English textile worker, they were as strange to Jewish descendants of previous generations whose curiosity led them to "Jerusalem." They were bewildered by the bearded men, some with ear-locks and the four-cornered ritual garment with fringes dangling loosely by their sides. The ritual slaughterer, reciting the appropriate prayer as he performed his art in the open street was no less an amazing sight. Preoccupied by the numerous other obligations practiced by traditionally observant Jews, the curious onlooker went unnoticed. But these scenes excited and disturbed members of the older community who at once flung their energies into bringing the Yiddish miniature of a Russian Jewish village into a framework of American *mores* and habits. "They deemed it their duty to provide for its educational and moral wants."

Although a synagogue, chartered in 1877, supplied the religious needs of the Jerusalemites, a school was opened by the Hebrew Education Society, where English and vocational subjects such as carpentry, cigar making, and sewing could be taught to the children of the immigrants. The Jerusalemites looked upon this well-intentioned undertaking as an intrusion in their community but, in spite of their resistance, a school building was erected and opened in 1879.[13]

Crowded quarters and the sweatshop system, two major aspects of emerging urban life, were absent in "Jerusalem." To the established Jewish community, "The locality was ill-chosen and lacked the essentials for a proper residence; its only advantage was the cheapness of the houses" on the extreme boundary of old Richmond. Lacking in spaciousness and the brighter accommodations of new housing, the colony found compensation in its self-sustaining economy, its homogeneity and its solidified religious practice and outlook.

In the three decades that followed the founding of "Jerusalem," vast changes took place in Philadelphia. Transportation was improved considerably when electrically-driven cars replaced the horse-drawn trams connecting Frankford, Richmond, and Kensington with the city's center.[14] Electricity replaced gas lighting in the new synagogue. Shopkeepers availed themselves of the new telephone service and greater communication was established with the older organized Jewish community. Lithuanian and Polish Jews eager to avoid the bustle of South Philadelphia had little difficulty in finding their way to "Jerusalem." In some instances they found their way with the aid of the Association for the Protection of Jewish Immigrants. In others, they were greeted by relatives when they disembarked at the Washington and Federal Street landing stations. Immigration agents at New York City and Baltimore directed newcomers to "Jerusalem" and the Richmond area had become a point of destination equal to that of an inland city.[15]

Accurate population figures for the original half square mile have not been determined, but 1,000 families representing approximately 4,000 residents were reported in 1908 by one Yiddish journalist who wrote the first account of "Jerusalem." [16] By this time the immigrants stepped out of their original quarter, reaching Richmond Street between Cumberland and Ann streets and north to Allegheny Avenue. In each instance they sought areas conducive to shopkeeping. The Jewish settlement, retaining its first enclave as a center for its religious life, spread over a huge rectangle that extended from Frankford Avenue to the Delaware River.

South Philadelphia

The independence that characterized "Jerusalem"—its two synagogues, its religious and vocational training schools, its local
charitable and mutual aid societies, and its economic stability—
separated it socially as well as geographically from the rapidly
developing South Philadelphia community almost four miles away.
South Philadelphia's immigrant settlement comprised three old
districts: Southwark, Passyunk, Moyamensing, and a portion of
Dock Ward, which was part of the original city. This lower part
of the city covered the territory south of Spruce Street and east of
Broad Street.[17]

Below South Street the districts were notorious for their high
crime rate, disease, and poverty. Before the war they were the
scene for the popular novels of George Lippard [18] and T. S.
Arthur [19] and after the war the source for sensational news stories
and the subject of dime novels. At one time the new immigrant
quarter was the hotbed for native Americanism and at another a
center for Philadelphia's antislavery movement. It was the heart
of the Irish Fenian Brotherhood, which planned to invade Canada
and wrest it from the English. No one who cherished his life
would venture into the neighborhood unprotected. The police,
inferior and undisciplined, either shuddered on their beats or joined
in the local corruption. Merchants and tradesmen seldom pressed
charges against local offenders for fear of reprisals.[20]

On the northern periphery of this rapidly changing district
were the homes of Philadelphia's old Negro families, all of whom
were residents of Lombard Street at one time or another. William
Still's "Underground Railroad Office"—later improvised as a synagogue—was near Seventh Street [21] and the two great Protestant
Negro churches, Mother Bethel and St. Thomas, rose to national
prominence in this area. The Negroes living at the eastern end of
Lombard Street were a buffer between the residential and mercantile district to the north and the underworld section to the south
dominated by Irish immigrants and a conglomeration of native
Americans. It was here that Octavius V. Catto, the young Negro
leader who sought to register blacks to vote under the new civil
rights legislation was one of a number of Negroes shot down in
cold blood in 1871.[22]

The immigrants who arrived in Philadelphia between 1878 and 1881 huddled together in the vicinity of Fourth and Lombard streets, less than a mile from the landing station. A mixture of Ukrainian, Polish, Galician, Rumanian, and Hungarian Jews found common cause with the Lithuanians who still outnumbered any single group coming from the Russian and Austro-Hungarian empires. Lithuanian domination continued until the spring of 1882 when the tide of immigration from southern Russia brought thousands of Jews to Philadelphia.

They poured into a section south of Lombard Street stretching from Second to Sixth streets and extending to Catherine Street. South Street, whose commercial liveliness was the product of Dutch and German Jewish enterprise, had an instant attraction. New and second-hand goods of every variety magnetized the immigrant at first sight. Peddlers' supply houses crammed with bargains that could be obtained on a week's credit and an emporia of rag and old clothes shops startled many whose battered satchels and wicker-baskets were filled with similarly doubtful treasures. Crockery shops, china shops, and pawn shops were wedged between stables and furniture stores. Its bazaar-like appearance stirred up memories of the Ukrainian marketplaces similar to the Odessa *tolchuk* which had been torn asunder by pogromists. Fifth and South, intersected by Passyunk Avenue, had emerged as an important commercial center and soon became the envy and an ambition of the street hawker and pushcart peddler who stood awed by the great Snellenburg clothing store that peered out triangularly from Passyunk Avenue.[23]

Familiar signs in Hebrew characters designated where kosher food could be bought. Other signs, lettered in Russian, Polish and Yiddish, advertised bath houses. Innumerable courts, alleyways, and lesser streets divided the area into small rectangular blocks. Wooden frame houses of three and four rooms abounded in the neighborhood. They could be quickly rented by those who had little funds. Prior to the organization of the Association for the Protection of Jewish Immigrants, the newcomers wandered aimlessly in quest of a countryman, and the Jewish shop owners provided information and direction to the stranger. But the search for lodging was frustrating and led only to wornout, unsanitary, rat-infested wooden frame houses identical to those described by W.E.B. DuBois in his study, *The Philadelphia Negro*. Not until the Association opened a wayfarers' house was the problem reduced. Inexpensive housing that was comfortable and sanitary was not to be easily found.[24]

By 1881 the housing shortage in Philadelphia was acute but no recognition of this was made by the city government. On the contrary, the general belief was that Philadelphia led the nation in building improved housing and its checkerboard plan was described as a tourist attraction. Speaking before the Philadelphia Society for Organizing Charity, Addison B. Burk stated:

> Philadelphians are pretty well accustomed now to being twitted about their mathematically straight streets, crossing each other at right angles, about their red and white houses, so much alike that strangers cannot tell one block from another, except by the names of the streets. But he laughs best who laughs last, and Philadelphians dwell in their cleanly, separate dwellings, with complacency, and study the health bulletins that tell them theirs is one of the healthiest cities in the world, without envying their neighbors who think that outside decoration is the only or chief end of architecture.[25]

But the truth was that the external appearance of the old housing, some of which was built in the late eighteenth century but most of it in the style of the 1830s, varied as much as the habits and manners of the immigrants. The city was still subject to cholera and most hospitals had segregated typhus wards.[26] Burk's reference to the neat rows of housing was to the new homes built after the Civil War and how they could be successfully financed by the building associations whose interests he was anxious to promote.

In the hands of the new occupants the old housing was quickly transformed. House fronts were converted into shops emblazoned with signs in Hebrew characters. Handicraftsmen, umbrella repair men, and cobblers, where they did not have shop fronts, practiced their trade on the front steps so that they could be seen by prospective customers. Improvised stands made of barrels and boxes served as counters across which barter and trade were carried on. These miniature retail establishments were the forerunners of Fourth Street's pushcart curb trade.[27]

Lesser east-west streets, Lombard and Bainbridge, were fronted by overhanging corrugated awnings that extended from the walls of the house to the curb, elevated by iron poles. The awnings offered shade and protection from sun and rain, and the poles became hitching posts and display racks for "old-clothesmen," who paid rent for the use of this meager space. Hazardous and a barrier to firemen's ladders in time of emergency, the metal awnings persisted into the twentieth century until their removal was ordered by the city.

Not all of the houses followed a uniform plan, as it is generally believed. Nor were they of the same size or constructed of the same materials. They were consistent only in their irregularity. Some were built of brick, many of wood; one roof was flat and another was pitched. Some had overhanging eaves, others were at sharp angles. Window glass was still hand-made, shutters were commonplace, and iron gratings covered the apertures of cellar entrances. Descriptions that typified certain east-west streets could not be applied to the uniform faces of row housing on north-south streets.

The interiors of small houses contained a front parlor and a kitchen in the rear of the first floor. Two bedrooms occupied the second floor and an occasional attic was reached by a blind and precipitous stairway. Gas lamps supplied illumination but more often naptha lamps were the source of light. Heat came from the parlor stove. There was no plumbing and cold water was supplied by the communal hydrant on the outside.[28]

In the decade that followed the great immigration, striking contrasts in the spreading Jewish quarter were apparent. Spruce and Pine streets, lined by ancient shade trees, once the residential quarters of old Philadelphia families, were supplanted by well-to-do and successful Jews from Russia.[29] When the Pennsylvania Railroad opened a series of modern stations along the Main Line and to Chestnut Hill, old Philadelphians yielded to the inviting suburban surroundings within and beyond the inner city, making possible the occupation of homes on Spruce and Pine streets.[30] As a result, non-Jews launched the first major movement away from center city Philadelphia. Where the three- and four-storey houses were not occupied residentially, they were converted into meeting halls, lodge headquarters, funeral parlors, and organizations that provided health services, mutual aid benefits, and temporary shelter. Adding diversity to this melange were mission houses, vegetarian, anarchist, Zionist, and ultra-orthodox centers. In the heart of today's Society Hill, the first orthodox synagogues of East European Jews were consecrated and by 1893 forty-five places of worship were reported in a half square mile area south of Spruce Street.[31]

Unlike Port Richmond's "Jerusalem," Society Hill was within the historic section of the old city. Nearby were the banks, the maritime and insurance offices, the steamship agencies, the mercantile institutions, and the cultural centers identified with the founding of the United States.

Less than a few minutes walk south of the original Society Hill tract arose one of the vilest Jewish immigrant neighborhoods. Alaska, Gaskill, and Kater streets were notorious for their decaying wooden "bandboxes," the offal and animal excrement encrusted in their wooden sidewalks and cobblestone alleyways. Because of these conditions, several Christian women chose Alaska Street as the site of the University Settlement House in 1893.[32] Gaskill Street reeked of similar filth and its inhabitants were as diverse in their occupations as they were in their backgrounds. At Third Street, Feinstein's saloon and money-lending office was a favorite spot of the river front Irish, and at the Fifth Street end was the home of Rabbi Eleazer Kleinberg, a Vilna *dayan* of pronounced Hebrew scholarship and the first influential East European rabbi to settle in Philadelphia.[33] At the corner of Fifth and Gaskill, William Wheatley's old Dramatic Hall was turned into a Jewish center before it was leveled and replaced by an orthodox Hungarian synagogue.[34]

A study of seventy-five houses encircling the Kater Street block revealed a total of 688 residents consisting of 142 families of whom 372 were adults and 316 children. The houses contained 496 rooms or an average number of 6.6 rooms to each house, with 9.17 persons to the house. The city average was 5.4 persons, the Negro average was 5.73, and only one Italian-occupied block, with an average of 9.88 persons to the house, exceeded the Jewish block average.

In the Jewish block of "75 houses, there were 86 water closets and 22 privies" whose quality and working order were in constant doubt. Eight bathtubs were in the 75 houses "of which 3 were only used in the summer."[35] In some blocks away from the main streets, one privy provided for local needs. Major Moses Veale, the Board of Health Officer, stated that, "There are in the small streets and alleys between Delaware Avenue and Fifth Street, South Street and Carpenter Street, 1763 small houses of from two to six rooms each, occupied by about 14,100 persons, principally Italians and Russians (Jews), an average of about eight persons to each house, having a breathing space of not over 200 cubic feet. In one small three-room house there were 16 persons who slept in two rooms 8 x 10 x 7. . . ." [36]

Five private bathing establishments were operated and patronized by Jews in this part of South Philadelphia. In addition, the Public Baths Association at Fourth and Gaskill was actively used by Jews, more so than any other immigrant group. Enforcement of public health regulations, maintaining decent plumbing and good water accommodations, was difficult as long as the city fathers looked upon foreigners as a blight.[37] Health and sanitation laws were enforced only when the city was threatened by cholera, small-pox, diphtheria, typhus, or ship fever. Tuberculosis, with a high incidence among Jews, attracted the serious attention of the medical profession but little was done to abate its spread. And homes whose upper floors were converted into sweatshops were looked upon as the breeding ground for a disease that was diagnosed as incurable.[38]

In one of many investigations of the sweating system in 1892, John B. Lennon described a typical Jewish sweatshop, condemning the residents as well as their work place. "These old houses have very poor plumbing arrangements and the connections with the sewers are miserable and the houses are just as unclean and untidy as it is possible for that class of people and they seem to like dirt as well as anyone I know of, and you will find them in these rooms, where they will have their work benches and many of the employees when they lie down to sleep will lie right down on the bench, and their closets, to which the women and children have to retire if they wish to use a closet, in many cases is directly connected with the same room or in a hall where the—well, the stench and conditions are terrible." [39]

Surrounding the Jewish slum were the slums of Slavic and Italian immigrants. South Street's commercial attraction for Jews was equalled by Washington Avenue's invitation to Italian laborers. Along this broad avenue ran the track line that once carried Union soldiers to the South. Freight was hauled from the Delaware River docks to the Schuylkill River and to points south and west. The railroad had become part of the Pennsylvania Railroad system, which was in need of cheap labor. The Pennsylvania promoted the American Steamship Line whose ships were built by Cramp and were reaching out to Italy to attract as much as possible the lucrative immigrant traffic to the port of Philadelphia. Those who came directly to the city under the auspices of the Pennsylvania quickly found employment with the railroad.[40] Immediately west of the Jewish settlement, the Italians made their homes, displacing some of the native-born and vying with other immigrants for homes. On Fitzwater Street, the Italian presence was emphatic.[41] To the south, thick settlements encroached upon the Jewish boundary competing for supremacy. One block was inhabited by Jews and another by Italians.

Flanking the Jewish quarter east of Second Street and further south, east of Third, were the homes of Poles, Ruthenians, and a small enclave of Irish. In this immediate vicinity they found employment as soap boilers and foundrymen. In the warehouses that overlooked the river and extended as far south as old Wicaco, a variety of unskilled Slavic hands were employed. Housing along the waterfront in and around Gloria Dei or Old Swedes Church was historically as important as any in the city. Squat two-story homes with slate and tin roofs, lingering from the previous settlements, were divided between Poles and Jews.

Polish and Lithuanian immigrants made permanent their settlement in the South Philadelphia section about 1907, shortly after Russian Jews brought the first hospital into this part of the city. Many of the Poles bought their homes from Jews but would not resell or rent to Jews, but only to their countrymen. They were motivated by the establishment of the Church of the Sacred Heart at Third and Wharton and Archbishop Ryan's insistence that the parishoners remain in the immediate area.[42]

Each immigrant group learned to concentrate in a low rental area. Although their occupations differed and they were separated by language and religion, the immigrants sought the cheap accommodations where work was available and places of employment could be reached without the cost of transportation.

Aware of the inadequate and worn-out housing, the United Hebrew Charities called the attention of its members to a plan for providing "the worthy poor, clean and well ventilated homes, at a moderate rent, away from degrading and contaminating influences." In 1884 its official report stated with regret that, "Nothing has been done as yet in this direction."[43] A plan was projected by the United Hebrew Charities to assist in making such homes available. Under the auspices of the Charities, a program of purchasing homes in different sections of the city that could be rented cheaply

to the "worthy and industrious poor" with an option to purchase
the homes was proposed. One of the conditions of the lease was
thorough cleanliness, and if this condition were to be violated, the
tenant would be evicted. Besides, it would be a step in removing
the immigrants from huddling "in the thickly-populated, plague
festered localities of the city." [44] Respectable surroundings offered
a model for emulation and would precipitate the Americanization
of the Jewish stranger from Russia. But the plan was shattered by
the weight of continued immigration. As regret for the failure to
implement this program turned to consternation, the pleas of the
Charities' presidents addressed in lady-bountiful English were repeated year after year. When there were as many families in a
house as there were rooms, or when the United Hebrew Charities
had to find shelter for 115 families in a single day, its energies were
diverted by immediate needs and its financial resources drained by
the complexity of an irreducible problem. Aggravating the housing
shortage was the visual response to the "sight of human beings by
the hundreds, unkempt, careless, destitute, more like the animal,
[it] is a thing to which we as Jews have never been accustomed
until within a recent period." [45] And who the "worthy" were
remained undefined. The older Jewish community was itself confused. The self-sustaining Jerusalemites were criticized for living in
an "ill-chosen section of the city" and the South Philadelphians
looked upon with dismay for huddling in a dense ghetto-like area
whose low rental made it a first attraction.

Housing in South Philadelphia worsened as the density of the
immigrant population increased. Early in 1893 a city-wide movement was launched to efface the slum and upgrade the condition of
the immigrant. Two laymen, Walter Vrooman, a Christian Socialist,
and Charles W. Caryl, an erratic social worker who was placed in
charge of the University Settlement House on Alaska Street, spear-
headed the encounter with the slum.[46] Under the idyllic name of
the Model Dwelling House Association, a number of Christian
clergymen were induced to support the plan. Rabbi Joseph Krauskopf, inspired by the recent emphasis given to the concept of social
justice by the Reform movement in Judaism, joined his Christian
brethren in the common crusade for better housing.[47]

The purpose of the Model Dwelling House Association was to
erect an apartment-style building at Twelfth Street and Washington
Avenue. It was to have separate rooms, fireproof staircases, an

ample water supply for each family, and light and ventilation for every room. Play space for children, a communal library, and an adjoining park were planned to provide recreational and cultural facilities. Krauskopf became an ardent supporter of the scheme and successfully enlisted the help of others. Pledges amounting to more than $50,000 were quickly directed to his attention. Felix Adler of the Ethical Society of New York came to Philadelphia to solicit good will for the undertaking, "urging the scourge of the preacher, and not encomiums of the philanthropist." The United Hebrew Charities warmly approved the scheme but took no corporate action. Joseph G. Rosengarten, a gentleman historian of a prominent Jewish family active in elite Philadelphia circles, spoke in behalf of the Beneficent Building Association. In its twenty-five years, the Association had accomplished little in the way of improving housing, yet its spokesman opposed the new-style building as impractical.[48]

Rosengarten's opposition was meaningless in the face of the sudden and unexplained withdrawal of the Protestant clergy, one of whom stated—referring to Krauskopf—that it would be impossible to work with a Jew. Overnight the grand movement collapsed. The newspapers that endorsed a better housing program in January 1893 condemned the undertaking nine months later. The clergy, who at first envisioned its activity as carrying forward a precept of the social gospel, now advocated strict Bible preaching as a solution to the evils of the city. Walter Vrooman, one of the original organizers of the Conference of Moral Workers, was discredited; the other, Charles W. Caryl, whose instability and erratic habits became a matter of public knowledge, fled the city.[49] Another strike by Jews in the tailoring trade protesting their unwholesome living conditions brought about further disaffections.[50] But the City Council became frightened. The fear of a cholera epidemic similar to the one that struck Philadelphia in 1869 was revived when news reached the city that the disease had spread to European ports of embarkation and might be carried across the Atlantic.

Before the fall of 1893, the City Council under pressure of these apprehensions appropriated the necessary funds to improve sanitation and drainage. The sewage system was revised, cement and asphalt paving covered the cobblestoned streets; alleyways were flushed and disinfected regularly, and receptacles for garbage were made available.[51] Following the collapse of the Model Dwelling

House Association, the United Hebrew Charities struggled to re-
move South Philadelphia families from the slums "to healthy
dwellings by assisting such parties with part of the rent for a short
time." A severe winter hampered the work of the Charities and
only a few families were assisted. The financial crisis that swept
the nation in 1893 diverted the funds of the Charities to other
needs and kept the program from being effective.[52] Various private
and commercial ventures had meanwhile improved the face of the
South Street area. The Hungarian Jews acquired the site on which
stood William Wheatley's Dramatic Hall and built an edifice at the
northeast corner of Fifth and Gaskill. During 1894 a number of
buildings were demolished on South Street to make way for store-
front buildings with apartments above them.[53] But housing remained poor and inadequate in spite of these minor changes. When
the Octavia Hill Association was formed in 1895, launching a
program of housing reform, the fusion of Christian and Jewish
efforts was not obstructed by anti-Semitism or the differences
between Jews of Russian and German background.

In 1894, twelve years after the arrival of the *Illinois* with its
band of Jews fleeing Russia, the Jewish population of South Philadelphia had risen from 300 to an estimated 30,000. They lived
in an area of six wards, the First, Second, Third, Fourth, Fifth and
Seventh, which covered 2.322 square miles. By 1907, after many
had moved to other parts of the city, the Jewish population of
South Philadelphia was estimated at 55,000. The Negro population of the same wards was 18,000, the Italians 28,000 and
Christian Slavs comprised less than 10,000. The remainder consisted of 50,000 Irish, German and native-born Americans of
various European backgrounds.[54]

North of Market Street

The third area of original immigrant settlement with the second
largest concentration of Russian Jews was north of Market
Street. Its background and development was in sharp contrast to
"Jerusalem" and the thickly populated quarter of South Philadelphia. It included the former district of the Northern Liberties
bounded by the Delaware River and Sixth Street and from Vine
north to Laurel Street, the northern boundary of William Penn's
"greene country towne." From here the Jewish population flowed

into lower Kensington and swept along historic Germantown Avenue. Second Street, a main north-south thoroughfare, cut through the heart of the Liberties, which at one time was the center of colonial Philadelphia Jewry. Later it bristled with the largest concentration of German Jews. With the coming of East European Jews, the residential pattern was extended to the areas north of the early settlement. Jews could claim an historic association with the Northern Liberties and its surroundings for more than two centuries. No other city in the United States had an equal residential counterpart.[55]

In the middle eighties the Russian incursion into the Northern Liberties was discernible. Bordering on Noble Street, where the freight lines of the Pennsylvania Railroad cut through to the Delaware River marking the course once taken by the Cohocksink Creek, wooden houses that were little more than shanties of one or perhaps two stories became the homes of the new residents. The skein of interconnecting courtyards and alleyways filled up rapidly with Russian Jews and extended east to New Market Street.[56] Here the abandoned synagogues of German Jews became the religious edifices of the Russians. North Second Street had its own vast market place and head-house which corresponded to the one on South Second Street. To the Jews of the Northern Liberties these streets held the same social and economic importance as the lively corner of Fifth and South streets.

Although the two neighborhoods were within comfortable walking distance, they were divided by the industrial and commercial market places that swept through the center city. Decay and impoverishment were as evident in one place as another. Prostitution involving many Jews was to be imbedded here for many decades,[57] tenderloin and hobohemia rooted itself nearby and numerous mission houses to save fallen souls sprang up within the new immigrant settlement. Dime museums, store-front spiritualists, rapid tattoo shops and gypsy fortune tellers thrived on the edge of the Northern Liberties. Nearby Elfreth's Alley, the residence of a number of colonial Jews, and Orianna Street, not far from the last home of Benjamin Franklin, were engulfed by sweatshops. Quaintness, grandeur, and the historic associations of the neighborhood temporarily vanished. Yet the Northern Liberties and its environs was in some ways more fortunate than its South Philadelphia neighbor. Its population was not as dense, and, while it was pocketed with "bandboxes," much of its old housing was far superior to that in the corresponding older section below Lombard Street. It quickly reflected its independent character by establishing separate health services, mutual aid societies, and institutions similar to those that arose in South Philadelphia at the same time.[58]

Franklin Street, which ran north from the square of the same name, was built up with rows of attractive limestone, brownstone and brick homes. At the turn of the century many of its residents felt compelled to move west of Broad Street and as far north as Columbia Avenue. As many were inclined to remain with the incoming immigrants. One Jewish writer did not share the view of those who remained behind and unmasked the cleavage between the Germans and the Russians:

> We quit the Franklin Street house in 1902. In that year almost every old family in the block moved away, many of them, like ourselves, to the new residential quarter in the western part of the town. A blight had hit the street in the form of a diaspora from the ghetto. With the arrival of the first few families, we Untouchables smiled tolerantly at their scheitels (ritual wigs worn by married women), their matted beards, and their Talmudized customs. We treated them distantly and with condescension, and a few of us hoped we might be able to freeze them out.

They were not frozen out, for according to the same writer it was more profitable to sell their homes to the immigrants.[59]

Not all of the older residents fled. Louis Edward Levy, president of the Association for the Protection of Jewish Immigrants, members of the prominent Sulzberger family, and others disregarded the social implications of remaining in an immigrant neighborhood.[60] Many preferred the convenience of the established Jewish shops that spread across Girard Avenue and up and down Marshall Street. The Jewish storekeeper of German background, unwilling to begin anew, remained on the site where he first entered business. A handful preferred the locale in order to carry out the program of immigrant settlement in that part of the city. Not until the end of the First World War did the Jews of German background disappear from the original Northern Liberties. By this time many of the Russian Jews from each of the three settlements also had begun to focus their sights on greener fields. But they left behind an almost solid Jewish neighborhood.

Housing conditions in Philadelphia were vastly different from those of other metropolitan port cities. The contrast between New York and Philadelphia was especially great. Of all the evils with which Philadelphia had to contend, it was spared the tenement house system. Philadelphia's growing fame as a "City of Homes," a description that was first used in 1881,[61] ranged from the "bandbox" type to the Georgian mansion. Between these two extremes were blocks of row houses that gave rise to the "City of Homes" concept. The row house was a dominant architectural theme in spite of its many variations, and block after block of mass-produced houses built of brick and stone became typical of late-nineteenth-century Philadelphia. More properly it should have been called "The City of Row Houses." This peculiar feature of Philadelphia housing led the *Philadelphia Press* to acclaim the city's workman as one of the best housed in the nation even though it had "dark and wretched" slums.[62] But immigrant slum housing was totally disproportionate to the boast of the *Philadelphia Press*.

Cheap and unimproved housing, population density, and the slowly rising status of the immigrants, emerging from the ranks of the poverty prototype, contributed to the first major movement away from the areas of original settlement. At the beginning of the twentieth century, Philadelphia was in the midst of a major real estate boom.

Children of the immigrants of the eighties were maturing, families were combining their financial resources, and new immigrants were eager to rent or buy what others were anxious to leave behind. Advertisements in the Yiddish press offered the services of the first Russian-Jewish real estate brokers.[63] Urban technology was precipitating city-wide changes. Transportation to all parts of the city was being reorganized after the last horse-drawn tram made its final run on Callowhill Street in 1897. The subway-elevated train had begun to carry passengers from the Delaware River to Delaware County, connecting the center city with all parts of West Philadelphia.

South Philadelphia shopkeepers, men and women in the professions so long denied them, and those who no longer felt it necessary to live in the vicinity where they were employed, took advantage of opening neighborhoods and new housing. A small down payment coming from the combined family fund, or recourse to a building and loan society—the immigrants established their own cooperative loan societies—made possible the negotiation of a thirty-year mortgage usually at 6 percent. This enabled the immigrant to move into one of the single row houses fronted by an enclosed porch, with a private entrance and a meager back yard. After 1900 more and more homes were lit by electricity. Gas ranges for cooking gradually replaced the wood and coal kitchen stove. Hot-air heat, another new housing innovation, added comfort, while sanitary plumbing was improved by vitreous enamel and china toilets.

Following the main business thoroughfares, the immigrants reached the neighborhoods opened to them. First they moved along Ridge Avenue, which brought them to Strawberry Mansion, nestling along the Schuylkill River. In a northwest thrust they crossed the Schuylkill from center city, moved along Lancaster Avenue, and settled in the Parkside area within sight of a chain of buildings where the Centennial of American Independence was only recently celebrated. These were looked upon "as beautiful and healthy neighborhoods." [64] By 1910 the lower part of Wynnfield offered both old and new housing to those who could afford it. Meanwhile, sufficient numbers found their way to Southwest Philadelphia to establish a number of outstanding synagogues and Jewish communal institutions. A separate movement north brought a substantial number of Jews to Logan, particularly east of Broad Street.

These five scattered areas of second settlement, begun prior to the First World War, represented more than a step toward better housing: it was a major transformation that spread Jews throughout a large section of the city. However, the largest number of immigrants came to rest in South Philadelphia and there they remained until the mid-twentieth century.

NOTES

1. Anthony N. B. Garvan, "Proprietary Philadelphia as Artifact," in Oscar Handlin and John Burchard, eds., *The Historian and the City* (Cambridge: MIT Press, 1963), p. 199.
2. J. Thomas Scharf and Thompson Westcott, *History of Philadelphia, 1609–1884* (Philadelphia, 1884), 1:433, 487, 492 and 612.

3. Lewis R. Harley, *Boundaries of the Incorporated Districts, Boroughs and Townships of Philadelphia County Included in the Act of Consolidation of February 2, 1854* (Philadelphia, 1908). Joseph Jackson, *Market Street, Philadelphia* (Philadelphia, 1918) provides information on innumerable buildings and houses that were erected in the eighteenth century and survived far into the nineteenth.

4. Scharf and Westcott, *History*, 1:718.

5. *Historical Facts about the North Side of Chestnut Street, Eleventh to Twelfth Streets* (Philadelphia, 1940?), pp. 3–4; see photographic insert of Chestnut Street in 1864.

6. *Chronicle of The Union League of Philadelphia* . . . (Philadelphia, 1902), p. 304.

7. Rachel Wischnitzer, *Synagogue Architecture in the United States* (Philadelphia, 1955), p. 67.

8. Federal Writers' Project, *Philadelphia, A Guide to the Nation's Birthplace* (Philadelphia, 1937), pp. 73–74; Charles J. Cohen, *Rittenhouse Square, Past and Present* (Philadelphia, 1922), *passim*.

9. Lorin Blodgett, *The Industries of Philadelphia as shown by the Manufacturing Census of 1870, Compared with 1860 and Estimates for 1875 and 1876* (Philadelphia, 1877), pp. 1–30 for a discussion of the city's industries and pp. 31–33 for tables of dwellings erected between 1863 and 1876.

10. All references to "Jerusalem" are drawn from three sources: David B. Tierkel, "Jerusalem in Philadelphia" in *Philadelphia Jewish American*, Nov. 13, 1908 [Yiddish]; Moses Freeman, "Jerusalem in Philadelphia or Jew Town," in *Fifty Years of Jewish Life in Philadelphia* (Philadelphia, 1929), pp. 10–16 [Yiddish], and Maxwell Whiteman, "A Journey to Jerusalem," in *Jewish Exponent*, Mar. 13, 20, 1964.

11. Henry S. Morais, *The Jews of Philadelphia* . . . (Philadelphia, 1894), p. 108 for the Dutch synagogue, Bené Israel, founded in 1857 at Fifth and Catherine Street.

12. Scharf and Westcott, *History*, 1:838 and 3:2339.

13. *Report of the Hebrew Education Society of Philadelphia for the year ending April 1, 1885* (Philadelphia, 1885), pp. 5–13. This section also contains pictures of the interior and exterior of the Lark Street Industrial and Day School Buildings. Quotations in the previous and subsequent paragraphs are also from this source.

14. Federal Writers Project, *Philadelphia*, pp. 143–45 for a survey of transportation development.

15. *Annual Report of the Association of Jewish Immigrants* from 1885 to 1918. The name was later changed to the Association for the Protection of Jewish Immigrants.

16. Tierkel, "Jerusalem in Philadelphia" provides this population estimate.

17. Edmund J. James, ed., *The Immigrant Jew in America* (New York, 1907), p. 304.

18. George Lippard, *The Quaker City; or, the Monks of Monk Hall* (Philadelphia, 1844) and *The Killers, a Narrative of Real Life in*

Philadelphia (Philadelphia, 1850). Also Roger Butterfield, "George Lippard and His Secret Brotherhood," *Pennsylvania Magazine of History and Biography* 79 (July 1955):285–309.

19. Timothy Shay Arthur lived at 721 S. Tenth Street in the midst of the immigrant settlement and many of his temperance tracts are based on the Philadelphia locale. S. Austin Allibone, *A Critical Dictionary of English Literature and British and American Authors* . . . (Philadelphia, 1871), 1:71.

20. *Sunday Mercury,* Aug. 10, 1890, for an interesting account of the Jewish immigrant quarter.

21. *Ledger and Transcript,* Sep. 23, 1885, for reference to Liberty Hall as a temporary synagogue.

22. W. E. B. DuBois, *The Philadelphia Negro* . . . (Philadelphia, 1899), pp. 40, 58–60; Scharf and Westcott, *History* 1:837.

23. *The Philadelphia Jewish American,* May 8, 1908, contains a lengthy article in Yiddish on housing, economic and other conditions facing Russian Jewish immigrants over a period of decades.

24. Morais, *The Jews of Philadelphia,* pp. 225–26 for the Wayfarers' Home at 218 Lombard Street.

25. Addison B. Burk, *The City of Homes and its Building Associations* . . . (Saratoga, N.Y.: [n.p.], 1881), p. 1.

26. Maxwell Whiteman, *Mankind and Medicine, A History of the Albert Einstein Medical Center* (Philadelphia, 1966), pp. 130–43 for health and medical problems among immigrant Jews.

27. *Sunday Mercury,* Aug. 10, 1890, published a series of photographs of the South Philadelphia area revealing these scenes and the state of housing. Louis Edward Levy, publisher of the *Mercury* and president of the Association of Jewish Immigrants developed the half-tone process by which these photographs were reproduced.

28. Ibid., and Henry McCulley Muller, *Urban Home Ownership. A Socioeconomic Analysis with Emphasis on Philadelphia* (Philadelphia, 1947), pp. 74–75.

29. James, *The Immigrant Jew,* p. 52.

30. Edwin P. Alexander, *On the Main Line, The Pennsylvania Railroad in the Nineteenth Century* (New York, 1971), passim.

31. The manuscript list of synagogues dated 1893 is in the papers of the Association of Jewish Immigrants in the possession of M. Whiteman.

32. Samuel McCune Lindsay, *Civic Club Digest* . . . (Philadelphia, 1895), p. 171 for background and founding of the University Settlement.

33. *Jewish Exponent,* April 22, 1891, on Kleinberg.

34. *Ledger and Transcript,* April 11, 1888, for the purchase of Wheatley Hall from the German Catholic Literary Association. The new congregation was Emunath Israel. A new building was erected and remained in the hands of the congregation until 1960. See Philadelphia *Evening Bulletin,* May 31, 1960.

35. James, *The Immigrant Jew,* pp. 306–7.

36. *The Record,* April 17, 1893 for Veale's statement.

37. Solomon Solis-Cohen, "Water Filtration," in *Philadelphia Polyclinic* (Philadelphia, 1896) 5:117–18 on the campaign to purify the city's water supply.

38. Whiteman, *Mankind and Medicine*, pp. 59–61.

39. *Report of the Committee on Manufactures on the Sweating System* (Washington, 1893), p. 213 for Lennon's testimony.

40. *Philadelphia Jewish American*, May 8, 1908.

41. James, *The Immigrant Jew*, p. 53.

42. *Philadelphia Jewish American*, May 8, 1908.

43. *Fifteenth Annual Report of the Society of the United Hebrew Charities of Philadelphia* (Philadelphia, 1884), pp. 10–11.

44. Ibid., *Sixteenth Annual Report* . . . (Philadelphia, 1885), p. 12.

45. Ibid., *Twentieth Annual Report* . . . (Philadelphia, 1889), pp. 15, 27; *Twenty-Fourth Annual Report* . . . (Philadelphia, 1893), p. 13.

46. Harlan B. Phillips, "A War on Philadelphia's Slums: Walter Vrooman and the Conference of Moral Workers, 1893," *Pennsylvania Magazine of History and Biography* 76 (January 1952):47–62. For additional background on Vrooman, see Ross E. Paulson, *Radicalism and Reform, The Vrooman Family and American Social Thought* (Lexington, Ky., 1968), pp. 89–91.

47. *Ledger and Transcript*, Jan. 9, 1893, for the announcement of Krauskopf's participation.

48. Ibid., Feb. 20 and 22, 1893, published a list of subscribers, most of whom were members of Krauskopf's congregation and a description of the building plan which was opposed by Rosengarten, who was also a contributor of the fund. *The Record*, May 8, 1893, reported that $56,000 was received for the project. *Twenty-Fourth Annual Report of the Society of the United Hebrew Charities of Philadelphia* (Philadelphia, 1893), p. 13.

49. Phillips, "A War on Philadelphia's Slums," pp. 58–59.

50. Maxwell Whiteman, "The Cloak Makers Strike of 1890," *Jewish Exponent*, Oct. 16, 23, 1964.

51. Phillips, "A War on Philadelphia's Slums," p. 61.

52. *Twenty-Fourth Annual Report of the Society of the United Hebrew Charities of Philadelphia* (Philadelphia, 1893), p. 13.

53. *Philadelphia Inquirer*, Oct. 13, 1893, on the new clothing stores erected by Leopold and Schwarzschilder at Sixth and South Street and *Ledger and Transcript*, May 5, 1894, "Old buildings give way to stores and apartments."

54. *The Record*, June 1, 1894, estimated the Jewish population at approximately 30,000 and James, *The Immigrant Jew*, pp. 51–52 provides figures for the year 1907.

55. No history of greater Philadelphia has taken these facts into account. Owing to the concentration of Jews in this district, Philadelphia's first congregation, Mikveh Israel, was built at Sterling Alley near Third and Cherry Street in 1782 where they had resided for more than forty years. See, Edwin Wolf, 2nd, and Maxwell Whiteman, *A History of the Jews of Philadelphia from Colonial Times to the Age*

of Jackson (Philadelphia, 1957), pp. 114–21. The nineteenth-century Jewish institutions built by immigrants from Germany has not been estimated, but three major congregations had their beginnings here. See Morais, *The Jews of Philadelphia*, p. 77 for Congregation Rodeph Shalom, p. 90 for Keneseth Israel, and p. 99 for Adath Jeshurun.

56. James, *The Immigrant Jew*, pp. 53–54 defines this area briefly. (The synagogue structures mentioned in n. 55 were all acquired by Russian Jews.)

57. Difficulty in obtaining specific information on prostitution other than locating the areas on Callowhill Street and Wood Street east of Franklin Street, were overcome by the private correspondence and reports prepared for Louis Edward Levy of the Association of Jewish Immigrants prior to 1912.

58. Emily W. Dinwiddie, *Housing Conditions in Philadelphia* (Philadelphia, 1904), *passim*, but especially the statistical aspect of health, sanitation, and population in the New Market Street section. North Fifth Street, between Parish and Girard avenues housed no less than ten different Jewish societies founded at this time which were still in existence in 1960 when razing of the area was begun.

59. Philip Goodman, *Franklin Street* (New York, 1942), pp. 3–4.

60. Levy lived at 907 N. Franklin Street until his death in 1919 and Judge Mayer Sulzberger lived at 1302 Girard Avenue until his death in 1923.

61. See n. 25.

62. *Philadelphia Press*, April 21, 1893, cited in Phillips, "A War on Philadelphia Slums," p. 59.

63. See n. 23 and *The Philadelphia Jewish American*, June 4, Aug. 7, 1908, for real estate advertising.

64. *The Philadelphia Jewish American*, May 8, 1908, on second areas of settlement.

Richard A. Varbero

12
Philadelphia's South Italians in the 1920s

The ethnic experience in American cities was a product of the interaction of the immigrant culture and the American environment. For Italian immigrants in Philadelphia, the 1920s were a time of transition in their adaptation to American society. During that period Philadelphia's public schools and Catholic churches provided key points of contact between the urban villagers from Southern Italy and the urban society of Philadelphia. An examination of Italian participation in education and religious life can illuminate the Italian experience in the city.

Neither the Italian community nor the educational and religious institutions of Philadelphia should be seen as monolithic, however. Within the Italian community there were important differences between those who had migrated from Northern Italy and those who had come from Southern Italy. There were also class differences within the large migration from Southern Italy. The minority of upper-class and middle-class families often shared a quite different attitude toward American educational institutions and had skills that allowed them to seize opportunities and thereby maintain their advantages as compared with the more impoverished and less sophisticated laborers who constituted the majority of the South Italian community.

Education and Immigrant Culture

Like other metropolitan centers in the aftermath of World War I, Philadelphia prepared to expand and reshape its educational system to meet the requirements of an increased school-age population. Despite fairly extensive school building and redirected programs, however, the city never adequately met the educational challenges of the 1920s. The reasons for this included limited funds, class and racial bias, a radical shift in the ethnic composition of students, and an atmosphere charged with post-war tensions.

The defeat of a school-bond issue in 1920 signaled a miserly policy toward school expenditure throughout the decade. In 1922, for example, it was estimated that Philadelphia needed 25 additional schools and $15 million more to supplement an original post-war school expansion program of $4 million. Yet at no time during the 1920s did the city rise above its position as next to lowest among large cities in per capita expenditure per child for education. Only Baltimore ranked lower. Although approximately 100 schools had been replaced after the turn of the century, many unsafe elementary schools still existed in South Philadelphia in 1930, some even without indoor toilet facilities or play space.[1]

The thrust of Philadelphia's public secondary education was increasingly directed toward vocational training during the 1920s.[2] While vocational training of the young was appropriate, especially in the industrial city, the school leaders thought it was most appropriate for children of immigrants and Negroes. Since the largest rate of increase in the school-age population was among these groups, modified school programs were in large measure a reflection of prevailing attitudes toward them. The assumption was that the future occupational roles of immigrant and Negro children were to be oriented to their working-class backgrounds. For example, the President of the School Board, Simon Gratz, lamented the fact that too many boys in high school were selecting academic rather than manual training or trade courses. Gratz pleaded for a much larger number of men trained in trades and mechanical pursuits, since that was "the work they were to follow in active life." Superintendent of Education Edwin C. Broome echoed the same sentiment when he suggested that the object of education was "to prevent children from becoming misfits in the world of industry." There is no evidence that these remarks were directed to the children of Philadelphia's elite.[3]

South Philadelphia, in particular, attested to the changing ethnic and racial composition of the school system in the 1920s. The South Philadelphia wards (one, two, three, four, twenty-six, thirty-six, thirty-nine and forty-eight) housed much of the obsolescent school plant. Here lived crowded colonies of Philadelphia's minorities. Russian Jews and South Italians joined the older resident Irish; in all, at least nineteen different nationalities were represented.[4] Blacks, long a significant and growing minority, stretched in a broad east-west corridor on both sides of Washington Avenue. In some cases, Negro families migrated as far into South Philadelphia as the vicinity of Sixteenth and Mifflin Streets before reaching areas of Italian residence.[5]

The post-war mood, which emphasized 100 percent Americanism and distrust of immigrants, had its affect in Philadelphia, where it was assumed by many that aliens were responsible for street crime, vice, and bootlegging. This mood found expression in the school system through a vigorous Americanization program. Taking root in the pre-war period, it was nurtured in the fervor of the war-time crusade, and bloomed in the hysteria of the Red Scare. Vocal patriots, in such diverse groups as veterans' organizations, the YWCA, and charitable societies, were determined to stem the tide of Bolshevism and anarchism. School programs, both day and night, stressed Americanization. Added to the functions of educators in Philadelphia, then, was the imperative to make the students 100 percent American, as well as useful.[6]

The immigrants, in turn, did not remain indifferent to neighborhood hostility nor to the thrusts at homogenization. Writers in the Italian weekly, *La Libera Parola,* for example, reflected disenchantment with the incessant hammering of Americanization in the schools and press. This resentment was summarized by one community spokesman, Dr. Leopold Vaccaro, who bitterly noted that

> The ideals preached by the Americanization teacher do not coincide with the attitude of the gang boss, the native union man, the fellow workingman, who, although compelled economically to work with the alien, would not voluntarily have him as a neighbor. Theory and practice are not synonymous.[7]

Philadelphia's educational program, then, had also to account for community pressures, immigrant sensibilities, and ethnic hostilities, in addition to other considerations.

How, then, did the children of Italian immigrants react to the institutional apparatus that was increasingly designed to assimilate them into American society? No assessment of the phenomenon can be made without consideration of the attitudes toward education by the *contadini*. The vast bulk of *contadini* males and nearly all females were illiterate. Claims of loyalty to the nuclear family and economic necessity overrode educational aspirations. Education was regarded as accessible only to the upper classes. Primary schooling in Southern Italy was a brief, even unnecessary interlude in the life of the young male, and women received even less consideration. The traditional educational pattern of the unskilled immigrant, therefore, was at odds with the compulsory education laws in the United States.[8]

Two broad generalizations describe the Italian educational experience in the 1920s. First, most of those Italo-American youths who completed high school and, especially, those who went on to college, were the children of the Italian middle and professional classes. Comprising a minority element in the ethnic community, the Italian middle class consisted generally of doctors, lawyers, pharmacists, community bankers, real-estate agents, journalists, musicians, artists, and school teachers. This aggregation of *prominenti* was supplemented by a contingent with especially marketable skills, and included, among others, custom tailors, barber-supply manufacturers, wholesale and retail store owners, and meat and produce dealers. Lower in the social order of the community, but important, were a large number of tailors and barbers. While such occupations were not esteemed in terms of American values, the skills each represented were significant in the Italian subculture. Tailors and barbers were higher in the socioeconomic scale and were more education-oriented than were unskilled laborers.[9]

A second and related generalization is that the children of the Italian laboring class, the *contadini,* did not pursue extended education to the same degree as did either the Italian middle class, skilled tradesmen, or their white peers in the public school system. Although there was an increasing tendency for laborers' children to attend school through graduation between 1918 and 1932, this development was gradual, not precipitate.

South Italians of all classes were aware of the socioeconomic potential inherent in extended education, especially as it related to professional occupations. Traditional avenues of economic mobility in Italy were formed in the venerable professions of medicine, law, and pharmacy. In the United States the class-conscious Italian middle class perceived that extended education also helped preserve old-world status roles. Despite the leveling effect of impoverishment and the noisy democracy of Philadelphia's "little streets" and row houses, schooling helped maintain the class barriers that land ownership or family status had accorded in the *Mezzogiorno*. Middle-class parents were also motivated to educate their children, in part, to maintain the distinction between the crude, unlettered *cafone* and those higher in the social scale of the South Italian villages. Family pride, class rank, and education were inextricably linked in the American city.

The large bloc of the South Italian laboring class in Philadelphia was no less ambitious, no less affected by considerations of family advancement, than was the middle class. Indeed, some *contadini* proudly managed to produce a *dottore* or *avvocato*. Long accustomed to accepting their socially inferior role fatalistically, however, the Italian laboring class subordinated unrealistic social aspirations to immediate economic gain. In fact, the *contadini* in the city had to be dissuaded from economic exploitation of their school-age children.

School census and graduation data support this hierarchical class model and its gradual breakdown. The test case in Philadelphia was South Philadelphia High School, or "Southern." It was the only public high school to serve school districts two, three, and six in South Philadelphia. Not until 1934 was there a parochial high school established in that area to attract Italian youths.[10] Equally important, South Philadelphia contained the preponderance of children of Italian immigrants in the city, although the number of Italian students had increased markedly throughout the school system. To illustrate: children, aged six to sixteen, of an Italian-born father, were the largest national bloc in the city in 1930. They numbered 48,761, or 14 percent, of the school-age population (see table 12.1). By contrast, the next largest national bloc in the city (also prominent in South Philadelphia) was the Russian (a surrogate for Jewish). Russian Jews comprised 33,139, or 9 percent, of school-age children. More than 66 percent, or 32,273, of the Italians were located in the South Philadelphia School Districts two, three, and six, as compared to 12,722 Russian-Jewish children. The only comparable areas outside South Philadelphia were School Districts four and eight, which contained 4,623 and 3,374 children of Italian parentage respectively (see table 12.2).

Children of Italian parentage had replaced Russian Jews as the

TABLE 12.1   Nativity Distribution, Children 6–16, 1930

	FOREIGN-BORN PARENT		FOREIGN-BORN, AGED 6–16
	Number	Percentage	Number
United States	203,215	58.58	—
Italy	48,761	14.05	1393
Russia	33,139	9.55	989
Poland	17,487	5.04	285
Ireland	11,573	3.34	—
Austria	6,091	1.76	—
Germany	5,966	1.72	788
England	4,237	1.22	—
Scotland	1,938	.56	—
Hungary	3,260	.94	133
Lithuania	2,970	.86	—
Rumania	1,736	.50	165
Norway/Sweden	811	.25	—

SOURCE: *Annual Report of the School District of Philadelphia, 1930,* table 13, p. 321

largest immigrant bloc during the period 1914–27 because of a higher birth rate among the Italians.[11] Foreign-born Russian Jews outnumbered Italians 80,959 to 68,156 in 1930, but the higher Italian birth rate helped account for the increasing presence of Italians, especially in the lower city. Another important factor in South Philadelphia was the beginning of the Jewish migration to

TABLE 12.2   Distribution of School-age Population (6–16) with an Italian-born Father, 1930

District	Number	Percentage
1	1,296	3.81
2 *	10,924	32.02
3 *	16,782	45.46
4	4,623	13.56
5	2,078	5.60
6 *	4,567	19.12
7	1,351	3.56
8	3,374	8.32
9	1,800	5.11
10	1,966	5.96
Total	48,761	14.05

SOURCE: *Annual Report of the School District of Philadelphia, 1930,* table 13, p. 321
* South Philadelphia

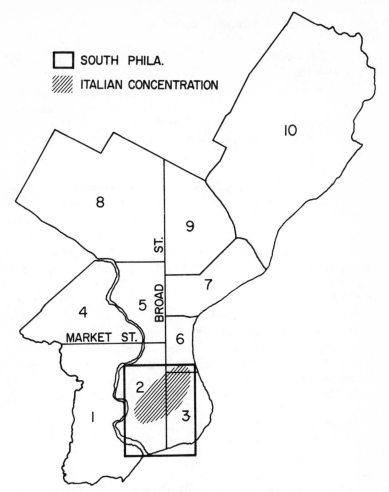

FIG. 12.1   Philadelphia school districts, 1930.

other locations in the city. A Philadelphia Housing Association Survey showed a drop of 41 percent in the number of Russian Jews in South Philadelphia from 1920 to 1930. The "far more stable" Italians decreased by less than 2 percent in the same period.[12]

In view of the large and increasing number of Italian school-age children in South Philadelphia over the decade, the Italians should have constituted a significantly increasing proportion of graduates from South Philadelphia High School. Statistics show otherwise. The percentage of Italian students did rise from roughly 5 percent of the total graduating class in 1918 (9 males in a class of 161; 2 females in a class of 67) to roughly 28 percent in 1932 (127 males in a class of 457; 56 females in a class of 330), but the rate of increase and the absolute number of Italian youths were less than their school-age constituency in South Philadelphia warranted. The 1930 class still graduated 170 Jews out of a total of 350, or nearly 50 percent. In fact, not until 1941 did Italians reach 49 percent of the graduating class at "Southern," a more representative performance.[13]

Inadequate school attendance at the high school level can be accounted for largely by the persistence of traditional attitudes toward schooling. One critical statistic involves the disproportionately large number of working children with an Italian-born father (see table 12.3). In 1930, Italian children constituted the largest number (2,041, or 30 percent) of employed white children aged fourteen to sixteen in the city.[14] In South Philadelphia, 1,574 Italian youths aged fourteen to sixteen were employed in a variety of occupations, mainly in the clothing industry, messenger service, and office-boy categories. Italian youths in Districts two, three, and six constituted 53, 67, and 36 percent, respectively, of employed children. Both the city-wide and South Philadelphia figures of employed Italian youths represented more than the *combined* city-wide total of the Russian and Polish blocs. Clearly,

TABLE 12.3   Employed Children Aged 14–16 by Nativity of Father, 1930

School District	Italian		Russian		Polish	
	No.	Percentage	No.	Percentage	No.	Percentage
1	31	12.5	16	6.45	8	3.23
2 *	381	53.44	4	.56	5	.70
3 *	980	66.85	196	13.37	18	1.23
4	88	36.51	20	8.30	2	.83
5	96	27.38	25	5.83	24	5.60
6 *	213	36.16	65	11.13	86	14.60
7	57	4.8	32	2.70	285	24.01
8	64	15.76	3	.74	90	22.17
9	63	8.97	11	1.57	8	1.14
10	68	8.84	13	1.69	278	36.15
Total	2041	30.24	385	5.70	804	11.91

SOURCE: *Annual Report of the Board of Education: 1930*, table 15, p. 323
* South Philadelphia School Districts

this data is consistent with the Italian peasant tradition of youthful economic exploitation and rejection of extended education.

Conversely, analysis of the backgrounds of many graduating students over the period 1918–32 supports the conclusion that they stemmed primarily from the middle-class and skilled groups. Admittedly, not all parents' backgrounds have been obtained, but the available materials and impressionistic evidence confirm the relationship between background, status, and extended education in the Italian subcommunity.

The middle-class orientation of many South Italian students can be inferred by another, less direct, approach. The preponderance of Italian students during the early 1920s was enrolled in the academic curriculum. In many cases, students were preparing for college. South Philadelphia High School, in fact, enjoyed a high reputation for its academic quality, second only to the showcase institute in Philadelphia, Central High School. Yet academic training and college preparation ran counter to the *contadini* orientation. An explanation for those who remained in school hinges on their middle-class values. Analysis of the backgrounds of Italian professionals who graduated from high school during this period also supports this conclusion.[15]

It is significant that by 1941 the number of Italian graduates in the vocational or commercial programs at "Southern" exceeded the number of academic graduates.[16] This tendency represented a long-range convergence of the utilitarian values of immigrant culture with the school system's increasing vocational emphasis, as well as with the diligence of the Bureau of Compulsory Education. Phrased another way, the children of the *contadini* attended school more persistently when parents became convinced that the school served to offer immediate occupational training, rather than generalized education or college preparation.

Adult education also reflected both the persistence of immigrant values and the gradual adjustment to American values. The 1930 Census indicated that 25 percent of Italian-born males (over 17,000) were illiterate, a figure exceeded only by the Azore Islanders and the Portuguese. Only Poles and Lithuanians had a comparable rate, both nationally and in Philadelphia. Yet, significantly, the age group ten to twenty-four contained but 3.3 percent illiterates in comparison to the age groups twenty-five to forty-four (18.9 percent), forty-five to sixty-four (37.2 percent), and over sixty-five (54.4 percent).[17] Although compulsory education had drastically reduced illiteracy among Italian-Americans in the age group ten to twenty-four, adults continued to require educational opportunities to become proficient in English and to learn the skills of reading and writing that were necessary in a complex urban society.

The ethnic distribution of adults in evening elementary school showed that Italian participation was second only to Russian Jews. More than any other ethnic group, however, the South Italian adults in evening school had a high ratio of men to women in both elementary and high school classes. Data for 1922, for example, showed 448 males to 68 females in the evening elementary school; in the evening high school, the figure was 951 males to 68 females. By comparison, Russian-Jewish females outnumbered males 940 to 796; the Polish ratio was 325 males to 227 females. The total evening school enrollment showed 1399 Italian males to 130 females (a ratio of ten to one); the Poles, 384 males to 205 females. This latter statistic suggests male domination among the Poles, but not as overwhelmingly as that of the Italians.

Uneven educational development among the South Italians verifies the persistence of vocational attitudes. Only gradually would traditional values toward schooling be altered.[18]

Italians and the Catholic Church

A second fundamental point of intersection of South Italians with the larger community was the Catholic Church. Nominally Catholic, the immigrants quickly learned that their traditional understanding of the Church was sharply at variance with religious practice in the American Church.[19] The Irish-dominated hierarchy and clergy agreed that the South Italians threatened to disrupt the established Catholic churches. From the time of the Third Plenary Council in Baltimore in 1884, the "Italian problem" agitated the minds of churchmen.[20] In Philadelphia the problem still persisted in 1918. For several decades thereafter the ruling Irish continued to regard South Italian religious practices as alien to universal Catholic beliefs.[21]

In 1884, one church served Philadelphia's then small colony of

Italian immigrants: St. Mary Magdalene de Pazzi. Located in South Philadelphia, in the heart of the growing Italian community at Seventh and Montrose, it was the first Italian Catholic church consecrated in the United States (1851). There is an irony in the fact that the first years of the church witnessed a degree of relative cordiality between the established Irish of the vicinity and the incoming Italians. The latter settled in the area around mid-century and the location served as a magnet for future immigrants. In fact, both the Irish and Italians collaborated on church committees between 1853 and 1883. Such names as Raggio, Malatesta, and Lagormasino were interspersed with those of Cochran, Sweeny, and Furey. In 1877, symbolically, John Raggio, a community leader, married Mary Leary Brown in the church to solemnize relations between Italians and Irish.[22]

It is worth noting, however, that these Italians were mainly Northerners, from Genoa and the Ligurian area, although there were already immigrants from the *Mezzogiorno* regions of Basilicata and Sicily. The church's famed pastor, Reverend Antonio Isoleri, was himself a Genoese. The long-lived cleric presided over the subsequent Southern invasion of the *contadini* after 1880 and witnessed the destruction of the truce that had temporarily united the worship of Italians and Irish.[23]

The impact of the Southern migration can be traced in the increasing number of national, or ethnic, churches. By 1920 ten national churches throughout the city had been established to handle the increased Italian immigrant population. Over the decade of the 1920s, five additional Italian community churches appeared (Chicago, by contrast, added none after 1919).[24] One more was created after 1930, Our Lady of Loretto, to serve a small section in West Philadelphia.

Thus the national parish had been established prior to the appearance in Philadelphia of Dennis Joseph Dougherty. Yet this churchman presaged a new era in the technique of immigrant assimilation in Philadelphia. Appointed Archbishop in 1918 and Cardinal in 1921, the indefatigable prelate became the principal architect of Philadelphia Catholicism until his death in 1951. Representing the conservative wing of the Irish Americanizers in the hierarchy, he imposed his firm will upon the Archdiocese; it bears his stamp still. The Cardinal's extended career in the city revealed his considerable talents as an ecclesiastical admin-

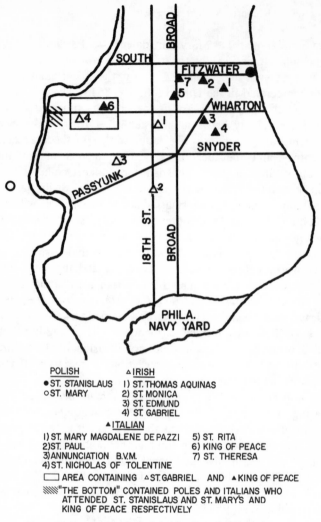

FIG. 12.2 South Philadelphia church dispersion.

istrator: his was a legacy of parochial schools, foundations, charitable works, and enriched coffers. As a bureaucrat, tempering rigid dogma with shrewd practicality, Dougherty excelled. But as a churchman, the Cardinal Archbishop's ability to convey a sense of warmth, charity, and human sympathy to the immigrants was limited.[25]

Cardinal Dougherty's principal achievement, as far as the South Italians were concerned, was to revaluate and restructure Archdiocesan policy toward Catholic immigrants.[26] He did this mainly by devising a carefully conceived dualistic church system. True, the canonical and national parish structure had existed historically.[27] But Dougherty adapted the canonical and national parishes to the unique features of Philadelphia and its immigrants. His experiment reflected his assessment of the Italians in the city; it embraced population density, mobility patterns, ethnic conflicts, intermarriage rates, and historically abrasive experiences. In brief, Dougherty charted a course of religious acculturation. In this context, Dougherty upgraded the immigrant ministry, created a base for an Italian-American priesthood, and autocratically suppressed resistance to his design. The rigid criteria of the self-supporting, puritanical Irish church was upheld as the model for the Italians. Realistic to a fault, Dougherty could not hope to make the Italians Irish, but he could at least attempt to make them respectable.

Many Italians recoiled from the austere mien and emotional parsimony of the Cardinal. Some stolidly resisted his policy to bring them the Sacraments of the Church in a universally approved manner. As late as 1933, in one flagrant case, parishoners publicly humiliated Dougherty by rioting in the streets in the notorious affair of Our Lady of Good Council. Members of the South Philadelphia church openly revolted when Dougherty ordered the church closed and directed parishioners to neighboring churches. Rumors had abounded concerning misconduct by the Italian priests of the Augustinian Order, but official church explanation was expresed in terms of "parish adjustment" as an administrative necessity. The Italians felt differently. In their ire they imprisoned one priest, menaced others, diverted funerals, cracked the church bell through incessant tolling, and threatened to burn the church down. Bands in the streets provided a background of the Italian and American anthems, as well as "Onward Christian Soldiers." [28] Extensive press coverage was given to this comic opera scenario, but the Archdiocesan organ, *The Catholic Standard and Times,* made no mention of the episode. Despite problems of this nature, Dougherty's program was reasonably successful in educating the Italians by the end of World War II. Success can be measured by the increasing number of Italian names in parish histories, including contribution lists. Counterpoised to the numerical increase, however, was the important intangible of leakage, continued male indifference, and Protestant proselytization. By 1932, the program to assimilate the South Italians into the American Church was well under way. But it had not made more than initial advances. The religious heritage of the South helps explain why.

South Italian religious practices were a reflection of traditional village values. Sectarianism, neo-paganism, superstition, and indifferent church attendance by males were among the key traits of this folk practice.[29] The historical legacy of the south of Italy was everywhere present. Remnants of the Greek, Byzantine, and Saracen invasions could be detected. South Italian Catholicism was patently syncretic. Furthermore, regional and village practices varied. A pantheon of saints and strikingly different Madonna figures suggest the varied accents given by the peasants to what was considered a universal religion. Even Christ was regarded by the peasants as less central to worship than the Madonna. Bereft of a well-ordered doctrinal comprehension, having little liturgical sense, the South Italian was implicated in ritualistic practices closer to cultism and classical pagan forms than to Roman practice. Carried to the United States, these syncretic folkways, supplemented by superstitiousness, male irreligiosity, and indifference to the financial needs of a lay-endowed institution, brought the South Italians into bitter conflict with the dominant Irish. Viewing the Italians with incredulity and hostility, the devout Irish did not consider Italians to be Catholic within their understanding of that term. A cultural clash was inevitable, and when it occurred it resounded with fury and invective. The South Italians were castigated from the pulpits and shunted off into basements and renovated buildings near the churches which the Irish had painstakingly built and sustained.[30]

The task before Dennis Cardinal Dougherty was many-sided. He had to reorder the religious priorities of the Italians by stressing self-sufficiency and the canonical role of the Church. Among the first of the steps taken was to encourage parochial school attendance by Italian youths. Although the colony school of Our Lady of Good Council claimed 1,500 elementary-age pupils in the early 1920's, largely because it was staffed by Italian-speaking nuns, Italians were notoriously lax in supporting such ventures financially.[31] (By 1930 the area had 5,149 children enrolled in parochial schools through grade eight.) Self-sufficiency was stimulated by the contrast of the dramatically inferior "national" parish with the successful Irish churches. The Italian churches had remained "the poorest and meanest in the city" mainly because large sums of money had been consumed in providing fireworks and a band for the procession ritual of village tradition—the *festa*. The emotional pageants were looked upon as idolatrous by the Irish generally. Dougherty sought ways to make the pageants vehicles of piety, and, importantly, to channel the funds into the Church rather than into the hands of opportunistic laymen.[32]

The Cardinal judiciously lent his presence to the Italian community when it translated faith into material achievement or when national rather than sectarian interest was involved. He gave his blessing when Italian-endowed institutions were commemorated, such as the Concordville Orphanage, sponsored by the Sons of Italy. Sanctioned affairs like the festive Columbus Day rallies in Fairmont Park drew his approval. When an individual Italian such as Henry De Bernadino showed uncommon zeal, he was rewarded with appointments to the Boards of Catholic charitable agencies.[33] These occurrences were rare enough during the 1920s, but the Cardinal's purpose was clear. His objective was to form a new orthodoxy among the Italians similar to that of the Irish.

Church organization, however, had to be adjusted to effect religious coherency and, at the same time, dampen Irish-Italian hostility. The bulk of Philadelphia's South Italians were contained in the South Philadelphia wards. East of Broad Street, bounded by Fitzwater, Snyder Avenue, and Fifth Street, the Italians were a majority. In other areas of the city, the Italians were minority elements, outnumbered by the Irish in every ward in which they appeared in any number (Wards twenty-two, thirty-four, thirty-eight, forty, and forty-four). Dougherty's parish organization reflected the pattern of Italian dispersion throughout the city. In areas of high Italian density, the Cardinal advocated the canonical or territorial parish.[34] Thus, the South Philadelphia churches of St. Paul, St. Mary Magdalene, St. Rita, St. Nicholas of Tolentine, and the Church of the Annunciation were designated territorial or neighborhood parishes. But each church was attended predominantly by Italians, and the "national" flavor was maintained.

Outside of South Philadelphia, in areas of lower Italian density, the national church was permitted to serve the relatively small enclaves of Italians within the proximity of territorial churches.

The largest of these settlements were in the thirty-fourth and thirty-eighth Wards (St. Donato in Overbrook; St. Mary of the Eternal in North Philadelphia). In such areas the immigrant church was maintained, as the hierarchy intended, to provide an intermediate step in the assimilation of immigrant Catholics. Neighboring canonical churches, largely Irish, were shielded from "the problem." Some of these national churches were tiny satellites of larger Irish churches, separated by cultural tradition from their ostensible co-religionists. Illustrative were the churches of Our Lady of Pompeii (North Philadelphia) and St. Michael of the Saints (Logan). These small sectarian colonies (Calabrian-Albanian and Venetian respectively) experienced the trials of the struggling immigrant church.[35]

Close relationship with the Irish were neither quickly nor easily formed. When the South Philadelphia Italians moved westward across Broad Street from the core community into solid Irish parishes such as St. Monica's, the theme of universality was emphasized. The mobile Italians learned they would have to bend to the iron will of the Irish ministry or return to the old neighborhood for mass. In fact, provision was made in some of the Irish churches for Italian language needs, but little more. The church historian of St. Monica's "proudly recorded the absorption of Italians without disharmony between people of different racial stocks," [36] but mention of the two key pastors of the church, Fathers John J. Walsh (1917–44) and Aloysius F.X. Farrell (1932–   ), wrests a sardonic smile from Italian old-timers.

When problems of ethnic adjustment developed from the Italians' westward migration in South Philadelphia, Dougherty was sufficiently flexible to create yet another national parish. This he did in 1926 with the establishment of Christ the King of Peace at Twenty-Sixth and Wharton streets.

As the Italians moved westward, along Reed Street, they fell within the orbit of St. Gabriel's Parish at Twenty-ninth and Dickinson streets. Some Italians had long occupied sections along Wharton Street, northwest of the large, well-appointed church, but they had never been comfortable with the inhospitable, laboring-class Irish who were visibly annoyed at "intruders" (Italians and Polish) from the adjoining territory. Some Italians were refused baptism and confirmation.[37] Typically, the Italians avoided the "Irish" church. Responding to the dilemma, Dougherty sanctioned the last of South Philadelphia's national parishes under Reverend William Pelosi. The small church received Italians who had moved beyond the boundaries of St. Rita's, St. Thomas Aquinas', and St. Edmund's.

The racially-mixed and ethnically diverse neighborhood now witnessed Italian rituals and pageantry common to the core community. On solemn occasions mourners amused Irish and Negro onlookers as they paraded through the streets in a traditional funeral procession behind a wheeled casket. An Italian brass ensemble provided a dirge. Although the adults were impervious, Italian youths were discomforted by the continuance of this village anachronism in hostile territory, especially when the eyes of their Irish peers were fixed upon them.

In other areas of the city, the minority status of the Italians permitted the tolerance of the national church under the supervision of well-instructed clergy. Dougherty's increasing emphasis was placed on upgrading the religious and administrative character of all immigrant churches. Italian priests were carefully screened as they came to undertake American assignments at the behest of the Cardinal. It was no accident that many of the priests were Northern in origin; some of them were the Reverends Biagio Giaz, Victor A. Strumia, Domenico Nepote, Matthew Amateus, and Giuseppe Lanza, all from Turin, and Reverend Eugenio Cassago, from Milan. The Southerners who arrived had flawless credentials, such as the Reverend Vito C. Mazzone, from Bari, and the Reverend Michael Pasto, from Foggia. Priestly vocations were fostered as well among Italo-Americans, such as the Philadelphians James V. Rosica and John V. Tolino. Young American priests were also trained for immigrant assignments and sent to the national and South Philadelphia churches "without feeling that they had been sent to a foreign mission." [38]

The decade of the 1920s was a transitional phase in the religious life of the Italo-American communities. The individualistic South Italians reluctantly adjusted to the American Church. Neither altogether pliable nor unresponsive, the Italians made an accommodation, but in their own fashion and with traditional reservations.[39] It is ironic that the highly criticized *festa* is still held in some of the remaining national parishes, albeit now as an acceptable form of piety. It is yet celebrated yearly in Hammonton, New Jersey, where Philadelphia's Italians gather to resurrect the past.[40] Time has wrought change among the children of the *contadini,* but the older customs linger. Cardinal Dougherty's program to win the allegiance of Philadelphia's *contadini* to a Puritanical version of Christianity was presented in terms of obedience and orthodoxy. These values, alien to the South Italians, were rejected by them, and this rejection explains their coldly deferential adjustment to American religious practice.

NOTES

1. *The Evening Bulletin,* May 10, 1920; July 6, 1922; Oct. 10, 1922; May 5, 1924; June 17, 1924; July 10, 1925; Jan. 21, 1930; *Annual Report of the Superintendent of Public Schools,* Philadelphia, 1925, p. 9; 1928, pp. 43–44; 1932.
2. *The Evening Bulletin,* Feb. 6, 1925; Oct. 14, 1929; Jan. 20, 1932.
3. *Annual Report of the Board,* 1920, p. 14; *The Evening Bulletin,* June 12, 1923.
4. *The Evening Bulletin,* Sept. 2, 1920; Nov. 12, 1924; Jan. 20, 1925; April 23, 1928.
5. B. J. Newman to Reverend C. E. Snowden, May 19, 1934. *Philadelphia Housing Association,* Temple Univ. Urban Archives; Donald W. Wyatt, May 10, 1934. *Armstrong Association of Philadelphia, PHA,* Urban Archives.
6. *The Evening Bulletin,* April 2, 1923; Dec. 10, 19, 1924; Aug. 19, 20, 24, 29, 1925; April 7, 8, 1921; June 23, 1922; April 17, 1923; June 19, 21, 1923.
7. *La Libera Parola,* Jan. 26, 1929.
8. Leonard Covello, *The Social Background of the Italo-American School Child* (Leiden: St. Martin's Press, 1967), pp. 241–329.
9. This model was reconstructed from Covello's *The Social Background; Boyd's Philadelphia Directory* (Philadelphia, 1914–34); Census Tracts; Italian-language newspapers; *The Italian-American Who's Who* (New York: The Vigo Press, 1937); Joseph W. Carlevale, *Americans of Italian Descent in Philadelphia* (Philadelphia: Ferguson and Company, 1954); and extensive personal interviews. Ernest L. Biagi was particularly helpful in clarifying class stratification in the Italian subculture.
10. A total of 84,472 children 6–15 were enrolled in parochial schools in 1930, while 234,861 were enrolled in public schools. In South Philadelphia the public-parochial ratio was as follows: District 2—21,907:9,550; District 6—16,736:5,359; District 3—28,210:5,149. As the density of Italians increased, so did the ratio of public to parochial school attendance. *Annual Report of the Board,* 1930, pp. 329, 330, 333, 338.

11. *The Evening Bulletin,* Feb. 23, 1932.
12. "Facts and Figures about South Philadelphia Teritory," *Philadelphia Housing Association,* 1943, pp. 3, 5. Urban Archives.
13. Data has been compiled from *Journals of the Board of Education,* Philadelphia, 1918–41, *passim.* Percentages refer to males.
14. Employed children of an American-born father numbered 2,440 or 36 percent. The city-wide figure for all children was 6,750 or 1.9 percent.
15. Illustrative are the following "Southern" graduates: Robert Sebastian, attorney, member of the Philadelphia School Board (father: custom tailor); Joseph Bongiovanni, attorney (father: medical supplier); Henry J. Tasca, Ambassador to Greece (father: dentist); Anthony DiSilvestro, State Representative, a Central graduate (father: journalist and editor of *La Libera Parola*).
16. *Journal of the Board,* 1941. Of 268 Italian graduates (549 total) 96 were enrolled in the academic curriculum, 172 in commercial and industrial courses.
17. United States Bureau of the Census, *Fifteenth Census of the United States: 1930.* Population II, pp. 1315, 1342, 1380.
18. *Annual Report of the Superintendent,* table 40, "Distribution by Nativity and Sex of All Pupils Registered," 1922; United States Bureau of the Census, *Fifteenth Census of the United States: 1930,* Population II, pp. 1066, 1087. While Italian male immigrants did in fact outnumber females statewide and in Philadelphia, census data do not present the overwhelming disparity shown in night-school attendance. The ratio of male to female was roughly ten to seven. Night-school attendance revealed the tenacity of patriarchial custom among the South Italians during the 1920s.
19. Representative accounts are Phyllis H. Williams, *South Italian Folkways in Europe and America* (New Haven, Conn.: Yale Univ. Press, 1938), pp. 135–39, *passim;* Robert F. Foerster, *The Italian Emigrant of Our Times* (New York: Russell and Russell, 1968; first published in 1919), p. 97; Covello, *The Social Background,* pp. 103–45; Edward C. Banfield, *The Moral Basis of a Backward Society* (New York: The Free Press, 1958); Humbert S. Nelli, "Italians in Urban America: A Study in Ethnic Adjustment," *International Migration Review* (Spring 1967), pp. 47–49. Also, *The Italians in Chicago, 1880–1930: A Study in Ethnic Mobility* (New York: Oxford, 1970), pp. 181–98.
20. Oscar Handlin, *The Uprooted* (New York: Grosset and Dunlap, 1951), pp. 131–32; Will Herberg, *Protestant, Catholic, Jew* (New York: Doubleday Anchor, 1960), pp. 136–71; Thomas T. McAvoy, C.S.C., *The Great Crisis in American Catholic History, 1895–1900* (Chicago: Henry Regnery, 1957), pp. 9–44. Henry J. Browne, "The 'Italian Problem' in the Catholic Church of the United States, 1880–1900," *Historical Records and Studies, United States Catholic Historical Society* 35 (1946): 46–72. Reverend John V. Tolino, "Solving the Italian Problem," *American Ecclesiastical Review* 99

(Sept. 1938): 246–56, "The Church in America and the Italian Problem," ibid. 100 (Jan. 1939): 22–32; "The Future of the Italian Problem," ibid. 101 (Sept. 1939); Rudolph J. Vecoli, "Prelates and Peasants: Italian Immigrants and the Catholic Church," *Journal of Social History* (Spring 1969), pp. 217–68.

21. Note Vecoli's citation of Aurelio Palmieri: "Il Clero Italiano negli Stati Uniti," *La Vita Italiana* 8 (February 15, 1920): 125. A suggestion of the Irish attitudes can be found in Thomas Sugrue, *A Catholic Speaks His Mind* (New York: Harper and Row, 1951), p. 48.

22. *Souvenir and Bouquet,* Recordo della Solenne Consecrazione della Chiesa Nuova di Santa Maria Maddalena de Pazzi, Philadelphia, 1911; Parish Records and Baptismal Certificates, St. Mary Magdalene.

23. *The Evening Bulletin,* June 4, 1926; *The Catholic Standard and Times,* April 15, 1932.

24. Nelli, *The Italians in Chicago,* pp. 93–94.

25. Hugh J. Nolan, "Cardinal Dougherty: An Appreciation," *Records of the American Catholic Historical Society of Philadelphia* 62, (Sept. 1951): 135–41. Richard J. Purcell, "The American Cardinals," ibid. 67 (Sept. 1946): 138.

26. Dougherty's career can only be reconstructed from external sources. I have created a model based on interviews with priests, laymen, Parish histories and the articles of Father John V. Tolino, cited above. Dougherty was a secretive individual, refusing even Monsignor Peter Guilday the privilege of writing a biography. My view is in no sense an official account.

27. Joseph H. Richter, "Conceptualization of the Urban Parish," in *Religion, Culture and Society,* Louis Schneider, ed. (New York: John Wiley, 1964), pp. 508–16; Robert D. Cross, "The Changing Image of the City among American Catholics," *The Catholic Historical Review* 48 (April 1962): 33–52. Note Cross's observation that the "national" parish was a device to permit immigrants to pay their "tuition in Catholicism."

28. *The Evening Bulletin,* May 21, 1933.

29. Christa Ressemeyer Klein, unpublished seminar paper, "Catholicism in Southern Italy and in the Philadelphia Italian National Parish: Its Sect-Like Characteristics," Univ. of Pennsylvania, 1968; Covello, *The Social Background;* Forester, *The Italian Migration;* Williams, *South Italian Folkways;* Vecoli, "Prelates and Peasants"; Nelli, "The Italians in Urban America"; Tolino, "Solving the Italian Problem"; "The Church in America," *passim.*

30. Vecoli, "Prelates and Peasants," p. 125; Parish History, Saint Michael of the Saints (1926).

31. *La Libera Parola,* July 8, 1922; *Il Progresso Italo Americano,* June 30, 1922.

32. Tolino, "Solving the Italian Problem," pp. 249–55.

33. *The Evening Bulletin,* Oct. 12, 1923; Oct. 13, 1924; *La Libera Parola,* Jan. 3, 1931.

34. Tolino, "The Church," p. 29; "Solving the Italian Problem," p. 252.
35. Parish History, St. Michael of the Saints, *Souvenir* (Philadelphia, 1926). *Twentieth Anniversary*, St. Michael of the Saints, 1944. Parish History, Church of Our Lady of Pompeii, *Twentieth Anniversary*, (Philadelphia: n.p., 1934).
36. Parish History, *St. Monica's Fifty Years Old*, 1895–1945, (Philadelphia, 1945), pp. 96–97.
37. Interview with the families Cesale and Cozzolino. Interview with Miss Estele Kletkotka.
38. Tolino, "Solving the Italian Problem," pp. 252–55. Personal interviews.
39. Tolino, "The Future of the Italian-American Problem," *passim*. Personal interviews: Ernest DiGiuseppe, Ernest L. Biagi, Joseph Bongiovanni, Robert Sebastian.
40. Gaeton Fonzi, "A Show of Faith," *Philadelphia Magazine* 61 (Sept. 1970): 78.

Recurring Themes
Mark H. Haller

Despite the variety of topics covered in this book, at least two themes continually recur. One is a comparison of the adaptation of ethnic groups to Philadelphia—an examination of how the values of newcomers interacted with the institutions of a growing city. The second is the relationship of social change to crime and violence in the city. Out of the heterogeneity of ethnic groups, the contrasts of wealth and poverty, and the opportunities to escape the supervision of church and family in the anonymity of the city arose group violence, youth gangs, street crimes, prostitution, and gambling. The problem of "law and order"—the search for methods of social control—has been an enduring theme in America's urban centers.

Ethnic Groups

In their treatment of the ethnic experience, the various chapters suggest that, in many ways, it is more illuminating to examine the differences rather than the similarities among the diverse groups that settled in Philadelphia. Ethnic groups arrived in the city during different periods of its development; each group—because of language, religion, or color—faced a different reception and therefore a somewhat different environment. But perhaps more important in explaining the diversity of ethnic experiences, each group brought a differing set of skills, expectations, and cultural values. The particular ethnic experience resulted from an interaction between the city's institutions and the cultural values of each group.

This diversity can be seen even in the varying adaptations of family life to the city, as shown in a government study of Philadelphia families in 1910, for instance. While most families exhibited considerable residential mobility, Italians more than any other

277

group continued to live not only in the same neighborhood but even in the same house. As Richard Varbero suggests in his chapter on the Italians, this remained true into the 1920s, at a time when many Jews were abandoning South Philadelphia for other parts of the city. In 1910, furthermore, although living in congested neighborhoods and under relatively impoverished conditions, Italian families also had the smallest proportion of women working outside the home. Thus economic need did not triumph over the Italian view that daughters and wives were to remain under the protection of adult males in the family. But for Italian boys the same strictures apparently did not apply, for, as Professor Varbero has pointed out, Italians in the 1920s were the group with the highest proportion of working teenage boys.[1]

Polish women also remained at home, but within the city's Polish population in 1910 there was a disproportionate number of men as compared to women. Over half the Polish families took in boarders, and the women therefore supplemented the family income as boarding-house keepers. Black women were more likely than any others to be working, either at home (keeping boarders or doing laundry) or outside the home (often in service occupations). Within black families, too, there was most likely not to be a husband present, so that the woman was often the sole breadwinner. This situation appears to be a continuation of Theodore Hershberg's finding that, during the pre-Civil War period, the city had an often devastating impact on the stability of the black family. Thus, although each ethnic group during its early years experienced relative poverty and congested living, what this meant to the family organization of each was different.

Ethnic groups also displayed considerable differences in the types of jobs and patterns of social mobility exhibited by adult males. As Caroline Golab emphasizes in her chapter on the Polish experience, the employment skills and the ways that immigrants were recruited for jobs were crucial factors in explaining why particular immigrant groups settled in particular cities and in explaining their locations within the city.

Dennis Clark, in his chapter on the Irish, describes how some Irishmen rose from construction laborers to construction contractors, while other Irishmen—in Philadelphia, as elsewhere—found a path to success in urban politics. Jewish males, unlike Irish,

Poles, and Italians, largely bypassed factory and blue-collar work in favor of activities such as peddling, junk dealing, and mom-and-pop stores. Such activities required long hours for often meager returns, but, unlike much blue-collar work, could lead to retailing and other white-collar jobs. Ownership of real estate in ethnic neighborhoods was another way that a few members of ethnic groups sought economic betterment and security. In his chapter on housing, John Sutherland points out that this was a field into which both Italians and Jews were moving by the early twentieth century.

Finally, W. E. B. DuBois, in his book *The Philadelphia Negro,* found that for black men in Philadelphia in the mid-1890s opportunities for upward mobility were uniquely limited. Of black males gainfully employed, nearly 40 percent were in menial service positions as janitors, domestics, hotel workers, waiters, messengers, bellhops, and the like. Only 2 percent (as compared to 4.2 percent of the total Philadelphia population) were in the professions, of whom ministers were the most important. Blacks, although American-born and even Philadelphia-born, shared with new immigrants the lowest economic position and were, in addition, shunted into positions with the least possibility for advancement or dignity.[2]

Ethnic institutions and even a recognition of common ethnicity were often a creation of life in the new world. Many immigrants, on arrival, had little notion of loyalties beyond village or province, but in the cities of America their common language and their need to unite for self-help broadened their sense of ethnic identity. For some Italians, a sense of being Italian developed in South Philadelphia, where the Irish controlled the Catholic Church and Italian ignorance of the English language forced them to turn to their countrymen in seeking jobs. Immigrants also brought Old World hostilities with them. In the streets of Philadelphia in the 1840s and 1850s, the Irish Protestants (Orange Men) and Catholics renewed their traditional hatreds. Many of the pre-Civil War anti-Irish riots were led partly by Orange Men. For Jews, the situation was still different. Although Jews in the nineteenth and twentieth centuries migrated from a variety of nations—including Germany, Poland, and Russia—they did not become part of a German, Polish, or Russian ethnic group. Despite tensions between the earlier and the later arrivals, their common religion, their shared religious persecution in Europe, and perhaps a sense of early common origin in Palestine—all underlay development of a Jewish identity in the city. Thus, the ways that immigrants forged a feeling of common identity varied from group to group.

Detailed studies of residential patterns in American cities indicate that the concept of the ethnic ghetto—defined as a neighborhood with a population predominantly of a single ethnic group—needs to be reexamined. While an ethnic group sometimes dominated a block, it seldom constituted even half the population of a particular neighborhood in Philadelphia. Even blacks, prior to World War I, lived in areas in which half or more of the population was white. Only with the greatly increased black migration of World War I and the growing residential discrimination by whites did the modern, compact black ghettoes emerge. In addition, rapid residential mobility meant that population was seldom stable in any part of the city, as Stuart Blumin's chapter documenting the high residential mobility of the city's mid-nineteenth century population demonstrates. In short, ethnicity cannot be defined in terms of stable residence in homogeneous ghettoes.

Instead, a concept of the ghetto is needed which takes account of the perception that parts of the city "belonged" to particular ethnic groups, even though most members of the ethnic group may not have lived there. The ghetto had symbolic importance: it was the place where the restaurants, special stores, churches, and social clubs of a particular ethnic group clustered. It might have meaning not only for those living there but also for other members of the group who once lived there and who returned to visit friends, to take part in religious or social life, and to shop for ethnic food.[3]

An ethnic group, then, can perhaps best be defined by two characteristics. One is a sense of common values and belonging, usually involving a common place of origin, common past experience, similar religion, or shared language. A second characteristic is the intimate social interaction of its members. An ethnic group was the group within which a person chose a spouse and selected his drinking companions. It was the group which set standards of childrearing and religious practice.[4]

If an ethnic group consisted of persons with a common social life and sense of belonging, then recent immigrants were not the only ones to form ethnic groups. The city's blacks, generally excluded from the social life of all white groups, created a rigidly separate social life of churches, benevolent societies, and other characteristic ethnic-group associations. So did the city's Quakers, with schools, meetings, and benevolent societies. As the city became increasingly black, Catholic, and Jewish, the white Protestants—by continuing to marry among themselves and to interact within their own churches and social clubs—became an ethnic group. Bruce Laurie, in his chapter on the fire companies, traces some of the beginnings of Protestant ethnicity. The predominantly Protestant fire companies, by insisting upon temperance as a rule of the company, differentiated their life style from that of the Germans and Catholic Irish, effectively excluded them from the Protestant companies, and thus turned their companies into native white Protestant social clubs. In short, ethnic groups—defined broadly—were an important means by which Philadelphians came to organize life in their populous and complex city. The social organization of the city became a mosaic of ethnic groups.

Urban Crime and Violence

In complex ways, the crime and violence of American cities were rooted in the diversity of ethnic groups, the gaps between rich and poor, and the uprooting of peoples that was part of the urbanizing process. It is necessary to understand the social structure and social changes in the city in order to understand the sources and locations of various criminal and violent activities.

American seacoast cities in the period after the Revolution were basically commercial centers, linking the growing economic activity of the new world with the markets and manufacturing of the old. In 1790 Philadelphia was still the largest among them. Despite their small populations, they were cities, not agricultural towns, and thus had the full range of occupations and class stratification that accompanies commercial activities. As seaports, they had sailors and longshoremen to work on the ships and docks—along with the groggeries, cheap rooming houses, and prostitution that everywhere formed a part of seaport life. The city also provided livelihood for a range of skilled and semi-skilled laborers and craftsmen: carpenters, wheelwrights, shoemakers, and so forth. Among the professionals were ministers, teachers, doctors, and lawyers. There were a variety of commercial occupations, from shopkeepers and clerks to wealthy merchants. The range of occupations—and the resulting inequality of wealth and status—already characterized

Philadelphia by 1800, as John Alexander explains in his opening chapter.

During the massive growth of Philadelphia in the nineteenth century, the city underwent significant changes in the arrangement of its business and residence districts. At the beginning of the period, businesses and residences tended to be mixed together. To the extent that the poor tended to cluster, they were found chiefly on the cheap or vacant land on the periphery, where shanties and small residences might be built, still leaving the poor within walking distance of the major commercial area of the city. Of course, while the poor were partly pushed to the outskirts, it is also true that they were drawn there by manufacturing activities and some of the early factories. As several chapters, including those by David R. Johnson and Bruce Laurie, make clear, the peripheral blue collar neighborhoods became the centers for teenage gangs and skirmishes among fire companies, as well as lower-class groggeries, gambling houses, and prostitution.

By the time of the Civil War, Philadelphia was beginning to turn itself inside out. Population grew rapidly, requiring the opening of new residential areas no longer within easy walking distance of the old city. Concurrently, the development of the horse-drawn omnibus and streetcars, as well as commuter railroads, made it possible to live away from the congestion and dirt of the center city and to commute daily. Furthermore, the expansion of warehouses, business offices, financial institutions, and even factories within the old city impinged upon the residences that had once been there. It was primarily middle-class and upper-class groups that could afford the costs of building new homes and the costs of commuting. Germantown rapidly ceased to be a separate village and became a bedroom neighborhood for the city. In the 1860s, Philadelphia's elite built an inner city neighborhood around Rittenhouse Square (west of Broad Street), but by the early twentieth century increasing numbers were moving to the "main line" suburbs west of the city.[5] As a result of these population movements, the same areas in Southwark and Kensington that had been peripheral slums in the 1830s and 1840s had, by 1900, become the inner city slums that concerned the city's housing reformers.

During the transformation of the city, the central business district also reoriented itself. In the early nineteenth century, the city —businesses as well as residences—was spread along the Delaware

River. Almost no building had occurred west of Seventh Street. As Philadelphia grew into a modern metropolis in the late nineteenth century, the business district became less dependent upon the harbor. Instead of extending north and south along the River, the business district moved west along Market, Chestnut, and Walnut Streets. Although warehouses remained and expanded near the River, other commercial activities—banks, department stores, newspapers, office buildings, and government buildings—rapidly relocated. The movement westward was symbolized by the construction of the massive new City Hall at the intersection of Broad and Market Streets in the 1870s (completed in 1881).

In Philadelphia, as in all other major cities, the areas around the expanding business district were characterized by a diversity of marginal uses including warehouses, skid rows, cheap rooming houses, and slum dwellings, as well as a wide variety of vice and entertainment. By the 1890s the area of Philadelphia north of Market Street and east of Broad Street contained the city's skid row, Chinatown, and "tenderloin" district. The skid row concentrated in the eastern portion of the district, near the river and the warehouse district. Living there were a mixed group of homeless men: runaway teenage boys, young men with seasonal and uncertain employment, tramps and beggars, and older men living in the area because of its cheapness and, sometimes, because of the camaraderie. In this area were flop houses, cheap restaurants, saloons, employment agencies, missions, and the other facilities that everywhere were part of the "hobohemias" of the city.[6]

Within Philadelphia's so-called "tenderloin" (extending from Market Street north to Callowhill, especially in the area from Ninth to Eleventh Streets) lay the center of entertainment and nightlife of the city: burlesque theaters, cabarets, dance halls, prostitution, and gambling dens. For many religious and civil leaders, of course, the open prostitution in the area constituted its most shocking aspect. One investigator in the 1890s estimated that some 300 houses of prostitution were open for business in the tenderloin. A more careful investigation, undertaken in 1913 after a police crackdown, was still able to find well over 100 parlor houses in the area, plus street walkers and girls working from apartments or soliciting in cabarets. There was a second area of prostitution in the old Southwark district at the southern edge of the central city. This district, extending for several blocks around

South and Fourth Streets, was largely a lower-class vice area, servicing sailors and other lower-class patrons—unlike the tenderloin, which provided a range of quality for a variety of customers.[7]

Gambling, vice, and entertainment were closely tied to the ward organizations of the city's dominant Republican Party. A number of influential politicians and officeholders owned or held interests in the gambling syndicates, saloons, and other entertainment facilities. The police, of course, were also tied to the syndicates, received substantial payoffs, and, like the police in all the major cities, had an official policy of tolerating vice and other illegal activities within the tenderloin district. Indeed, so tenacious were the interrelationships that Philadelphia was among the last of the large cities to maintain a segregated vice area. During World War I, when the armed forces attempted to clean up the major cities so that soldiers on leave might remain "fit to fight," federal investigators under Raymond Fosdick found Philadelphia to be one of the most dangerous cities for the morals of the troops. As the Philadelphia *Inquirer* noted in April 1918:

> Police have not conducted a single raid on any of the immoral establishments listed by the Fosdick Commission. Local authorities have failed to clean up the situation because of the connection between responsible officials and those who profit from crime. Secretary of the Navy Daniels, thus, feels Philadelphia alone of the big cities has failed to provide a wholesome atmosphere for the soldiers and sailors.[8]

The thriving vice and entertainment districts affected the ethnic and lower-class communities of the city in many ways. To begin with, the areas abutted on or were located along the business streets of the inner city slums. Investigators who knew the vice districts of New York and Chicago were astounded at the degree to which vice and family residences intermingled in Philadelphia. Some 1,542 school children, for instance, lived in the fifteen blocks of the city's tenderloin in 1913. Many parents, then, had to raise their children in an environment of vice and corruption. The statement of a sixteen-year-old messenger boy provides some idea of the attitude of a street-wise youth of the slums:

> All the women in the houses telephone to the office when they want something. We run errands for them, buy chop suey, take messages, buy things for them, and do anything they want us

to. . . . Things are mighty dull right now. It's all on account of that damn Mayor [Rudolph] Blankenburg we got in office now. He's closing all the houses up. It makes business bad for us and bad for everyone. Now that everything is closed up the pimps are getting desperate because the women don't make enough money for them to gamble with. So they rob the men as soon as the women go to bed with them. . . .

The pimps are taking to selling opium and cocaine, too. Before the police were so strict, the night messengers used to do that business, and we made a little money out of it, too. But now that the women don't make much, the pimps are making something on the side. . . . The place I got most tips was on the station-house calls. When a woman was locked up, she would call for a messenger, and he would hunt up her friends to get bail. I used to overcharge them on the service, and I always got a good-sized tip, too. You see when a woman's in bad like that, especially in jail, she don't care for money, so that when you say a dollar for a service that costs fifteen cents it makes no difference to her. . . .

We messengers certainly get free shows. I have seen women all naked in bed. I go right up to the rooms.[9]

The gambling, vice, and entertainment activities were also tied to ethnic life by providing jobs and paths of mobility for members of several of the city's ethnic groups. In Philadelphia, as in other American cities, discrimination against blacks meant that opportunities as prostitutes, pimps, maids, and musicians in the vice districts were among the most attractive open to them. As in other major cities, the Irish apparently played a crucial role in the late nineteenth century in organizing gambling and arranging political protection. By the twentieth century, however, Jews and Italians begain to rise rapidly in the world of organized crime. By World War I, Jews were crucial figures in the organization of vice activities in Philadelphia. During the 1920s, ambitious men of Jewish, Italian, and Irish background seized the opportunities presented by prohibition and led the bootlegging syndicates of the city. A grand jury investigation in 1928, initiated after a series of assassinations in a bootlegging war, found that Max ("Boo Boo") Hoff—fight promoter, saloon keeper, and operator of a major gambling casino in the city—was the city's leading bootlegger, presiding over a largely Jewish syndicate. Michael ("Mickey") Duffy led another bootlegging syndicate. And in South Philadelphia a number of Italian bootlegging gangs arose, perhaps the most famous being the one associated with the Lanzetta brothers. The grand jury found that the bootleggers were closely tied to politicians and to the police, many of whom had incomes far in excess of their salaries. At least until the 1930s, organized crime, politics, police, and some elements from the ethnic communities were closely interrelated in Philadelphia.[10]

Although group violence—or rioting—probably reached its peak in Philadelphia from the 1830s through the 1850s, group tensions that escalated into violence remained a characteristic of Philadelphia life. In analyzing rioting, the chapters of this book distinguish between two patterns. Michael Feldberg analyzes patterns of instrumental rioting, in which the group violence had a specific, limited goal and was employed as a bargaining tactic within an ongoing dispute. A second pattern of group violence, described by Bruce Laurie in his chapter on the fire companies, might be termed expressive violence. Such violence, rooted in cultural and ethnic differences of the city, expressed general antagonisms among groups but seldom had a specific purpose and was therefore often less controlled and goal-oriented. In American cities, instrumental violence has been most likely to characterize economic or political disputes; expressive violence has been most likely to characterize ethnic and racial antagonisms.

In Philadelphia after the Civil War, labor disputes often escalated into violence. Usually such clashes arose when employers attempted to defeat a strike by hiring strikebreakers, and the strikers in turn attacked the strikebreakers in order to force the company to halt its operations. Two incidents, in particular, stand out.

With the decline of business during the depression of the 1870s, railroads announced wage cuts in the spring of 1877. Workers struck, demanding a restoration of wages. In city after city, the strikers, augmented by sympathizers among the unemployed, attempted to bring the railroads to a halt; clashes between workers and authorities escalated into the burning of railroad and other business property and pitched battles between troops and workers. Philadelphia, as the headquarters of the Pennsylvania Railroad and of the Philadelphia and Reading, was a command center for corporate strategy during the days of violence in July. Yet Philadelphia itself remained relatively quiet. The mayor, who had gained considerable popularity in 1872 when he personally led the police against striking employees of the gasworks, again took personal charge of the police and called for federal troops. He banned public gatherings; and the police, backed by troops, attacked gatherings of workers and dispersed them with clubs on four consecutive days in July. On the fourth day the fighting was particularly bitter in the working-class Kensington neighborhood.[11]

One of the most notable strikes in the city's history was begun February 20, 1910, by streetcar motormen. Strikes by streetcar workers in American cities were often especially violent. When companies hired workers to man the streetcars during strikes, the cars were burned and vandalized or the driver attacked, so that it was nearly impossible for the police to provide adequate protection. In Philadelphia, newspapers reported violence almost immediately in the Kensington neighborhood:

> Cars wrecked and burned and their crews forced to flee in terror were some of the incidents which marked a series of riots which began . . . soon after the strike was declared.
>
> On Kensington Avenue, where the worst disturbance occurred, firemen had to go to the aid of the police with streams of water in order to disperse a mob that jammed that thoroughfare for blocks.
>
> In Tioga rioters destroyed a car after dragging passengers from it. . . . One of the latter was seriously injured by a brick. Only by liberally using their riot sticks were the police able to restore order.

The Director of Public Safety appointed 3,000 special policemen and soon called for reinforcements from the state police. The situation was complicated by the fact that there was a strike of steelworkers in the city at the same time. When the city moved to indict labor leaders for inciting to riot, labor unions responded with a call for a general strike of all workers in what one union leader called "a general uprising of the people." By March 9 union leaders declared, probably with some exaggeration, that 125,000 men were out on strike. Sporadic and often severe rioting continued, and a number of deaths occurred. Despite mediation efforts by Senator Boies Penrose and "Sunny" Jim McNichol, the construction contractor and political leader, the company remained adamant in its refusal to submit the dispute to arbitration. By the end of March, however, the general strike was called off, and the motormen and the company settled in for a long war of attrition.[12]

The railroad strike of 1877 and the general strike of 1910 were only the more prominent of a series of strikes, often accompanied by confrontations of police and strikers. In most cases, the strikers' goal was to increase their bargaining strength by stopping the operations of the company. They resorted to violence in part because there existed no legal framework for settling the disputes by requiring that employers recognize unions and that the parties bargain in good faith. Thus, for the strikers, their jobs and their union's existence were often at stake during a strike. Beyond this, the violence of American labor relations both reflected and increased the social distance that separated many workers from employers and other well-to-do groups. Many members of the well-to-do groups perceived strikes—and the accompanying violence—as seditious and dangerous uprisings of the poor that had to be put down with force.

Despite the many ethnic tensions in Philadelphia in the post-Civil War decades, the city's blacks were the major object of ethnic violence. Blacks, disenfranchised in Pennsylvania before the Civil War, faced resistance in their efforts to regain the right to vote. With the passage of the Fifteenth Amendment to the U.S. Constitution, the blacks of Philadelphia held a mass meeting and parade in February 1870 to celebrate their enfranchisement. Octavius V. Catto, a black civic leader, led the parade. But in October 1871, during the municipal elections, there was a good deal of violence, especially near the black areas of residence in South Philadelphia. On election eve, a black was killed at Eighth and Bainbridge Streets. The next day, rioting in two South Philadelphia wards led to the death of two blacks, including Octavius Catto.[13]

In July 1918, however, Philadelphia experienced its major anti-black riot. Beginning with the influx of blacks to northern cities during World War I, perhaps 10,500 blacks annually flocked to Philadelphia. This forced an expansion of the area of traditional Negro settlement along Lombard Street, and many of the more established blacks began to move south into the thirty-sixth Ward west of Broad Street, convenient to the war industries across the Schuylkill River in West Philadelphia. The Irish were the major white ethnic group in this area. During early 1918 several blacks were attacked, their homes stoned, and their possessions burned when they attempted to move into homes in the areas west of Broad Street. Then on Friday, July 26th, Mrs. Adelia Bond, a

Negro probation officer for the county court, was sitting outdoors on a hot summer night. A crowd gathered in front of her new home in the 2900 block of Ellsworth Street and began to throw stones. When Mrs. Bond fired a pistol into the air, a melee occurred during which a white youth was shot. Police soon brought a halt to the rioting.[14]

Saturday was a time of sporadic brawls, during which a white man, allegedly shot by a black, was the first fatality. On Sunday and Monday, the rioting was intense and spread to ever wider areas of South Philadelphia. The mayor closed all saloons in the area and ordered pawn shops not to sell weapons. The police, largely white and recruited from the areas where they served, devoted much of their energy to disarming and arresting blacks. By Tuesday, with the onset of rain, the rioting abated. But the tensions created by expanding black ghettoes have remained a continuing part of Philadelphia's history in the twentieth century.

Violence, then, has long characterized the city's history, and the issue of law and order has often dominated local politics. According to Russell F. Weigley in his chapter on the Civil War period, this was certainly true from 1855 to 1865. Yet, as David R. Johnson makes clear in his chapter on the patterns of crime, formal efforts to control violence and crime have often involved an incorporation of criminal or violent elements into the formal political or law enforcement machinery. Youthful gangs were often recruited into the police and played an influential part in local politics. Organized crime—gambling, prostitution, and the bootlegging of the 1920s—had close ties to political factions and local police. As a result, city government and the police have often acted as much to coordinate and regulate criminal activity as to suppress it. In a society in which criminal groups were influential in many areas of the city and in which law enforcement was locally controlled, this development was doubtless inevitable. Yet the close connection that has existed in American cities between crime, politics, and the police may well help to explain the fact that American cities have the highest level of street crime and violence among modern nations.

NOTES

1. Statistics from the 1910 study are from an unpublished research paper by Barbara Klaczynska. She is studying the history of woman labor in Philadelphia.
2. W. E. B. DuBois, *The Philadelphia Negro: A Social Study* (Philadelphia: Schocken Books, 1967), chap. 9.
3. The discussion here has been aided by reading Howard P. Chudacoff, *Mobile Americans: Residential and Social Mobility in Omaha, 1880–1920* (New York: Oxford Univ. Press, 1972), chap. 5.
4. The argument here is generally compatible with that in Milton M. Gordon, *Assimilation in American Life: The Rôle of Race, Religion, and National Origins* (New York: Oxford Univ. Press, 1964), chap. 2.
5. The relocation of the elite is described in E. Digby Baltzell, *Philadelphia Gentlemen: The Making of a National Upper Class* (New York: The Free Press, 1958), chap. 9.
6. Information on skid row from Professor Leonard Blumberg, Temple Univ., who has been engaged in a long-term study of Philadelphia's skid row inhabitants.
7. Frank M. Goodchild, "The Social Evil in Philadelphia," *The Arena* 15 (March 1896): 574–86; Vice Commission of Philadelphia, *A Report on Existing Conditions. . .* (Philadelphia, 1913).
8. *Inquirer,* April 18, 1918.
9. Vice Commission, *A Report,* pp. 79–80.
10. See typewritten copy of the Special August Grand Jury (1928), in Committee of Seventy papers, series 3, folder 1, in Urban Archives, Temple Univ. For journalistic accounts of Italians, see Jim Riggio, "Tales of Little Italy," *Philadelphia Magazine* (March 1971), pp. 73 ff., and Greg Walter, "One Man's Family," ibid. (Sept. 1969), pp. 59 ff.
11. Robert V. Bruce, *1877: Year of Violence* (Chicago: Quadrangle, 1970), esp. pp. 194–96, 232–33, and 308.
12. Philadelphia *Bulletin,* Feb. 11-March 26, 1910. Quotations from Feb. 20 and March 3.
13. J. Thomas Scharf and Thompson Westcott, *History of Philadelphia* (Philadelphia: L. H. Everts, 1884), 1: 836–37.
14. Marion Stepansky, "The Philadelphia Race Riot," research paper, Spring 1969.

Contributors

John K. Alexander, a member of the Department of History at the University of Cincinnati, is completing a study of the poor in Philadelphia from 1760 to 1800. The chapter in this book is one of several articles he has published based upon his research.

Stuart M. Blumin, who teaches at the Massachusetts Institute of Technology, has published other articles on geographical mobility in nineteenth-century Philadelphia. More recently, he has completed a book on the transition from rural to urban social organization in a nineteenth-century American town.

Dennis J. Clark is Associate Director at the Samuel S. Fels Fund in Philadelphia and has published many books and articles on American cities. His book, *The Irish in Philadelphia,* is to be published by Temple University Press.

Michael Feldberg, a member of the History Department at the University of Massachusetts in Boston, has special interests in working class and ethnic cultures in America. His chapter in this book is drawn from a larger study he has completed on riots in Philadelphia in the nineteenth century.

Caroline Golab is currently a member of the Departments of History and Urban Studies at the University of Pennsylvania. Concerned with immigrant adaptation to urban America, she has completed a major study of the Poles in Philadelphia, from which her chapter in this book is taken.

Theodore Hershberg is a member of the History Department at the University of Pennsylvania and Director of the Philadelphia Social History Project. He is currently involved in an extensive comparative study of blacks, Irish, Germans, and native Americans in Philadelphia in the nineteenth century. His chapter in this book is the first of many publications to result from this project.

David R. Johnson, a member of the Department of History at Louisiana State University in New Orleans, is interested in the history of urban crime and police in the United States. His chapter in this book is drawn from a larger study comparing the development of the Philadelphia and Chicago police in the nineteenth century.

Bruce Laurie is primarily interested in understanding preindustrial working-class culture. A member of the History Department at the University of Massachusetts, he has completed a major study of working-class life in antebellum Philadelphia.

John F. Sutherland, a member of the History Department and Director of the Institute of Local History at Manchester Community College in Connecticut, is completing a study of housing reform in Philadelphia.

Richard A. Varbero, a historian at the State University College in New Paltz, New York, specializes in urban and immigration history. His chapter is taken from a larger work that he is completing on the Italian experience in Philadelphia.

Russell F. Weigley, a member of the Department of History at Temple University, has written a number of distinguished books on military history, including *History of the United States Army* (Macmillan, 1967). He has also had a continuing interest in Philadelphia history and from 1962 to 1967 was editor of *Pennsylvania History: Quarterly Journal of the Pennsylvania Historical Association.* His chapter on Philadelphia during the Civil War reflects his two major scholarly concerns.

Maxwell Whiteman is Archivist and Historian at The Union League of Philadelphia and has served with numerous organizations to encourage the study of Pennsylvania history. He has written several books and is co-author with Edwin Wolf, 2d, of *The History of the Jews of Philadelphia from Colonial Times to the Age of Jackson* (Jewish Publication Society of America, 1957). He is currently working on a history of Eastern European Jewish immigrants in Philadelphia.

Index

Abbott, Edith, 189
Abolitionists, 10, 159–61, 237; black, 112; census by, 113, 115; society of, 112, 117, 156, 158, 237. *See also* Riots
Addams, Jane, 4, 184, 189
Adler, Felix, 245
Alaska Street, 241, 244
Allegheny Avenue, 236
Amateus, Matthew, 271
Americans in Progress, 4
American Republican Association, 73, 75, 79, 80
American Steamship Line, 242
Andrews, John, 82
Ann Street, 236
Anti-abolitionists, 114. *See also* Riots
Anti-slavery. *See* Abolitionists
Apple Tree Alley, 18
Arch Street, 90–91, 155
Arthur, T. S., 237
Association for the Protection of Jewish Immigrants, 236, 238, 248
Association of Journeymen House Carpenters, 72
Atlantic Oil Refineries, 220
Auburn Street, 233
Aurora, 25
Austrians, 206

Bainbridge Street, 104, 239
Baldi, Charles C. A., 191, 192
Baldwin Locomotive works, 219
Baldwin, Matthias, 72
Baldwin, Roger, 189
Baltimore and Ohio Railroad, 213
Baltzell, Edward Digby, 3
Baptists, 121
Bedford Street, 91

Beneficent Building Association, 245
Benjamin Franklin Parkway, 147
Bernstein, Yehzekiel, 233–35
Biddle, Charles John, 14, 164–66
Biddle, George W., 166
Biddle, Nicholas, 73
Biddle family, 160–61
Blabon Oil Cloth Works, 219
Blacks: abolitionists, 112; artisans, 117; attitudes toward, 164–65; census of, 113, 115; children, 256; churches, 120, 237; convention movement, 111; crime, 19, 20, 96; disfranchisement, 112, 114, 288; economic situation, 114; education, 21, 122; ex-slaves, 118–19; families, 119, 278; female-male sex ratio, 115–16; free-born, 118; French, 20; housing, 90, 178, 179–80, 186; population, 10, 111, 159–60, 246; occupation, 124–25, 208, 210, 224, 226, 279; opportunity for, 9, 111, 116–17; revolt, 13; segregation, 7; social life, 280, 281; societies, 121–22; soldiers, 167. *See also* Riots, anti-black
Blankenburg, Rudolph, 285
Bond, Adelia, 288–89
Boston's Immigrants, 4
Bridesburg, 219
Briggs, Asa, 145
Bristol, Pa., 233–34
Broad Street, 91, 104, 158, 159, 219, 232, 237, 248, 269, 280, 283, 288
Broad Street Subway, 214
Broome, Edwin C., 256
Brown, John, 158
Buchanan, James, 162

293